Tourism Social Science Series
Volume 18

Tourism Social Media: Transformations in Identity, Community and Culture

Tourism Social Science Series

Series Editor: **Jafar Jafari**

University of Algarve, Portugal
University of Wisconsin-Stout, USA,
Tel: + (715) 232-2339; Email: jafari@uwstout.edua

The books in this Tourism Social Science Series (TSSSeries) are intended to systematically and cumulatively contribute to the formation, embodiment and advancement of knowledge in the field of tourism.

The TSSSeries' multidisciplinary framework and treatment of tourism includes application of theoretical, methodological, and substantive contributions from such fields as anthropology, business administration, ecology, economics, geography, history, hospitality, leisure, planning, political science, psychology, recreation, religion, sociology, transportation, etc., but it significantly favors state-of-the-art presentations, works featuring new directions, and especially the cross-fertilization of perspectives beyond each of these singular fields. While the development and production of this book series is fashioned after the successful model of *Annals of Tourism Research*, the TSSSeries further aspires to assure each theme a comprehensiveness possible only in book-length academic treatment. Each volume in the series is intended to deal with a particular aspect of this increasingly important subject, thus to play a definitive role in the enlarging and strengthening of the foundation of knowledge in the field of tourism, and consequently to expand the frontiers of knowledge into the new research and scholarship horizons ahead.

Tourism Social Science Series
Volume 18

Tourism Social Media: Transformations in Identity, Community and Culture

ANA MARÍA MUNAR
Copenhagen Business School, Denmark

SZILVIA GYIMÓTHY
Aalborg University, Denmark

LIPING CAI
Purdue University, USA

United Kingdom • North America • Japan
India • Malaysia • China

Emerald Group Publishing Limited
Howard House, Wagon Lane, Bingley BD16 1WA, UK

First edition 2013

Copyright © 2013 Emerald Group Publishing Limited

British Library Cataloguing in Publication Data
A catalogue record for this book is available from the British Library

ISBN: 978-1-78190-213-4
ISSN: 1571-5043 (Series)

ISOQAR certified
Management System,
awarded to Emerald
for adherence to
Environmental
standard
ISO 14001:2004.

Certificate Number 1985
ISO 14001

INVESTOR IN PEOPLE

Contents

Chapter 1

Tourism Social Media: A New Research Agenda

Ana María Munar
Copenhagen Business School, Denmark

Szilvia Gyimóthy
Aalborg University, Denmark

Liping Cai
Purdue University, USA

INTRODUCTION

Advances in information and communication technologies (ICT) have brought unprecedented opportunities and challenges to tourism as an information-intensive industry. Currently the Internet is evolving into a web of increasingly interactive communication platforms, which is once again transforming the virtual landscape of tourism. The emerging "Web 2.0" is claimed to be more participatory and inclusive, as it allows users to create, publish, and comment on digitized content worldwide. It provides a new generation of technological tools, enabling users to develop online communities and networks by collaborating and distributing Internet content and customizing applications (Vickery & Wunsch-Vincent, 2007). Web 2.0 is inherently collective; it is no longer just an informational medium, but a technology that nurtures, augments, and modifies social interactions and communication (Weinberg, 2009). As such, the information age has gradually become the social age.

Tourism Social Media: Transformations in Identity, Community and Culture
Tourism Social Science Series, Volume 18, 1–15
Copyright © 2013 by Emerald Group Publishing Limited
All rights of reproduction in any form reserved
ISSN: 1571-5043/doi:10.1108/S1571-5043(2013)0000018003

The progression of a collective Web 2.0 has led to the emergence of new tourism cultures and practices. Tourists receive and share information online and form virtual communities on a whole array of social media software. These encompass a variety of different types of ICT tools and take many different forms. Some of the most popular ones are wikis, blogs and microblogs, social networks, media sharing sites, review sites, and voting sites (Stillman & McGrath, 2008; Zarrella, 2010). Tourists share their travel images on Flickr, upload videos to YouTube, write personal stories on Travelblog, provide reviews on TripAdvisor, and publish updates about their tourism experience on Facebook. Hence, the participatory web has enabled new kinds of tourism interactions (such as electronic word-of-mouth), which complement and expand the experience of physical travel in diverse ways. For example, virtual communities such as Wayn or Dopplr focus especially on exchanging content to facilitate the planning of the journey, and by doing so they also encourage sociability and virtual knowledge sharing among members.

Social media emphasize the role of fantasy and imagination as part of a fluid tourism experience. This implies a virtual, emotional, and imaginative mode of travel, preceding as well as running parallel with the actual physical journey. On the other hand, everyday life and work issues gradually infiltrate the days on the road. As long as wireless network hubs make it possible, tourists are eager to regularly keep in touch with their friends, families, peers (and sometimes, work) back home. This fluidity blurs modernist dichotomies neatly differentiating between everyday life and nonordinary tourist behavior, between home and away, or work and leisure. However, as Jansson's (2002) study on the mediation of the tourism experience suggests, this virtual layer does not lead to the "end of tourism" and physical travel, but instead inspires and enriches the "on-location" experience. Perceptions and knowledge of tourism are conceived along the spatial activity of actually visiting places; however, it is equally shaped by the experience of mediated, simulated, and imagined space (Campbell, 2005). Social media provide new channels for the production and circulation of meaning in the tourism experience and imagination.

In this sense, tourism social media can be regarded as a novel form of collective value creation. They provide a fast-evolving technological structure shaping tourism cultures on and offline. The extensive creative effort of tourist-generated content and peer-to-peer reviews benefits other tourists with updated and (seemingly) impartial online information. Social networks and online communities provide tourists with information as well as pleasure, entertainment, appreciation, and status. Furthermore, social media sites have the potential to alter power relations (Shih, 2009), and tourism organizations are now confronted with the challenges of communicating with customers amidst media influences they have little or no control over. A new paradigm of marketing communications is on the rise (Mangold & Faulds, 2009) that entails not only the incorporation of social media in the promotional mix, but also requires a new way of strategic thinking. Social media reviews and user-generated content are believed to be independent of commercial agendas, giving them a new dimension of credibility and legitimacy. Many marketers are overwhelmed with these challenges or lack a full appreciation or knowledge about the potentials and character of social media (Mangold & Faulds, 2009; Merman Scott, 2011).

TOURISM SOCIAL MEDIA RESEARCH

The changing virtual landscape of tourism has received increased attention by tourism scholars. There is an emerging interdisciplinary field of study attempting to describe this phenomenon and to understand its consequences on tourist decisionmaking, behavior, and strategic communications. As such, social media are approached mostly from a business administration perspective, where contemporary studies on tourism and information technologies (IT) are informed by frameworks developed in management and marketing theory. This has resulted in the dominance of a (post) positivistic methodological approach in articles and textbooks (Sigala et al., 2012) and the emergence of research networks (such as the International Federation for Information Technologies in Travel and Tourism or the ENTER conferences), driven by an applied business research agenda. Taking the benefits of a "first-mover" advantage, these networks have developed into a densely knit, closed circle of actors who hold key editorial and advisory positions. These communities are similar to academic groups (Tribe, 2006) as they perpetuate one particular ontological view on technology and tourism and often act as gatekeepers of research production and distribution. Arguably, contemporary IT studies in tourism are still at a stage similar to the first, advocacy phase of tourism research in general (Jafari, 1990). This stage is characterized by a methodological hegemony, where studies of tourism social media are seldom inspired by relevant theoretical advances from other social science disciplines (such as anthropology, sociology, or geography). Nor is there a tendency to adopt critical or interpretivist schools of thought in research agendas, leaving important aspects of tourism social media unexplored. To substantiate this claim, three main streams of contemporary research can be pursued.

The first stream is characterized by exploratory research of social media sites and content and provides classifications according to types of tourism and its activities (Pudliner, 2007; Volo, 2010), type of genre, tourist-generated content, and the tourism experience (Kaplan & Haenlein, 2010; Munar, 2011; Tussyadiah & Fesenmaier, 2009), and types of tourists and country of origin (Enoch & Grossman, 2010; Wenger, 2008). These cataloguing approaches are useful to develop a comprehensive vocabulary to address a new phenomenon; however, rigid taxonomies and prematurely determined ontological structures may equally undermine theoretical sensitivity.

A second stream of research examines the relationship among social media, decisionmaking, and information search. The research of Mack et al. (2008) suggests that blogs are not as credible as word-of-mouth and that they act as complementary tools for market communication. Huang et al. (2010) provide an empirical test of a travel blogger's intention model and conclude that there is a positive relationship between blogging and a positive view of the ads of the site. Consumer-centered research approaches are also adopted in other studies of electronic word-of-mouth and location-based services (Lee & Tussyadiah, 2010; Tussyadiah, 2012) and articles that analyze tourists' behavior on review sites and recommendation systems (Bronner & de Hoog, 2011; Yoo & Gretzel 2008; Zhang et al., 2009). Moreover, scholars have examined the impact that social media sites have on travel information search and choice of destination (Fotis et al., 2012; Jacobsen & Munar, 2012; Xiang & Gretzel, 2010) and indicate the increasing role that electronic word-of-mouth plays in consumer decisionmaking processes (Litvin et al., 2008). While acknowledging these contributions, it can be argued that they do not go beyond the descriptive mapping of consumer behavior. It is time to adopt a more "techspressive" (Kozinets, 2008, p. 870) approach to studying sociotechnical systems, acknowledging the role of technology in individuals' self-realization and in collective identity projects. Technology is a mediated emotional landscape; nevertheless, the hedonic and emotional dimensions of ICT have received poor attention among tourism scholars.

A third stream of research takes a supply-oriented perspective, dealing with the challenges that tourist-generated content represent for destination marketing organizations and tourism firms. Munar (2011, 2012) presents a model of generic strategies used by these organizations to interact with the virtual world of social media. Other studies describe patterns of technology adoption of the industry and discuss the challenges that tourism organizations face when wanting to use social media for communication, promotion, or product development (Ayeh et al., 2012; Hvass & Munar, 2012; Schmallegger & Carson, 2008; Xiang & Gretzel, 2010). Finally, there is also evidence of novel approaches scrutinizing the collective, virtual value creation between providers and consumers, for instance on festival social media (Larson & Gyimóthy, 2012).

Challenging Unquestioned Assumptions

Studies of tourism social media are fraught with a number of underlying assumptions, which have developed into list of truisms reiterated in the introductory sections of most articles on this matter. As unreflected orthodoxy and assumptive mantras may hinder conceptual development and novel thinking, there is an urgent need to identify and reassess the most "die-hard" truisms. For instance, social media are often claimed to epitomize a more transparent and trustworthy web. The Web 1.0 represents a virtual sphere dominated by the content of firms and organizations, while the Web 2.0 empowers individual users around the world previously dominated by the content of organizations (Brogan & Smith, 2009; Shih, 2009). Increased participation of end users has the potential of altering previously established power relations. However, the claim of consumer sovereignty is challenged by ample examples of identity theft by media (Poster, 2006) or disputes over ownership of digital content uploaded to social media platforms such as Facebook (Aspan, 2008). It is also possible to question the reliability and trustworthiness of anonymous content. For instance, fake reviews and profiles on TripAdvisor are other problematic practices revealing a paradoxical balance act between transparency and necessary control mechanisms. Interactive media is a double-edged sword that provides opportunities for emancipation and socialization and for increased control and monitoring (Munar, 2010a).

Moreover, it is problematic to deem the Web 2.0 as a domain free of commercial interests. Ooi and Ek (2010) question the altruistic motives of peer-to-peer review sites and suggest that there exists a commercial motive behind most social media platforms. When aggregated, positive travel stories posted on TripAdvisor become valuable commercial assets and rhetorical ammunition in market communication. This exemplifies the tension between the ambition to achieve commercial success and the desire to maintain the illusion of a noncommercial domain.

A common assumption in the literature is the understanding of the web as an enabler for democracy and democratic communication. However, use of and participation in the Web 2.0 phenomenon takes for granted access to ICT and the acquisition of technological skills and an appropriate level of e-literacy. Use of and access to ICT, termed the digital divide in literature, varies greatly throughout the world. There is also a socioeconomic and generational divide to be taken into consideration (Prensky, 2001; Tapscott, 2009). Despite the increased popularity of social media platforms, critical perspectives show that not everybody is a writer or enthusiastic information sharer. Social media are claimed to promote the wisdom of crowds, but increasingly there is a debate on the merit and the quality of the user-generated content available, for example, citing the lack of depth and superficiality of tourists' contributions (Volo, 2010; Wenger, 2008).

Social media brings democratization and establishes new forms of social segregation, inclusion, and exclusion in the tourism system. Furthermore, while the majority of researchers prefer to think of web content as instantaneous and ephemeral (with microblogging as a conspicuous example), the information posted on collective platforms becomes permanent and can be retrieved. The tension between real-time communication culture and digital archiving systems creates new challenges related to the management of user-generated information, authorship rights, and data-management rights. It also demands a new reflectivity by users when building their virtual identities or uploading and sharing content on these new media.

Accordingly, this book embraces critical and reflective approaches to understanding the characters and implications of tourism social media at a 7greater depth. While recognizing the pioneer contribution of tourism management scholars to this field, the authors question established discourses and the assumptions presented above about social media, including truisms about equality, transparency, reliability, and customer sovereignty. By analyzing the structures, social rules, and cultural values of these new technological platforms, the chapters of this volume reveal how social media influences, augments, and transforms tourism interactions and relationships. By doing so, this work does not simply question dominant assumptions about new media, but also contributes to the existing field of knowledge by offering a broader methodological toolbox to better comprehend virtual relationships and digital content in tourism.

Theoretical Approaches for Digital Age Tourism

The evolution of technology and its impact on social change is a recurring theme in the social sciences. Research has focused on the role that technological development plays in, one, the relationship between individual agency and sociocultural structures and, two, in the provision of value and meaning in society. Technology and lately ICT play a crucial role in the different accounts of modernity and postmodernity (Bauman, 1998). The Internet provides new opportunities that change how people behave and make sense of their lives. The Internet and the web, as agents of social change, have been studied from many different perspectives: first, in relation to globalization processes (Hand, 2008); second, focusing on the digital divide, diversity, and power relations (Kirkpatrick, 2008; Kleinman, 2005); third, with regard to the construction of personal identities and virtual communities (Poster, 2006); fourth, examining changes in space-time constraints and cultural perceptions of body (Basu, Mok & Wellman, 2007; Schwanen & Kwan, 2008; Shaw, 2008); and, fifth, from a historical and sociological standpoint (Castells, 1997[1996], 2001). Furthermore, recent books have examined the impact of social media and web communities such as Facebook, YouTube, and Twitter on both society and on the marketplace (Qualman, 2009; Weinberg, 2009).

Some of the theories that critically elaborate on the relationships among sociocultural change, economic development, and technological transformation are liquid modernity (Bauman, 2000), information age, network society, and Internet cultures (Castells, 1997[1996], 2001), risk society (Beck, 1993, 2000), disembedding and reembedding of social relations (Giddens, 1990), communicative action (Habermas, 1984, 1987), social distinction and cultural capital (Bourdieu, 1984), actor network theories (Law & Mol, 2001), and complexity theory (Burnes, 2005; Byrne, 1998). These theoretical essays and conceptual frameworks have been widely used to examine many different types of cultural phenomena in society and are increasingly applied to the study of tourism (Pritchard et al., 2011; Tribe, 2006, 2009). However, they have so far been bypassed by researchers investigating the virtual world of tourism social media.

Mediated Encounters and Relationships

Interactive digital technology is dramatically changing tourism encounters and relationships. Social media has transformed the way in which businesses can interact with their customers. Users can now be involved in product development in radical new ways, which go well beyond the idea of "outsourcing" or "disintermediation." Tourists' value creation on the web changes power and responsibility relations in production processes and alters the value chain in tourism. This situation also impacts business-to-business relations and the way in which business compete. The evolution of a site such as Expedia is a clear example of this transformation, as well as the online and self-service strategies pushed by low-cost airlines such as Ryanair. At the same time, the possibility of communicating with customers on a real-time basis provides new opportunities for tourism organizations in their communication strategies, for example, as effective tools in the management of crisis.

The traditional relationship between host and guest is also being altered. CouchSurfing and the peer review site of TripAdvisor exemplify the transformative power of social media. The former, a user-based community where hosts offer free accommodation, promotes alternative and noncommercial intercultural encounters and social interaction. The latter is a review site for hotels, destinations, and attractions, which, despite its openness, is dominated by tourists' contributions and lacks local voices.

Online communities do not follow the structure of markets or hierarchies. Social media empower the customer-to-customer dimension and change the rules of the touristic marketplace. Moreover, social media are based on the establishment of alternative and nonmonetary reward systems (Brogan & Smith, 2009). For example, some of the most popular general sites for video and photo sharing are Flickr and Youtube. Many of the images on these sites have a "real-life" approach, without any or only a minimum degree of manipulation. The large diversity of video films available presents a kaleidoscopic image of destinations that stands in deep contrast to traditional dominant tourist images of destinations as presented by tourism or the cultural industry and that have usually played a relevant role in the marketing of destinations.

The ubiquitous web also modifies the relationship among destinations and between destination and place. A phenomenon like Google Earth, combined with review sites such as TripAdvisor, provide real-time online communication on places and surpasses traditional organizational channels of information about the destination, such as those provided by destination management organizations. ICT have altered local–global relationships. Tourists can see and read travel blogs, reviews, updates, and videos from around the world. Poster (2006) observes that the territoriality of the subject is minimized in digital culture, but not eradicated. Thanks to the Internet, the supply of tourist-generated content is global but consumed and produced locally. Social media sites act as a tool to make sense of and structure the excess of information (Qualman, 2009). Altering local–global relationships, social media provide a mobile virtual layer of information and storytelling. These platforms transform the perception of space and function as a mobility enabler. The sharing of information is omnipresent and public, however, the production and the interpretation of meaning remain personal and context specific to a particular sociocultural setting.

Emerging Theories and Practices

This collection treats the emerging technological phenomenon of social media from multidisciplinary perspectives.

Part I: Expanding the Theoretical Landscape
This stage-setting part of the book consists of conceptual chapters taking as their point of departure social science theories and examines the relationship between technology and sociocultural change in tourism. This contributes to expanding the field of academic inquiry in social media by applying and critically assessing theoretical concepts and frameworks in order to understand this empirical phenomenon in greater depth.

So far very few scholars have attempted to theorize the communicative patterns of social media. Chapter 2, "Tourism Social Media as a Fire Object" by Richard Ek, presents a stimulating essay on the necessity of an ontological paradigm shift in social sciences. Following in the footsteps of actor-network theorists Law and Mol (1994), Ek stresses the importance of alternative, messier ways to conceptualize and approach the societal and the trajectories of societal phenomena. One such challenging ontology is fire spatiality: a societal topology whose shape is achieved and maintained through the relation between different forms of presence and absence. The metaphor of fire is also omnipresent in the discourse on social media; its "explosive spreading," marketers' efforts to "canalize it," being unable to fully "control" or "tame" it. The chapter discusses the potential of using the fire topology and its attributes to better comprehend the diffusion and development of communication of social media within tourism.

Chapter 3, "Paradoxical Digital Worlds" by Ana María Munar, addresses emerging social media cultures and sociotechnical practices through the theoretical lens of Habermas' (1984, 1987) communicative action. The chapter analyzes the paradoxical role of interactive technologies as forces for the reproduction and transformation of tourism. Munar shows that the virtual space of social media reproduces inclusion and exclusion patterns of tourism physical worlds, but also challenges the settled lifeworld of tourism and raises new questions about the goodness, justice, and value of travel. She discusses the relationship between new media and processes of colonization of personal relations and life-spaces. Social media are both an agent of commercialization of everyday practices and an agent of de-commercialization of activities previously dominated by the market. The chapter reveals the ambivalent potential of these media as communicative technologies for emancipation but also as technological tools for hierarchization, control, and exploitation.

Symbolic convergence theory offers a relevant theoretical departure to address the complexities of social media communications. Chapter 4, "Symbolic Convergence and Tourism Social Media" by Szilvia Gyimóthy, suggests that the predominant mechanistic and behaviorist ontological framework in social media research results in a lack of awareness about the inherently social nature of tourism consumption and Web 2.0 communications. Gyimóthy stresses the urgency of acknowledging the sociality and narrativity of social media and explores the potential of an alternative analytical framework informed by symbolic convergence theory. The linkages between tourism social media, virtual communities, and symbolic convergence processes are illustrated by examples of postings and dialogue strings taking place on the Facebook fan site of an established music festival. These examples highlight the significance of symbolic communities in shaping the tourism experience and the festival concept against the backdrop of contemporary trends in consumer culture.

Changes in consumer culture also have consequences for destination management. Chapter 5, "Social Media Sites in Destination Image Formation" by Raslinda Mohd Ghazali and Liping Cai, proposes that existing theoretical models of destination image are outdated in the context of globalization and advances in IT, particularly the emergence of social media sites. The authors advocate a new conceptual model that builds on the seminal work by Gartner (1993) and that of Tasci and Gartner (2007), and extends the existing understanding of destination image formation. The model posits that, with the social media sites as the agent, an overall cognitive image of a destination can be formed by the overlap and intersection of provision and evaluation of cognitive and affective information by and among suppliers, consumers, and third parties.

Chapter 6, "Sustainability and Tourism Social Media" by Adriana Budeanu, critically assesses the claim that social media may play an important role in implementing tourism sustainable policies. The chapter reveals how, much like tourists' attitude in practice, the virtual interest of individuals in the sustainability of tourism provision or consumption is in its infancy. It discusses how the types of involvement enabled by social media reshape institutional relations and raises some concerns regarding social media as practical tools for developing and maintaining sustainability. To the claim that social media cause a power shift from institutional to individual actors, Budeanu responds that they add a new regime of social power in tourism, while the challenge for authorities remains to identify the best use and to design suitable incentives to capture the benevolent support of the crowds for sustainable goals.

The critical scrutiny of social media and their rapidly developing affordances will make it possible to revisit contested concepts of human interaction in cyberspace: equality, anonymity, transparency, democratization, hybridization, and publicity culture. Beyond this theoretical exercise in Part I, the book also aims to reflect upon the consequences of Web 2.0 on commercial and social relationships in a variety of practical and empirical contexts.

Part II: Practices and Empirical Dimensions
The chapters in this part present several empirical essays studying the transformation of tourism interactions and the impact of social media. A wide array of tourism interactions and relationships are analyzed on micro-, mezo-, and macro-levels, paving the way to revisit theoretical models of tourism encounters. This collection of essays addresses both customer-oriented aspects, such as the mediated tourist experience on social media sites, as well as managerial issues of how to integrate social media into marketing and organizational communication.

Chapter 7, "Inspiring Design: Social Media from the Beach" by Mads Bødker and David Browning, argues that the affordances of mobile technologies to assist tourist experiences are limited. The design of mobile guides and information systems, or mobile social media, is rooted in the assumption that tourism revolves around spectatorship and guided sightseeing activities (and thus lacks the acknowledgement of the tourist as an active creator). Taking their point of departure in the performative ontology of tourist activities, the authors argue that viewing the tourist as networker can be a useful trope in designing innovative social and locative mobile technologies. The chapter presents ethnographically inspired field-work at a popular destination in Australia, using a particular form of video ethnography (EgoPoint-of-View). This reveals tourists' dynamic construc-tions of destinations or sites as social places, while interacting with and participating in local physical, social, and cultural topologies. The chapter further demonstrates how analysis of egoPOV data produces artifacts that can be used to shape a design space, which supports the design of social and locative information technologies in keeping with the networker model.

The social dynamics of travel-related online communities are often based on other commonalities than travel reviews, such as a passion for films of books. Chapter 8, "The Virtual Fan(g) Community: Social Media and Pop Culture Tourism" by Maria Lexhagen, Mia Larson, and Christine Lundberg, investigates the behavior of online fan cultures related to the Twilight saga and its impact on travel motivation and behavior. They demonstrate that social media have added a new dimension to popular cultural tourism that goes beyond enhancing tribal connections among members of fan communities. New locations may become attractive for fan tourists as they develop emotional ties with destinations based on associations with dramatic events or characters.

Making sense of tourist experiences, however, often happens in retrospect. Chapter 9, "Digital Social Construction of a Tourist Site: Ground Zero" by Can-Seng Ooi and Ana María Munar, drawing inspiration from Bakhtin's (1981) chronotopes, shows how spatial and temporal structures are being negotiated. By adopting a netnographic approach, Ooi and Munar examine the confessionary tales of tourists visiting the contested site of Ground Zero and discuss new forms of technologically mediated authenticity. Through a systematic analysis of tourists' narratives and sociotechnical structures of TripAdvisor, this chapter provides insights into an emerging virtual tourism culture, where tourists are layering new meanings to historical sites, and are contributing to the rewriting of local histories, all as part of glocalization.

Chapter 10, "Tourism Social Media and Crisis Communication: An Erupting Trend" by Kristian Anders Hvass, studies the affordances of Internet technologies and social media as a crisis communication tool. It describes Scandinavian Airlines' use of new media platforms and micro-blogs to communicate with stranded passengers during the 2010 volcanic ash crisis. By combining the social mediated crisis communication model and situational crisis communication theory, the chapter identifies a new pattern of communicative practices to alleviate crisis impacts. The case explains the success of the airline in integrating social media in managing the crisis by portraying its organizational structuring and online learning processes transcending firm boundaries.

Chapter 11, "Web 2.0 Innovations in Events: Human Resource Management Issues" by Pamm Kellett and Anne-Marie Hede, explores how the adoption of social media platforms impacts organizational design, culture, and human resource management. Based on a cross-sectional study of 12 event organizations, they demonstrate that social media affects event workers by creating role overload and ambiguity. The authors identify three types of social media innovation adopters: spontaneous activists, spontaneous reactors, and organized initiators and discuss the implication of these on human resource management.

Chapter 12, "Identity and Social Media in an Art Festival" by Fabrizio Montanari, Annachiara Scapolan, and Elena Codeluppi, investigates the role of social media through the lens of identity and social identification with an art festival. Drawing on the literature on temporary organizations, organizational identity, and the empirical case of an Italian festival, Fotografia Europea, the authors investigates how festivals communicate their central and stable characteristics to audiences by adopting social media-based communication strategies.

Part III. Future Perspectives

The volume concludes with the presentation of "Critical Digital Tourism Studies" by Ana María Munar and Szilvia Gyimóthy, and with Toby Miller's chapter. In an eclectic and highly personal essay, Miller argues for a change of agenda in the way tourism relates to media studies. First, he describes and contrasts two key phases of media studies, identifying the dominant perspectives and weaknesses of both. While Media Studies 1.0 conceptualizes audiences as passive consumers, Media Studies 2.0 acknowledges the agency of media consumers and the coproductive character of communication. This overtly naive perspective paints a picture of a deregulated, individualist, and truthful world of media where amateur opinion makers on social network sites defeat dictated, controlled, professional messages, hence altering the ways in which tourism sites and destinations are presented. Miller recommends media and tourism scholarship to progress toward a new, dialectical 3.0 perspective, integrating the black-and-white binaries of Media Studies 1.0 and 2.0. This agenda may open up new avenues of understanding power balances between media audiences and tourism authorities, the social and environmental impacts arising from this struggle, and the issue of media labor.

CONCLUSION

Social media add further dimensions to the tourist experience and provide new channels for communities to socialize and communicate about tourism. They represent a new form of mediating tourism realities, giving voice to personal reflections rather than representing the travel or the cultural industries. Virtual community platforms and online content posted by fellow tourists help other peers make sense of tourism. The reading, viewing, and making of digitized content ease the access to the experience of touristhood so that this experience increasingly not only takes place as a contrast to everyday activities but also in many different contexts.

Late modernity is characterized by high media intensity and saturation. Through the web, the world of tourism has gained access to a vast amount of constantly updated information from multiple sources. The question remains whether this increase in the speed, intensity, and extent of available information will eventually lead to a more human and sustainable tourism development. Social media contribute to expanding the communicative landscape of multimedia societies. Modern individuals are profoundly sociotechnical subjects (Lash, 2002). It is in the interface between the technical and the social that individuals define their identities, express their political beliefs, socialize and form attachments, and interact with the physical world around them. However, beyond aesthetic and hedonic pleasures and social recognition, the promises of new communication channels as tools for human emancipation are still to be proven.

Social media appear as a novel channel for social organization and political mobilization. Nevertheless, the exposure to massive amounts of fragmented information may not be equal to insight, wisdom, or justice. It is still to be seen whether this highly fragmented and ubiquitous public communication space can result both in public mobilization or entertainment and in political and legislative initiatives resulting in increased social welfare and equity. The existence of millions of people enjoying videos of laughing babies on YouTube or updating their personal status on Facebook or Twitter, brings memories of the famous "bread and circuses" of the Roman empire. Social media promise enlightenment but provide new ways to get public recognition and appeasement through entertainment. These new technologies have the potential to start a communicative revolution and to be emancipatory tools, but they may also end up being worldwide digitized circuses.

The question is how the massive amount of information and content displayed online can be transformed into insights that may help to solve some of the main issues that tourism and the world community are facing today. Tribe (2002) suggests the need for a stronger coupling between reflection and action in tourism and an increased commitment to achieving the good of tourism societies. This task also demands research to understand technical development and its impact on one's relationship to the worlds of tourism. This book aims to increase academic reflexivity on the technical world of social media. It advocates that critical thinking and sociopolitical engagement can be applied to examine the development of the web and its connection to tourism sociocultural practices.

Digitization has provided the academic world with an ever-expanding landscape of data and research material available on the web and through organizations' ICT. However, the analysis of the virtual world represents a challenge to traditional research methods and is characterized by the rapid change in the patterns of use and the fragmentation and massive amount of data related to the different objects of analysis. The Internet changes the way in which researchers conduct qualitative and quantitative enquiry. There is a need for tourism to develop new methodological insights to advance the field (Tribe, 2008).

The theoretical grounding, conceptual developments, empirical evidence, and interdisciplinary analysis presented in this anthology expand the actual research agenda in this field and shed light on some conceptual tensions and ambiguities in the present literature. The book also contributes to increasing research reflexivity in studies that use the web and online content as their sites and objects of study. An important theme to be found throughout the book is the acknowledgement of the complexity of research design and processes when addressing a fast changing information-saturated context. The different chapters critically examine the validity of traditional methods for the study of virtual worlds and new digital platforms. As such, the book offers a new venue for reflections about emerging methods and ethical issues of social media research.

PART I

EXPANDING THE THEORETICAL LANDSCAPE

Chapter 2

Tourism Social Media as a Fire Object

Richard Ek
Lund University, Sweden

ABSTRACT

Tourism studies have conceptualized social media as artifacts and networks of tangible objects based on neat distinctions and categorizations. These neat ontological distinctions and categorizations have been discussed within the academic field of actor-network theory. Several scholars have most significantly investigated the spatialities of messier ways of conceptualizing and approaching societal objects and the trajectories of societal phenomena. Efforts are being made to widen the ontological register that has traditionally dominated social science research, including tourism studies. The purpose of this chapter is to address and problematize the social media pertaining to tourism, focusing on a research project as analytical and methodological lens.

Keywords: Fire object; social topologies; spatiality; tourism ontologies; tourism social media

INTRODUCTION

As an empirical field of knowledge production, tourism studies have persistently directed scholarly attention toward how social and economic changes have influenced tourists' behavior, and how these changes in turn affect the business and management of this industry. Technological change

Tourism Social Media: Transformations in Identity, Community and Culture
Tourism Social Science Series, Volume 18, 19–34
Copyright © 2013 by Emerald Group Publishing Limited
All rights of reproduction in any form reserved
ISSN: 1571-5043/doi:10.1108/S1571-5043(2013)0000018004

has had a pivotal position, especially the development of information technologies. Tourism, and the travel industry at large, was quick to adapt to the possibilities offered by a growing electronic commerce. Information exchange and dissemination is now its backbone (Kanellopoulos, 2006). The change in information technology is regarded as substantial, particularly due to the rise in Internet usage (Yeoman & McMahon-Beattie, 2006). The structure of the industry as a whole has changed and continues to change in several ways. First, it restructures the consumer and demand dimension. Increasingly sophisticated information technologies empower the tourist by facilitating the identification, customization, and purchase of tourism products (Buhalis & Law, 2008). Second, information technology has been reducing costs and enhancing operational efficiency, with improved service quality as a business outcome (Alford & Clarke, 2009; Law, Leung, & Buhalis, 2009). Third, the accelerating use of information technology changes the industry fundamentally when it comes to global competitiveness, value creation, business strategies and practices, and, not the least, the representation and perceptions of tourism (Gretzel, 2011). In short, according to Buhalis and Law (2008, p. 610), the industry is facing a new paradigm shift when it comes to tourism demand, supply, and technologies.

At the same time, the perception and imagination of (information) technology remains a traditional one, in that technology is conceptualized as digital machines that are increasingly connected but are nevertheless distinct artifacts. There are clear-cut ontological distinctions among technology (networks of machines), economic management and business, and the social (tourists and their behaviors). In methodological terms, this traditional ontology results in a corresponding distinction. The research questions follow causal schematics, such as "How does the Internet influence the choice of tourist destinations?" (technology → social); and "How does interactive technology influence the management of hotel brands in a global hospitality context?" (technology → management). This is probably due to the fact that tourism studies, like social science in general, have primarily been occupied with tangible objects and doctored ontologies with neat distinctions and categorizations. The separation of subjects (people) and objects (artifacts) is perhaps the most important one in this context, since subjects (tourists, managers) use objects (technology) in different ways. Further, information technologies (technical devices such as computers) include special kinds of objects that are ontologically separated from non-technological objects such as guidebooks. In sum, mainstream tourism studies have generally reproduced the habitual Cartesian logic in which mind is separated from matter, culture is separated from nature, subjects are separated from objects, time is separated from space, and so on. Out of this worldview, technology has been conceptualized as a distinct set of materiality, machines, and artifacts that can be isolated methodologically as an object of research.

But there are alternative understandings of technology. The field of actor-network theory (ANT)—a strand of literature within the wider field of science and technology studies that is sometimes labeled sociological studies of science and technology—has scrutinized these habitual distinctions between nature and culture, humans and nonhumans, objects and subjects, etc. One key mission of ANT is to dissolve the distinction between the social and the material and present a network approach that does not reproduce the Cartesian worldview. Here, technology is not a distinct black box that can be attached to humans and other social beings or other kinds of materialities in conventional networks. Instead, heterogeneous networks of multiple sets of actors (organic, material, and immaterial) that constitute and stabilize what is called "society" (Latour, 2005) are given ontological precedence. Within ANT, Annemarie Mol and John Law (1994) have consequently questioned the neat conceptualization of tangible research objects and advocated alternative, "messier" ways of imagining, spatializing, and defining the societal and the trajectories of societal phenomena. The ambition is to create methodological approaches with the capacity to address non-tangible phenomena through a widening of the ontological register that has traditionally dominated social science and tourism research.

The purpose of this chapter is to address social media in tourism using the research of Law and Mol as an analytical and methodological lens, and consequently be able to avoid conceptualizing tourism social media in the habitual way of Cartesian logic. The intention is to introduce and explore what kind of new research questions can be asked if tourism social media are imagined as something not easily compartmentalized and tangible but as something more fluid and spatially more complex than a distinct "object in space". Although tourism scholars have made use of ANT to search for an alternative understanding of tourism (Jóhannesson, 2005; Ren, 2011; Van der Duim, 2007), tourism social media have not yet been examined from the perspective of an ANT-based ontology and methodology.

ANT-BASED APPROACH TO TOURISM SOCIAL MEDIA

The concept of Web 2.0, social media, has only been partly attended to within tourism studies. This is because it is a relatively new cultural media formation (dynamic, collaborative, and interactive websites in contrast to static, web-based home pages). The main difference is that in addition to allowing for communication, this technological set-up also facilitates other managerial aspects, such as service recovery, relationship marketing, and brand building (Buhalis & Law, 2008). Chan and Guillet define social media as "a group of Internet-based applications that exist on the Web 2.0 platform and enable the Internet users from all over the world to interact, communicate, and share ideas, content, thoughts, experiences, perspectives, information, and relationships" (2011, p. 347). Social media is thus a set of technological applications that can be used as tools (Parra-López, Bulchand-Gidumal, Gutiérrez-Tano & Diaz-Armas, 2011, p. 640). Social media are further divided into subgroups according to empirical functionality: blogs, social network sites, virtual worlds, collaborative projects, content community sites, and sites dedicated to feedback (Chan & Guillet, 2011, pp. 347–348). This division of social media into subgroups is arbitrary and overlapping due to the flexibility and fluidity of the medium, which exemplifies the difficulty of making empirical categorizations based on applicability. As a consequence, some of the most familiar concepts in social media become the basis for categorization. Often, the subcategorization is connected to familiar web-sites: "blogs and microblogs (Blogger and Twitter), social photo and video sharing (Flickr and YouTube), social sharing of knowledge (Wikipedia), social bookmarking (Delicious) ..." (Parra-López et al., 2011, p. 640).

Habitual Imaginations of Tourism Social Media

Metaphors are sometimes used to characterize the new social media. Xiang and Gretzel use the concept "online tourism domain," defining it as "a collection of links, domain names, and Web pages that contain texts, images, and audio/video files stored in hypertext formats" (2010, p. 180). The use of spatial and territorial concepts is common in attempts to conceptualize the Internet (the concepts cyberspace and virtual worlds). Some tourism scholars discuss the creation of a "virtual tourist community" (Wang, Yu, & Fesenmaier, 2002), thereby referring back to the habitual division into a group that shares something in common due to some kind of delimiting criteria (territorial, ethical, here functional) that neatly separates them from the "world outside." A "community" or a "domain" is then connected to the functional aspects of the different technical applications. The functional or role-based division between economy/management and social/tourist behavior is often reproduced through this approach.

On the managerial side, the language and logic of marketing are often applied, since the discourse on marketing is compatible with the phenomenon of social media. The common concept "word-of-mouth" is extrapolated to "electronic word-of-mouth" and addressed as a necessary practice to master in hospitality and tourism management (Litvin, Goldsmith, & Pan, 2008; O'Connor, 2010). Here the prefix "e" (as in e-tourism and e-business) indicates that the material world and its inhabitants can be claimed and controlled through the digital, electronic realm of other socio-material practices or tourism social media. Even though the empowering of the tourist is stressed, "...instead of, as in the past, the marketer dictating how information is presented and consumed, the user is now in control" (O'Connor, 2010, p. 755), the ontological division between management and consumer behavior is maintained in the sense that the tourist and the marketing actor are imagined as separate subjects of action and performance, even if their internal relationship is changed.

The bulk of the literature on tourism social media focuses on how the new technical tools and applications influence tourist behavior and have "implications for management." Here, even if the possibilities and changes that occur are given substantial importance, the tourist remains a tourist; a tourist subject that can be acted upon, a distinct subject that needs to be understood for business and competitive reasons (Lo, McKercher, Lo, Cheung, & Law, 2011). Blogging is presented as perhaps *the* new practice of the tourist subject, as it is the most popular form of social media (Thevenot, 2007). Spatialized as a "blogosphere" (Schmallegger & Carson, 2008), tourists' weblogs are given both cultural and promotional power (Pudliner, 2007), the utility and credibility of which have to be investigated (Mack, Blose, & Pan, 2008; Volo, 2010). Traditional analytical models from consumer behavior and service marketing literature are applied (Huang, Chou, & Lin, 2010; Zehrer, Crotts, & Magnini, 2011). The models and theories that are used are based on the premise that the consumer is a subject with a distinct psychology (consumer involvement theory, Huang et al., 2010) and cognitive expectations (the expectancy-disconfirmation paradigm, Zehrer et al., 2011).

In sum, it is safe to say that tourism scholars have, methodologically speaking, mainly approached social media from what Law (2004) calls a Euro-American ontology of "in-here" research statements and "out-there" realities that are reflected in the "in-here" depictions. This Western-based, culturally situated method assemblage is visual, perspectivalist, and in the continuation, reductionist, in that eventually a single account of "out-thereness" is stated (Law, 2004, p. 122). In order to come out with an increased understanding of the world, the messiness of reality has to be reduced, and a plethora of processes, forces, materialities, people, and other living creatures have to be transformed into the Other and made invisible. This is done through the mechanisms of dualism: human/nonhuman, knowing subjects/objects of knowledge, social/natural, active/passive entities (Law, 2004, p. 132). However, the Euro-American dualist ontology that Law criticizes has long been questioned and problematized within continental philosophy, such as the Frankfurt School and French post-structuralism, even though the Euro-American template is still more or less taken for granted in research and in other discursive arenas. As shown by Munar and Ooi (2012), these dichotomies are reproduced through and in the narratives and metaphors of tourists themselves and are displayed through different social media channels, such as TripAdvisor. The process of epistemological clarification is intertwined with the invisibility of the ontological register (it is assumed that the world has to be simplified in order to be understood and made explainable). The effect is that difference is reconciled and multiplicity avoided, in that a single version of reality becomes the "gold-standard" used to determine the nature of the single reality (Law, 2004, pp. 61, 53). In other words, "Euro-American method assemblage enacts—or seeks to enact, or understands itself, as being constituted in—a reality that is independent, prior, singular and definite" (Law, 2004, p. 131). An ontological template is constructed and followed: with a coherent world "out there," with processes, phenomena, and trajectories that can be registered, mapped, and explained as independent in relation to the scholar and his or her methods of investigation.

However, this reduction of what counts as reality is just about the methodology or metaphysics of social science, it is also about politics, or to be more precise, ontological politics. Ontological politics is the active, performative presentation of a particular version of the world as a more valid, or the only valid, take on reality (Law, 2004, p. 93). Law is thus a central representative of strong social constructionism. Method is never objective, neutral, or purely technical craft that just reports "what is out there." Method is the production of truths, realities, and presences, and at the same time, the production of non-truths, non-realities, and absences. But in order to unravel the black box of Euro-American metaphysical certainties, dualisms, and neat ontological categories, one needs to apply alternative spatial topologies.

The Spatial Topologies of Research Objects

ANT stresses the ontological symmetry within a collective of humans, nonhumans (other living beings), and objects such as texts, artifacts, and other materialities. It is the assemblages of this collective that really help to make social structures last and act at a distance (Latour, 1986, 1991). Actors are shaped in these collectives, since they are co-constructed *in* the networks, not *outside* the networks. It is the relations that perform agency (Callon & Latour, 1995). Spaces are also made out of the relations, from the materials that are brought together and mobilized (Murdoch, 2006). Using labels like "ANT 2.0" and "ANT and after," attempts have been made to expand the spatial sensitivity, ontologically speaking (Hetherington & Law, 2000), and show that the spatiality of the network ontology is not the only spatiality around. Depending on how objects are imagined, a specific spatiality is also unfolded.

What counts as a research object is up to the researcher. Usually, objects are imagined as physically graspable and/or can be conceptualized as a distinct practice (blogging, for instance). The object thus takes up volume in absolute space (or it takes place *in* space). However, an object may also be something more fluid and difficult to pinpoint, such as alcoholic liver disease (Law & Singleton, 2005). Thus. the project initiated by Law and Mol is an attempt to widen the ontological horizon that has habitually been dominated by a topographical view based on the Cartesian visualization of space as three-dimensional distance and place as a bounded locality. The topography of Euclidean space (stressing the contour, demarcation, and containment of space as well as its relief) must lose its primacy if one is to unfold the hidden, ontologically erased complexity and heterogeneity.

Mol and Law begin by declaring that Cartesian topography is only one form of social topology. Topology (stressing properties, relationships, interactions, and relations among relationships; Murdoch, 2006, p. 86) is a branch of mathematics that has been adjusted and used in a metaphorical sense, rather than in a strict mathematical way. In mathematics, topology is about the character of objects in space; to Law it is about the continuity of the shape of objects even if the object is stretched and bent. Topology concerns "the properties of geometric figures which remain invariant under bending, stretching, or deforming transformations, that is, transformations which do not create new points or fuse existing ones" (DeLanda, 2002, pp. 25–26). Thus, topology does not comply with Euclidean restrictions such as three dimensionality (Simonsen, 2004).

In essence, Law and Mol discuss four topologies (Law & Mol, 2001; Mol & Law, 1994). Initially, in Mol and Law, they execute their reading by discussing the first three social topologies: regions, networks, and fluidity:

> The "social" doesn't exist as a single spatial type. Rather, it performs several kinds of space in which different "operations"

take place. First, there are regions in which objects are clustered together and boundaries are drawn around each cluster. Second, there are networks in which distance is a function of the relations between the elements and difference a matter of relational variety. These are the two topologies with which social theory is familiar. (1994, p. 643)

The region is the first social topology. This is a "striated, Cartesian geographical space with demarcated zones and co-ordinates. It is the topography of the social in terms of differentiated regions, e.g. structures, systems, or fields based on territorialized and non-transformable objects" (Diken, 2010, p. 96). The spatiality of this social topology is the Euclidean absolute space. The network is the second social topology. Here, compared to the social topology of the region, proximity is measured by how the elements of the network hang together, rather than by physical distance. These two social topologies are the most dominant in social science research, including tourism studies. However, in order to break up the dominance of these two social topologies, Mol and Law present the third social topology, or a fluid topology:

Sometimes, we suggest, neither boundaries [emphasised in the topology of the region] nor relations [emphasised in the topology of networks] mark the difference between one place and another. Instead, sometimes boundaries come and go, allow leakage or disappear altogether, while relations transform themselves without fracture. Sometimes, then, social space behaves like a fluid ... We're looking at variation without boundaries and transformation without discontinuity. We're looking at flows. The space with which we're dealing is fluid. (1994, pp. 643, 658)

Fluidity indicates the absence of clear and distinct definitions in the relations or in the shape of the enrolled research objects, since the spatial relations are relentlessly becoming, shifting, and moving. The fluid space of the third topology is a realm of mixtures, generated by robust, but at the same time changeable and not very well defined, objects. The objects of fluid space are functionally fluid objects of a fluid spatiality that coexists with the prior two topologies outlined (1994, p. 663). Mol and Law conclude that the study of fluids will be a study of the "relations, repulsions and attractions which form a flow" (1994, p. 664). Later, Law suggests that in fluid space, no particular structure of relations or particular boundary around a research object is privileged (actually mobile boundaries are needed for some, but not all, objects to exist in fluid space). He also concludes that change is necessary if homeomorphism is to be achieved, although here change needs to be continuous rather than radical (2002, pp. 99–100). In fluid space, tourism social media do not simply consist of technical devices that can be transported through Euclidean space (into a specific region) or be connected to different networks. Tourism social media are here primarily a fluid research object that enacts heterogeneous practices into functionally differentiated performativities, such as identity construction, the expression of cultural capital, or political acts of resistance. In the social topology of fluidity, functionally speaking, tourism social media are not necessarily "touristic." It is not a static practice either, but a transformative, even plastic practice of human and nonhuman assemblages.

Although this chapter is not primarily about fluid social topology, it is still necessary to elaborate on it, since the fourth topology is outlined in contrast to the flow version (with its elemental affinity to water): fire space (Law & Mol, 2001, p. 615). In the fire topology, shape is both achieved and maintained through the relation between different forms of presence and absence. For instance, object presence depends on simultaneous absence, or rather the simultaneous absence of multiple others, and, as a consequence, has three attributes:

> ... [continuity] as an effect of discontinuity, continuity as the presence and the absence of Otherness; and ... continuity as an effect of a star-like pattern in this simultaneous absence and presence: this is what we imagine as the attributes of shape constancy in a topology of fire. Thus fire becomes a spatial formation alongside (and in interference with) Euclidean, network, and fluid space. To say that there is a fire topology is to say that there are stable shapes created in patterns of relations of conjoined alterity. (Law & Mol, 2001, p. 616)

In this strong social constructionist account, particular realities are enacted and produced by scholars' practices and a set of methodological inscription devices (Law, 2004, p. 21). The research object is thus assembled and crafted. Like representations, they are usually enacted "in-here" as a reality "out-there," but presented as something independent "out-there" (as, for instance, an increase of the phenomenon of "travel blogging"). Hence, there is a need to depart from the conventional perspectivalist ontology and admit that there is more than one side to the story: "We are dealing with *different objects produced in different method assemblages*" (Law, 2004, p. 55, original emphasis). There are relationships that have been made invisible in conventional research procedures. In the fire topology, some of these relationships are made visible because this social topology pivots on the relationship between the enactment of presence and absence:

> More specifically, it is the crafting, bundling, or gathering of relations in three parts: (a) whatever is in-here or *present* (for instance a representation or an object); (b) whatever is absent but also *manifest* (it can be seen, is described, is manifestly relevant to presence); and (c) whatever is absent but is *Other* because, while necessary to presence, it is also hidden, repressed or uninteresting. The issue, then, becomes one of imagining—or describing—possible ways of crafting method, obvious or otherwise. (Law, 2004, p. 144, original emphasis)

In the case of tourism social media, the social media are *per se* the enacted present phenomenon or practice. Technological devices, such as computers and viral networks, are enacted as manifestly absent. But what is absent as Other in this example? This is of course a tricky question, since it is difficult to discuss what has traditionally been neglected.

First, as Otherness is limitless, the fire topology is just another topology (among still to be discussed topologies). Law's reasoning is thus philosophically anchored in a post-structuralist critique of the metaphysics of presence (the tendency in modernist accounts to prioritize what is present on behalf of what is seemingly absent). Of course, not everything can be brought to presence, and absence is a precondition for presence (just as presence is a precondition for absence): "An object is a pattern of presences and absences" (Law & Singleton, 2005, p. 343). This approach is similar to the hermeneutical interplay between the part and the whole, in that it becomes the researcher's task to crystallize what is absent but is nevertheless still relevant, which in turn makes a difference to the shape and functionality of a specific research object.

To Law, for instance, in the calculations of aerodynamic formulas used to develop airplanes with a capacity to fly, the human test pilot and the density of the atmosphere are absent presences, invisible in the formalism but still necessary for getting the airplane in the air (Law, 2002). In tourism social media, money is not presented as something that is present, even though it is crucial for whatever social media practice is talked about. For example, going into an Internet café in Cairo requires money, not to mention buying the technological equipment in the first place. Tourism social media are generally something for affluent tourists, rather than for vagabonds forced into mobility by violence and destitution (Bauman, 1998). This should be seen in relation to another variable that is not present in accounts of tourism social media, namely the growth imperative of big corporations (which some might call greed). As Petersen (2008) insists, the Internet always operates within the confines of capitalism, and its architecture and design allows an oscillation between participation (the social in social media) and exploitation in the shape of the commodification of users and their work on different social media.

The world is thus created through the empirical account, rather than the empirical account being a declaration of an external reality. Many artifacts and materialities are enacted as Other because they are regarded as uninteresting or irrelevant, or are not taken into account because they are either taken for granted or too politically sensitive: "The implication is that Otherness takes a variety of forms. Those above—*routine, insignificance* and *repression*—are no doubt only three of the possibilities" (Law, 2004, p. 85, original emphasis). Thus, the reasonable question to ask is what kind of absent presences, or what is enacted as an invisible Other, could be "identified" in the case of tourism social media?

The Invisible Other in Tourism Social Media

First, it must be stressed that tourism studies are no stranger to ANT. Jóhannesson (2005) makes an early explicit and systematic call for the use of ANT in tourism studies, claiming that this input strengthens the possibilities to address the relational materiality of the social world and catch multiple relational orderings (Franklin, 2004). In a similar call, Van der Duim (2007) stresses that besides opening up new ontological horizons, ANT also opens epistemological panoramas, in that it points to how tourism should be studied (following the actors through a trail of associated heterogeneous elements and orderings, analytically imagined as tourisms-capes). Further, another call is made by Ren, Pritchard, and Morgan (2010), who, by approaching tourism research as a fractionally coherent practice (after Law, 2002), stress that tourism research objects should not be recognized as single versions of reality, but as several enacted objects. There is also a growing literature of case studies using ANT as an analytical and methodological lens (Arnaboldi & Spiller, 2011; Mordue, 2009; Paget,

Dimanche, & Mounet, 2010; Rodger, Moore, & Newsome, 2009; Tribe, 2010; Van der Duim & van Marwijk, 2006; Van der Duim, van Marwijk, Ndubi, & Fetene, 2006). In this context, the single contribution that deserves some elaboration is Carina Ren's (2011) study of the different enactments of a Polish cheese. The case by Ren displays how the Oscypek cheese (a smoked cheese made of sheep milk exclusively in the Polish Tatra Mountains) is enacted as multiple objects (as traditional cheese, tourism cheese, modern cheese, and unique cheese) within a tension field of presences and absences. Ren's ambition concurs with that of this chapter, namely to advocate "a higher sensitivity towards a radical ontology which performs tourism objects and realities in multiple ways" and in the process confront a simplistic understanding of tourism objects (2011, pp. 860, 876).

Therefore, if social tourism media are enacted as a fire object, constituted by the interdependent force of tension among presence, manifest absence, and absence as other, the crucial and interesting question is, what is made invisible through other processes? What is regarded as routine and thus made invisible, what is regarded as insignificant, and what is more or less consciously repressed? Something that is not very visible in the tourism social media account is the materiality of the information technology that makes social media possible in the first place. Is it that this materiality is taken for granted, or is it that the materiality of technology is not regarded as interesting in tourism research? In an ANT approach, this materiality is something significant that has to be addressed. If computers are considered, in practice a computer contains all the metals included in the periodic table, but primarily plastic, glass, iron, aluminum, and copper (Elstad et al., 1998, p. 20). In Africa, 2.5% of the iron ore is produced in South Africa (US Department of the Interior 2011, p. 22), Guinea is a world-leading producer of aluminum (Campbell, 2009) and, as is well known, Africa is an important producer of copper. Mining in Africa has become an increasingly discussed issue. There have been calls for mining codes, increased corporate social responsibility, a greater environmental concern and social legitimacy as a reaction to the very high corporate maneuver opportunities that have resulted from the political creation of a favorable environment for foreign investments in Africa (Adanhounme, 2011; Campbell, 2009). From a postcolonial perspective, it is possible to claim that mineral resources in the South/former colonies are produced and used to increase an Internet-based technology in the North/former colonial powers. Multinational corporations have been associated with all kinds of maltreatment (violence, environmental ravagement, etc.) as the former South is opened up to the world economy. To Banerjee, Chico, and

Mir (2009), this is an indication of a rising corporate imperialism that favors multinational companies at the expense of the environmental well-being of local places in the South.

In the case of tourism social media, an absent, unrecognized Other could consequently be the village in Ghana where the groundwater is polluted due to metal mining in the locality; metals that are used to produce portable computers that are in turn used by the blogging backpacker tourist to upload pictures of him- or herself in the countryside in Vietnam and to comment on the presence of an unspoiled and "authentic" rural culture and the hospitality of its inhabitants. Thus, in this reading, polluted water in Ghana is unfolded as topologically related to the carefree backpacker, but neglected in relation to tourist blogging—instead of being something that is made invisible or nonexistent, as it is in a topographical Euro-American method assemblage. In this conventional reading, the bad water in Ghana and the happy blogger in Vietnam are two independent research objects "out there"; the first being a research object of interest for development scholars or biologists, and the second a research object of interest for scholars interested in how tourists use social media.

However, seen as a fire research object, tourism social media appear as a heterogeneous network of materiality, technology, immaterial codes and binaries, and the practices of traveling people (just to mention some of the components in these actor networks). Further, its spatiality is performed through the assistance of absent Others, such as polluted water, ignorant transnational mining corporations, corruption among local authorities who look the other way, and a set of neoliberal regulations and governance constellations that are made possible by the power of global organizations such as the World Bank and the International Monetary Fund. Today's backpackers should not be able to upload pictures of themselves holding happy Vietnamese children in their arms via a technology that would have been manifestly or recognizably absent if it had not been for the aluminum mines in Ghana; mines that in their turn are managed in a way that creates corporate profits, including the managerial choice to not purify the water used in the mining process, resulting in polluted groundwater in the area. This is the practice of ontological politics, and the creation and representation of a single, purified, and neatly categorized tourism ontology: blogging back-packers as an increased phenomenon that changes the preconditions for the conduct of tourism and hospitality management.

The conceptualization of social media as a tool that is used in tourism (tourism social media as a practice) is thus the conduct of ontological politics. This relates to the imagination and presentation of tourism as something that is not political. However, as Adrian Franklin (2004) suggest, tourism is an ordering practice, a practice that is and creates the contemporary societal (rather than a phenomenon in society "out there" to study by scholars "in here"). Tourism "is not a decorative and superficial activity or even a compensatory activity for the ills of capitalism or modernism. Instead it relates centrally to modernity in a number of dimensions: politically, morally, technologically, and economically" (Franklin, 2003a, p. 38). However, this is another invisible and unacknowledged Other—the performative power of the politics of tourism social media. Tourism social media as a practice has implications and repercussions for destinations, for the management of hospitality organizations, and for the individual tourist, but not for the politics of society as a whole, as is commonly argued in tourism studies.

Something that is invisible, and which is perhaps also true for social media research in general, is the political contribution of (tourism) social media to the increased nonsociability of social media. To Bauman (2002), social media and digital mediated media, such as email, are ex-territorial forms of communication that give the impression of being social but are in fact nonsocial, since engagement in place is lacking (Franklin, 2003b, 2009). It may be that Bauman expresses an "old-fashioned" view of sociality as something that is either conducted face-to-face or not at all. Nevertheless, a "weak" or "loose" sociality is increasingly connected to a post-political condition in which politics is defined as economics or personal ethics, but not politics *per se* (Diken & Laustsen, 2005). When politics disappears (and implicitly also the societal) one becomes a consuming tourist rather than a politically engaged citizen. In this sense, tourism social media may not be social at all, but something that enhances loneliness, in that it increases the ephemeral character of social relations and the liquidity of modernity. In an extension of this, one could argue, following Diken (2007), that tourism itself is a nihilistic and post-political tendency in society. However, the nonsociality of tourism social media is repressed by scholars. In other words, it is Othered.

Claudio Minca (2012) addresses this dimension of tourism and its nonsociability. To Minca, processes of politicization are present but apparently absent (and are recognized in studies to an insignificant extent). A biopolitical element at the core of tourism becomes increasingly apparent as tourist manifestations are pervaded by a biopolitical logic. One such manifestation is an emphasis on touristic communities of different kinds, for example, in the marketing of destinations (meet the genuine locals) and practices by the industry, as well as in the ambitions to construct touristic imagined communities through tropes like *Lonely Planet*. Contemporary tourism seems to be obsessed with finding and creating tourist communities, although to Minca this is rather an indication of a missing community: "... what these temporary communities of strangers actually have in common is the fact that their accidental members share practically nothing, but they share this nothingness in the same place and in a similar way" (Minca, 2012, p. 22).

Contemporary tourism is rather a missing community; a highly organized staged experience of nothingness twisted into an intensive nostalgic imagination of a utopian tourist space detached from the history and geography of society—a post-historical community (imagined in movies like "The Beach") of nothingness that promises escapism and freedom from responsibility (Minca, 2012, p. 24). On the other hand, this responsibility could be argued to be the very cornerstone of community and society—individual commitment in local places and the people that live there—the foundational principle of democracy (Diken, 2012). Social media in a tourism context could thus be seen as an increasingly exhibitionist and voyeuristic practice (Munar, 2010a), that like a simulation, hides the absence of a background reality, is characterized by the lack of tourist communities, and is a marketing tool that can visualize a mirage, the tourist community. But social media perhaps also become a medium that actively takes part in the creation of the touristic missing community, in that through tourist social media people and places are put on display and exhibited in a way that reminds people of dead things in museums (Kirshenblatt-Gimblett, 1998). In that sense, it represents people smiling at the camera with nothing in common other than being in the same place at the same time, intensively attempting to behave as though there is a tourist community to address in the first place (Munar & Ooi, 2012).

CONCLUSION

It is difficult to outline a traditional research agenda regarding tourism social media from the perspective of strong social constructionism, as outlined in this chapter. Such an agenda would be counterproductive if it, for instance, fell back on habitual categorizations such as different sectors of the tourism industry, different phases of tourist behavior, or other common ontological distinctions. Some guidelines can be spelled out, however. First, habitual and traditional distinctions and categories, such as seeing "technology" as a distinct variable in an analytical model, or seeing technological devices as neatly limited artifacts, have to be truly scrutinized and questioned. While it is not certain that habitual ontological distinctions and imaginations should be rejected, their metaphysical and methodological limitations need to be discussed. Second, conducting exploratory research may not always produce good results, but is something that must nevertheless be encouraged. Instrumental and method-bound research has its long-proven value, as well as its limitations. In order to unfold interesting avenues of research in tourism, social media research has to be more experimental in character, in content, and in form (is it not possible to publish research on tourism social media in tourism social media?). Finally, there is a need to attend to the metaphysics of presence—critique and discuss that which is not immediately present in tourism social media but is nevertheless something that makes a difference or functions as an invisible precondition to it. This means going back to radical empirical approaches (like ethnomethodology) to address the present absence of neglected routines and taken-for-granted performances, as well as radical critical approaches (like the Frankfurt School), all of which are necessary to address the more or less consciously neglected aspects as a result of ideological and political sensitivity. Yes, these may be sensitive guidelines, but they are crucial if the scientific horizon in tourism studies is to be widened.

Chapter 3

Paradoxical Digital Worlds

Ana María Munar
Copenhagen Business School, Denmark

ABSTRACT

This chapter addresses emerging social media cultures and socio-technical practices through the theoretical lens of Theory of Communicative Action. This conceptual scene is used to explain the interplay between social media and tourism. It analyzes the paradoxical role of interactive technologies as forces for the reproduction and transformation of this industry. The chapter discusses processes of colonization of personal relations and life-spaces. The analysis shows the ambivalent potential of tourism social media as communicative technologies for emancipation but also as tools for hierarchization, control, and exploitation. Finally, further theoretical examination of technological development and tourism practices is sought.

Keywords: Lifeworld; Habermas; sociocultural practices; technology adoption

INTRODUCTION

There is an overarching interdependence between tourism and media. Increasingly, the tourism experience is reshaped by desire, imagination, and media as much as by physical travel itself (Crouch, Jackson, & Thompson, 2005; Jamal & Hollinshead, 2001). The emergence of the Web 2.0 and social media affect even more the way tourists plan, experience, and share their travels (Huang et al., 2010; Volo, 2010; Xiang & Gretzel, 2010). The key

Tourism Social Media: Transformations in Identity, Community and Culture
Tourism Social Science Series, Volume 18, 35–53
ISSN: 1571-5043/doi:10.1108/S1571-5043(2013)0000018005

characteristic of the Web 2.0 is that it enhances collaboration and sharing of information online. It is built around social media software, which makes it possible for people to communicate and form communities using their computers (Musser, O'Reilly, & O'Reilly Radar Team, 2007). Some of the most popular types of social media are wikis (Wikipedia), blogs (Travelblog), and microblogs (Twitter), social networks (Facebook), media sharing sites (Flickr, YouTube), review sites (TripAdvisor), and voting sites (Digg) (Stillman & McGrath, 2008; Zarrella, 2010). All these technological platforms allow tourists to create, upload, and publish individual experiences in a variety of digitized forms (Tussyadiah & Fesenmaier, 2009).[f] Social media are new communicative platforms with the potential to transform the way in which individuals share and make sense of their tourism experiences.[s]

Most studies of social media in tourism have examined this phenomenon from the consumer's perspective (Ayeh, Leung, Au, & Law, 2012). A stream of research has provided insights on the impacts of electronic word-of-mouth and user-generated content. Researchers have examined the credibility of blogs compared to traditional word-of-mouth (Mack et al., 2008), the relationship between blogging and positive sentiment toward websites' advertisements (Huang et al., 2010), the impact of social media sites on the Internet and on travel information searches (Xiang & Gretzel, 2010), and the increasing role that electronic word-of-mouth plays in the strategies of traditional marketers (Litvin et al., 2008).

Several contributions have focused on categorizing and examining digitized content, such as online reviews. Studies in this line of research have provided classifications according to types of tourism and its activities (Volo, 2010), typologies of tourists, types of technology adoption, and countries of origin (Enoch & Grossman, 2010; Gretzel, Kang, & Lee, 2008; Wenger, 2008). Bronner and de Hoog (2011) provide a study of motivational factors of tourists' knowledge-sharing behavior on review sites and introduce the term *e-fluential* tourist to describe active online contributors. A similar line of research has focused on a categorization of audiovisual contributions, such as Tussyadiah and Fesenmaier's (2009) study of online shared videos on YouTube. Several articles discuss the impact of new media on tourist decision making (Fotis, Buhalis, & Rossides, 2012; Jacobsen & Munar, 2012). Finally, some research studies have examined the challenges that tourist-generated content presents for destination management organizations and tourism firms (Ayeh et al., 2012; Munar, 2011, 2012; Schmallegger & Carson, 2008).

As can be seen from the research field depicted above, despite a growing body of knowledge, the majority of scholarly contributions are highly heterogeneous and of an exploratory character. Academic work focusing on theoretical or paradigmatic perspectives on tourism social media is unusual. Most of the contributions are related to management and marketing studies. Theoretical frameworks grounded in other social sciences such as sociology, political science, and geography, just to name a few, are seldom applied. Further, in the field of technology and tourism, research deals mostly "with single empirical studies while conceptual papers driving theory development and critique are rare" (Gretzel, 2011, p. 758). The dominance of specific management and marketing approaches in this field results in a partial understanding of the complex phenomenon of online communication and in the hegemony of discourses oriented toward market development, profit, and efficiency. There is a need to strengthen theoretical knowledge in this field and to address questions such as how new media transforms and is transformed by culture and society. This chapter aims to face this theoretic lacuna by adopting Jürgen Habermas' (1984, 1987) theory of communicative action to analyze how social media generate socio-technical practices that change relationships and eventually become constitutive of the everyday life of tourism.

Social media entail a radical transformation in the possibilities of human communication (Baym, 2010) and Habermas' theory of communicative action has been considered a major theoretical contribution to the understanding of the role of communication in human development (Giddens, 1987). Habermas' extensive work ranges from political science to sociology and epistemology and it has been widely applied across diverse disciplines. Although highly influential within European critical social sciences, his contribution is also a polemical one. His critical view on postmodernism especially has been the target of criticism (Delanty, 2005). Habermas' theories analyze the challenge that economic processes represent for democracy and human emancipation. He argues that the evolution of democracy depends on the revival of the public sphere and that communicative practices and media play a crucial role in this revival. Social media is a new dimension of the public sphere and Habermas' theories can help to provide a deeper understanding of this phenomenon.

Habermas' philosophy of social science, mainly his focus on critical knowledge and the emancipatory potential of social analysis, has influenced a stream of tourism research that reflects on knowledge production (Pritchard, Morgan, & Ateljevic, 2011; Tribe, 2006). Nevertheless, a review of academic papers that make reference to Habermas' work in tourism research shows that the use of the theory of communicative action is very limited (Spracklen, 2011; Tribe, 2006, 2009), especially in relation to information and communication technologies (ICT) in tourism. Alford and Clarke (2009) denounce this situation and the shortcomings of the dominance of a (post)positivist theoretical approach in the field of ICT and tourism, and advocate an increased use of critical theoretical perspectives, including Habermas' theoretical contribution.

The aim of this chapter is to use Habermas' theoretical framework to critically approach the technological and sociocultural phenomenon of tourism social media. To this end, the discussion presents Habermas' understanding of media in relation to the development of modern societies and explains how social media impact tourism understandings and relationships. Additionally, it discusses the ambivalent potential of tourism social media as communicative technologies for emancipation but also as technological tools for hierarchization, control, and commercialization. Finally, the chapter calls for further exploration of theoretical paths in the examination of technological development and tourism practices.

PARADOXICAL DYNAMICS OF TOURISM SOCIAL MEDIA

In *The Theory of Communicative Action,* Habermas (1984, 1987) proposes a paradigm for the social sciences based on the "mutual understanding between subjects capable of speech and action" (1987, p. 295). Social relations are developed thanks to people's ability to communicate through language with three main spheres of existence: the objective, subjective, and social worlds. Individuals interact with these worlds through communicative actions, which are processes of interpretation in which cultural knowledge is tested and "at the same time processes of social integration and socialization" (1987, p. 139). Communicative action takes place in a lifeworld, which is taken for granted and which allows individuals to perceive their world as accessible. Communicative rationality is essentially reflective criticism made of argumentations that are always open to revision (Giddens, 1987), and the concept of lifeworld plays a crucial role in the possibility of individuals to reach an understanding through communicative rationality:

> Insofar as speakers and hearers straight forwardly achieve a mutual understanding about something in the world, they move within the horizon of their common lifeworld; this remains in the background of the participants—as an intuitively known, unproblematic and unanalyzable, holistic background [...] The lifeworld forms a horizon and at the

same time offers a store of things taken for granted in the
given culture from which communicative participants draw
consensual interpretative patterns in their efforts of interpretation. The solidarities of groups integrated by values and
the competences of socialized individuals belong, as do
culturally ingrained background assumptions, to the components of the lifeworld. (Habermas, 1987, p. 298)

Communicative action is the medium through which the lifeworld as a
whole is reproduced. The lifeworld carries this task of social and cultural
reproduction through different functions: "the propagation of cultural
traditions, the integration of groups by norms and values, and the
socialization of succeeding generations" (Habermas, 1987, p. 299). Although
the lifeworld represents values and understandings that are taken for granted
by individuals, it is not static. The dynamic change between what is taken for
granted and what is taken up for critical revision happens through the social
mechanism of *a situation*, which is a segment of the lifeworld context of
relevance that is thrown into relief by themes and articulated through goals
and plans of action. Despite the relevance of the lifeworld, its very existence
is increasingly threatened by the evolution of modern social forms that entail
the diminution of communicative rationality and the increase in noncommunicative and instrumental rationality, for example, through the commercialization (market dominance) and the bureaucratization (state and
bureaucratic dominance) of social relationships.

Reproducing and Transforming Tourism through Digitized Worlds

Tourism social media is a constitutive part of the lifeworld of an increasing
number of tourists. Uploading messages on Facebook or photos on media
sharing sites has become a taken-for-granted communicative practice. The
relationship of social media technologies with the lifeworld is, however,
paradoxical. These interactive technologies help to reproduce but also to
transform tourists' lifeworlds, nurturing the dynamics of change indicated
by Habermas (1987). First, these media are channels for sociocultural
reproduction, they perpetuate established practices and attitudes of the
touristic lifeworld. They imitate, in virtual spaces, well-established features
of tourism in modern societies. Moreover, to engage in touristic activities
appears as "one of the defining characteristics of being 'modern'" (Urry,
2002, p. 2). As a central element of modernity and in everyday life

communication, many of the elements that compose the understanding of tourism are not challenged or questioned in online forums. Tourists communicate about their trips implying an understanding of what travel is, what a tourism product is, what it is to be a tourist, etc. Participants draw upon tourism sociocultural activities that have become established as part of the horizon of their modern lifeworld.

Research on virtual communities has identified the sharing of common frames of reference in relation to social norms, interests and goals, and sense of identity (Williams, 2009). For example, Adkins and Grant's (2007) study of an online community of backpackers suggests that participants draw on a common access to and knowledge of mundane backpacking experiences. In these online communities, there is a sense of a common cultural framework based on the everyday touristic backpacker experiences. These tourists share a common horizon of the lifeworld of backpacking that allows them to share consensual interpretative patterns. Tourists' digitized conversations draw upon established cultural tourism traditions and attitudes. The examination of tourist-generated reviews conducted by Munar and Ooi (2012) suggests that participants understand themselves as part of a community of fellow tourists who come together to create, share, and exchange information. Bronner and de Hoog (2011) identified social benefits and concerns related to solidarity, such as sense of belonging, group attachment, or being helpful as important motivation factors of online contributors.

The sharing of photos on media sites, such as Flickr or Facebook, are virtual practices that reproduce traditional tourism activities while demanding new technological competences. Digitized photos and videos have replaced the postcards and photo albums of the past. They keep tourists connected with the world at home and reproduce in virtual spaces traditional communicative practices about travel experiences. Tourists write personal travel stories and impressions and share them in different social media forums, for example, in blogging sites such as Travelblog or IgoUgo, without problematizing "tourism" or "being a tourist" as such. Their views and reviews posted on TripAdvisor are good examples of the taken-for-grantedness of some tourism elements:

> *Needless to say*, the Forbidden City is one of the great historical sites that we have on this planet (Forbidden City, Mr-Maggot; italics added).

> A visit here certainly makes you feel like you can check a box in your "Things to See Before You Die" list (Acropolis, uncvic).

The virtual space of social media reproduces inclusion and exclusion patterns of tourism physical worlds. Despite popular discourses on democratization and participation of social media, not everybody participates and shapes the digital tourism lifeworld. The world of digital technologies, as it also the case with the world of tourism, is only accessible for some. Bauman (1998), in his renowned book on globalization, denounced a global divide between tourists and vagabonds, between individuals with the right to mobility and leisure and those bounded to place. Tourists' social media participation demands the use of skills of complex modern everyday life such as consuming and shifting between media forms, producing, assembling, and deciphering multiple layers of texts and images (Campbell, 2005). Bauman's physical divide is mirrored in a virtual digital divide with the use of the Internet, with access to digital technologies and levels of e-literacy varying greatly throughout the world (Gursoy & Umbreit, 2004; International Telecommunication Union, 2009). The virtual digital divide is creatively presented in the art of Filippo Minelli. His art entitled "Contradictions" (Fig. 1) is a revealing and challenging collection of photos presenting "the gap between the reality we live in and the ephemeral world of technologies" (Pierce, 2008).

The second role of social media is that of transformation of the lifeworld of tourism. Social media communicative potential allows the dynamic

Figure 1. Facebook, Contradictions (Minelli, 2008)

establishment of situations and the problematization of what tourism is and should be. In social media sites, tourists can produce new situations by discussing and sharing novel issues from the "reservoir" of topics of the lifeworld of tourism. When uploading and downloading content about their holidays, tourists choose the elements that they want to transform into a situation, for example, when discussing the value of a natural site, denouncing commercialization tendencies, or sharing personal emotions related to the visit (Volo, 2010). The communicative potential of social media allows the settled lifeworld of tourism to be challenged. Tourists, through their online-created content, raise new questions about the goodness, justice, or value of travel. This entails an increased level of self-awareness about the touristic role (Campbell, 2005). Enoch and Grossman (2010) suggest how tourists' blogging problematizes tourism experiences by focusing on the negative aspects of life in India, disapproving of different cultural views on sexual relations and gender, or criticizing a cultural encounter with the host community. Tourists' reviews posted on websites challenge general views on heritage management traditionally concerned with the uniqueness and the cultural value of the sites. User-generated reviews show that tourists are just as concerned about sensory impressions, imagination, practical issues, and personal comfort in the immediate moment as they are about historical and cultural details (Munar & Ooi, 2012).

The emancipatory potential of social media challenges power relations in tourism. Blogs and their users are seen as powerful new agents in the touristic marketplace, acting as new intermediaries that change the rules of the game and challenge firms and organizations serving this industry (Huang et al., 2010). Increasingly, the diversity of digital images and stories about destinations challenge traditional ways of developing and building brands (Munar, 2010b, 2011). Thanks to this emancipatory potential, some studies portray social media content as wild or potentially dangerous. This literature advocates for improved management and marketing control (O'Connor, 2010; Schmallegger & Carson, 2008). However, controlling social media communication may turn out to be an impossible task. Web technologies provide global reach to the content created and shared by tourists (Qualman, 2009); and contrary to face-to-face social encounters, digital interactions introduce the possibility of anonymity and lack of personal accountability, such as an anonymous review posted on a review site such as TripAdvisor (Streitfeld, 2011).

Despite their emancipatory potential, social media are not neutral communication platforms. The sites have different ways to establish limits to the horizon of interpretation and to what can be introduced as a situation and thus problematized and reflected upon. Social media sites differ in their level of openness and control mechanisms (Baym, 2010). While wikis (like Wikitravel) are an example of open frameworks of communication where software design and structure are part of the discussion among users, other platforms such as social networks or review sites display a much higher level of control by the administrators (Munar, 2010a).

Despite the promises of participation by these media (Sandoval & Fuchs, 2010), social media administrators use interface design and regulations to limit communicative practices and to shape the horizon of communication. For example, on the review site TripAdvisor, tourists discuss openly their opinions on tourism products but are not allowed to question preestablished rating categories and typologies. The terms of use of the social network Facebook also limit the type of communication among users. For example, the site prohibits nudity or drugs consumption in visual content (Pariser, 2011). However, casual sex, binge drinking, drug use, and other prohibited behavior are relevant practices of some tourism experiences (Sönmez et al., 2006; Uriely & Belhassen, 2006). Tourists sharing experiences on social media sites conform to communicative limitations. These technologies incorporate new rules and frameworks limiting what can be represented and discussed. Besides the barriers set up by the administrators of the sites, Internet companies such as Google, Facebook, Yahoo, and Microsoft are increasingly accused of acting as gatekeepers of web content thanks to the use of personalized filters that show the Internet that these companies believe users want to see (Pariser, 2011). These filters provide the type of information that supports users' previously established interests and views, acting as a conservative tool that makes challenging viewpoints different from the users' cultural background more difficult to access.

Commercialization and Colonization of the Lifeworld

Habermas (1987) provides a detailed explanation of the role of mass media in his chapter entitled "The Tasks of Critical Theory." His analysis differentiates between "steering" media and other forms of mass media. Steering media, money, and power do not rely upon communicative practices. Money and power are tools that enhance objectifying (reification) processes and the technicizing of the lifeworld. In systems dominated by steering media, such as the market or the state, persons stop being individuals with a rich and complex lifeworld and are reduced to being members or consumers. Increased commercialization of social media means a diminution of communicative rationality and an expansion of noncommunicative and instrumental rationality. Eventually this development entails the dehumanization of society (Habermas, 1987, p. 308) and takes place when steering media colonizes the lifeworld. The colonization of the lifeworld happens

> to the degree that elements of a private way of life and a cultural-political form of life get split off from the symbolic structures of the lifeworld through the monetary redefinition of goals, relations and services, life-spaces and life-times, and through the bureaucratization of decisions, duties and rights, responsibilities and dependencies. (1987, p. 322)

Steering media and mass media are thus intrinsically different. The latter are generalized forms of communication, which still remain tied to the lifeworld/ communicative contexts and can allow communicative rational practices. But mass media is also different from face-to-face communication or word-of-mouth. Through mass media, communicative actors achieve a release of spatiotemporal specific contexts. These media have two main features. First, by being far removed from space and time, mass media allow access to messages in manifold contexts. Second, these media have an "ambivalent potential" (Habermas, 1987, p. 390); on the one side they establish new hierarchical structures and on the other remove restrictions for communication. The question to be examined is to what extent tourism social media represent a digitized form of mass media, contributing to the expansion of communicative action, and to what extent social media help to colonize the lifeworld by expanding the marketplace and objectifying personal relations and life-spaces.

According to Castells' (2001) analysis of Internet cultures, social media should be understood as an electronic type of mass media, which have two important characteristics. First, they are structured through free and nonhierarchical communication based on the free exchange of ideas (Lash, 2002). Second, they permit self-directed connectivity, which allows any person to connect to the web and publish his/her own information. Self-directed connectivity (Castells, 2001) is a tool for social organization, collective action and meaning, and allows individuals to express their identities and to create and maintain social relations online. However, Castells' arguments provide a partial view of social media development. An analysis of tourism social media shows that these communicative platforms have steering media features, such as customized advertising. Increasingly, there is a commercialization and monetization of the content produced by the tourists, which is transforming online communicative platforms into global virtual marketplaces (Cook, 2008; Dellarocas, 2003; Law, 2006; O'Connor, 2010).

The process toward an increased commercialization of new media, or the expansion of instrumental rationality (Habermas, 1987), has been described as social media exploitation (Andrejevic, 2011). It is characterized by the transformation of social and emotional resources into tradable capital. This process can be seen as that of *separation* in which previously non-tradable areas of the lifeworld (such as personal face-to-face communicative acts about travel experiences) become assets in the process of production. The process entails the colonization of the lifeworld. Thanks to digitization processes, what previously were private social experiences of knowledge sharing are transformed into global databases of consumer information managed and analyzed by tourism firms and organizations (Miller & Christakis, 2011; Munar, 2011). This results in the establishment of new property rights on tourist-created content, which benefits tourism social media firms. Related sites are not only public spaces for dialogue, they are "big business." Social network sites such as Facebook have a communicative dimension but equally a commercial dimension with users constantly being exposed to advertising. YouTube is a media-sharing channel for tourists and organizations alike that is increasingly used to promote destinations (Fesenmaier & Cook, 2009). TripAdvisor provides millions of reviews by users but at the same time is a sales channel and advertising platform for tourism firms.

Commercial sites adopt social media tools to expand the touristic marketplace. Popular sites such as hotels.com or expedia.com combine traditional e-commerce features with user-generated reviews and use these reviews as promotional tools on their sites. These sites' financial results show that social media are not only platforms for the free exchange of ideas and personal empowerment, as argued by Castells (2001), but increasingly, very profitable businesses (Buss & Strauss, 2009). Commercialization tendencies are enhanced by the trend of linking e-commerce channels to social media platforms. Lu, Zhao, and Wang (2010) suggest that increasingly, major virtual communities aim to transform their users into buyers and sellers. For example, consumer-to-consumer e-commerce is already the most successful e-commerce business model in China and Facebook and Twitter are used by airlines as sales channels (Hvass & Munar, 2010). The attention paid by scholars to how tourism marketers can benefit from such platforms (Xiang & Gretzel, 2010) is also an indication of the increasing commercial dimension

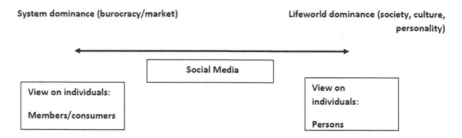

Figure 2. Commercialization and Emancipation of Tourism Social Media

of the media. The structural tension of the double nature of tourism social media is described in Fig. 2.

De-commercialization Tendencies and Emotional Influence

Social media are both an agent of commercialization of everyday practices (such as personal chats on social network sites) and an agent of de-commercialization of activities previously dominated by the market (user-generated travel guides on Wikitravel). Commercialization tendencies cohabit with communicative features that encourage non-monetized relationships and expand the reach of the lifeworld. An example of the expansion of the lifeworld in virtual space is CouchSurfing. This is a virtual community site that provides accommodation services for free and encourages a tourism experience rooted in lifeworld communicative practices, the sharing of personal information, interactivity with the local community, and establishment of a closer relationship between the host and the guest. CouchSurfing is also an example of the paradoxical double nature of social media. From its origins in 2003, its online community had a strong noncommercial identity, but in 2011 the site became a benefit corporation adopting a for-profit corporate model. Despite this change, CouchSurfing exemplifies the de-commoditization of host and guest relationships and how social media can alter taken-for-granted under-standings in this context. Tourism is not about gazing places (Urry, 2002) but an opportunity to participate in "creating a better world" and to "engage with the world in a whole new way" (CouchSurfing, 2011). The homepage of the community invites tourists to move away from traditional knowledge of places, the kind included in guidebooks, and to explore a noncommercial experience, which includes communicative interaction with the host community:

> Look up from that guidebook before you bump into a statue! There are millions of people who want to freely welcome you into their home and show you what it's really like where they live. (CouchSurfing, 2011)

Through a holistic understanding of hospitality, this community also transforms the understanding of the tourist as a consumer. The site announces that "You don't need to cross the sea to practice a second language or pick up a new cooking technique" (CouchSurfing, 2011). Hosting a tourist is hosting a teacher of foreign languages, a possible friend, and a cultural ambassador. Social media platforms rely on the management and sharing of users' influence. According to Habermas (1987), communicative media entail the use of either cognitively specialized influence (through the sharing of knowledge in wikis or blogs) or normatively specialized influence (information about what is good and bad about hospitality services in a review site like TripAdvisor). Social media adopt these two forms of influence of traditional mass media, but additionally they are also based on *emotional influence*. They are "techspressive" (Kozinets, 2008, p. 870) technologies that provide individual realization, mediated pleasure, and escape.

The language of the virtual world includes a new form of grammar that reshapes linguistic and semantic rules enhancing emotional communication. Social media communicative culture mixes new signs with traditional language structures and enriches textual communication with feelings and a sense of immediacy (Baym, 2010, p. 103). Examples of digital communicative practices are the use of the "like" sign introduced by Facebook or the popular "smiley." Tourists use emoticons to signal happiness or disappointment and informal language to share their feelings. They use blogging sites to share their feelings and emotions related to their travel experience (Volo, 2010). Social media sites are digitized databases displaying tourists' emotional narratives. Access to cognitive, specialized, and emotional influence provided freely by tourists has become a successful tradable commodity that is reshaping the touristic marketplace.

Fluid Time–Space Relationships and Transformation of Reference Systems

Communicative situations are related to different spatiotemporal and social reference systems (Habermas, 1987). First, in relation to space, individuals experience a space within their actual reach (a specific location such as a building or a room) and worlds within their potential reach (the city, region, country, continent, etc.). Second, from the perspective of time, it is possible to differentiate between the daily routine, the life history, the epoch, and so forth. Finally, from the perspective of a social dimension, there are diverse reference groups such as the family, the community, the nation, etc. ICT and electronic media represent a change in the spatiotemporal and social dimensions of the horizon of communicative situations. Communication through the web compresses time and space and establishes networks that are simultaneously local and global (Castells, 1996, 1997; Robertson, 1995).

Spatiotemporal Dimensions.   The tourism social media space dimension is not a physical place but a ubiquitous and fluid virtual touristic one. Digitized communicative practices differ from face-to-face communication or communication in traditional media, which have a common public space with historical shared bonds. Digital media expand the worlds under tourists' potential reach and networks of influence become dominated by strangers (T. Smith, 2009). Bauman's (2000) liquid modernity thesis suggests that the transformation of reference groups and the compression of time and space enhanced by ICT augur the end of the era of mutual engagement. Social media represent the diaspora of public space communication. Bauman's negative view on technological development is a form of determinism in which people are seen as passive recipients of a development that damages personal relationships (Baym, 2010). However, social forces influence the development and evolution of technologies (Castells, 2001).

The possibilities of web technologies are reworked and transformed by everyday life practices rooted in the lifeworld. Social media studies indicate that online communities break traditional bonds, and they also provide sociability, support, information, a sense of belonging, and social identity (Wellman, Boase, & Chen, 2002). Social media technologies allow the emergence of new types of reference groups such as virtual communities and online-based social movements (the open source movement) and contribute not only to the boundary breaking of the social worlds but also to the establishment of new solidarities and personal encounters across frontiers. Thanks to its vast reach, the Internet has allowed the emergence of tourism communities of strangers (Adkins & Grant, 2007). While physical communities have traditionally been built on extended kinship and shared culture, virtual communities are framed as a consequence of "intentional social interaction" (Williams, 2009, p. 4).

Social media allow tourists to be socially and emotionally present, although physically absent. This way, tourists interact in a complex landscape of intertwined physical and virtual communities. A tourist can share photos with colleagues, get an update about a friend's activities by text messaging, or ask a question to a virtual travel community, being active in a multitude of spaces from a singular place. Digital media diffuse barriers between the world of the destination and the world at home, and between physical communities and virtual ones. At the same time, tourism takes place through embodiment and physical space (Urry, 2003). The virtuality and nonspatiality of social media technologies provide another dimension to the content shared in the sites that contains reflections and knowledge about the experience and consumption of physical spaces.

The diaspora of communicative space dilutes national frontiers while raising other communicative barriers. Social media is a virtual prolongation of today's consumer society and of the different level of access to global mobility. The openness of the new media stands in contrast to new emergent stratifications based on immigration control and economic inequality and reflects the different privileges of "tourists and vagabonds" (Bauman, 1998, p. 78). Communicative participation in online space demands an intentional act to be part of tourism. However, intentionality and desire are not enough. Participation is highly dependent on material aspects of cultural reproduction, for example, specific technological equipment, and know-how. These demands shape new social divisions based on technology access and ICT skills, increasing the diversity of tourism practices (Gursoy & Umbreit, 2004). The digital divide also has a generational dimension, with younger generations most actively shaping the web (Prensky, 2001; Tapscott, 2009). Further, tourists may share their experiences in their national languages, such as Hebrew or Danish (Enoch & Grossman, 2010), contributing to limited and localized touristic virtual spaces.

Time is also radically transformed by digitization. Social media provide tools for instant communication (like chat forums), but most of the genres of tourism social media, such as reviews, blogs, travel diaries, or audiovisual contributions, do not aim to be synchronous communication. Digitized texts and visual images are stored, recalled, shared, and commented upon (Baym, 2010). Similar to the difference between oral and written communication, the digitization of tourists' narratives and word-of-mouth involves a relative canonization of tourism communicative practices. However, the massive amount of data recorded and the informality of the communication that takes place in social media (Qualman, 2009), provide a canonization of banalities, similar to the recording of daily talk (Munar,

2010a), which is very different from other types of formal, written tourism information sources such as guidebooks and travel reviews in traditional printed media.

Hierarchy, Control, and Reference Groups.   Mass media are characterized by an "ambivalent potential" (Habermas, 1987, p. 390). They establish new hierarchical structures and also remove restrictions for communication. Tourism social media entail major changes in communication channels and hierarchical structures (in the power relations between top-down and center–periphery). This feature results in changes in the way social control is executed. Contrary to face-to-face social encounters, digital interactions introduce the possibility of anonymity and lack of personal accountability, such as an anonymous fake hotel review posted on a site (Streitfeld, 2011). Social media can also be used for increased social control and monitoring (Baym, 2010; Munar, 2010a). For example, the publication of unfavorable, discreet disclosures on the web, including travel tales, can lead to employees getting fired. One example of this is the 13 crew members of Virgin Atlantic who were fired because they criticized passengers and the airline on Facebook (Vassou, 2008). Social media bring new risks that are characterized by being more difficult to manage for individuals and organizations. They are more diffused, multidimensional, and ambiguous. The Web 2.0 has become a new channel for the expansion of the World Risk Society (Beck, 1993). Researchers point to the need for tourism organizations to develop an increased reflexivity about these communicative tools (Xiang & Gretzel, 2010). However, because of the very nature of communication in social media, a systematic enforced repression may also be very difficult to exert.

Habermas suggests (1987) that the one-sideness of media can alter the potential of emancipation in communication networks. Media have different top-down communication patterns and central–peripheral dynamics. In social media, the tourist is the new centrality. These platforms allow a cacophony of voices but in many cases discourses of local communities are just missing (Munar & Ooi, 2012). In review sites or travel blogs, the conversation is one of tourists for tourists. These platforms contribute to a virtual touristification of place based on the view of the visitor. The tourist consumer is the new centrality and the locals are the new periphery of social media communication. Despite the dominance of tourists' discourses in social media, there are also examples of organizations using interactive technologies to tap into the knowledge of local residents. The destination management organization of the city of Copenhagen, Denmark, launched a campaign called "Your Copenhagen" inviting residents to upload stories and images of their city. This is an example of how tourist marketers try to adapt their strategies to electronic word-of-mouth and virtual communities (Litvin et al., 2008) and how knowledge of local residents has the potential to become a tradable resource of tourism organizations thanks to digitization.

Some critical perspectives challenge the community-building dimension of social media and examine the self-promotion tendencies and the lack of solidarity and empathy of web contributors (Williams, 2009). Tourists use social media as a new tool to enhance their ego-tripping experience (M. Smith, 2009, p. 261). Enoch and Grossman (2010), in their study of travel bloggers in India, indicate that "the impression which the reader gets from many of these journals is an absurd one: The Indians are conceived as the ones who prevent the journal writers from fully enjoying India" (p. 529). Virtual communities and networks also provide channels for increasing voyeuristic tendencies (Munar, 2010a) and the reaffirmation of tourists' socioculturally preconceived knowledge of the touristic places (Jackson, 2005). Additionally, social media allow easy and cheap media production but not all contents receive public visibility or influence (Sandoval & Fuchs, 2010).

"When we tell stories, we cannot avoid also saying indirectly how the subjects involved in them are faring, and what fate the collectivity they belong to is experiencing" (Habermas, 1987, p. 137). Social media provide opportunities to enter and establish new collectivities. It entails an expansion of the traditional "we," such as the nation, the workplace, or the family. In social media platforms, the "we" becomes a fluid community of cyberspace users. Here narrativity and storytelling reflect both upon the experiences of subjects involved in activities and on the collectivity of tourists as a whole. Tourism is an activity linked to identity construction and lifestyle (Jafari, 1987; Wang, 2000). Web users shape their identity (at personal and collective levels) also through touristic imagination and activities that are shared as part of presentable digitized stories of their travels. The impact of media expansion has also been noticed by other studies such as Campbell's (2005) "post-tourism" thesis and Haldrup and Larsen's (2010) emphasis on the afterlife of tourism experiences. In a digital age characterized by media proliferation and saturation, tourism is increasingly being imagined and "told" besides being "physically experienced." Social media mediate experiences and provide new layers of meaning and action in tourism.

CONCLUSION

The theory of communicative action helps to reveal the high complexity and the paradoxical nature of tourism social media. These are technological tools that help to shape the evolution of tourism in late modernity. Technological evolution is rooted in sociocultural practices and as such is embedded in a lifeworld of tourism practices. At the same time, technologies have the potential to transform social relations, attitudes, and understandings. The examination of the nature of these media showed that they have an ambivalent potential. Social media platforms help to reproduce under-standings and attitudes about the industry and the tourist that are taken for granted in the lifeworld of tourism practices, but they also have an emancipatory and transformative potential. Communication through participative and interactive digital media establishes new understandings of what tourism should be and transforms power relations and structures in this process.

Habermas suggests that the project of modernity entails the increasing colonization of the lifeworld by steering media such as money and power. However, the analysis of social media technologies shows that the evolution of modern societies is not linear but multidimensional and highly complex. Social media have a revolutionary and transformative potential in relation to the touristic marketplace. Thanks to digitization of knowledge and influence, these technologies commercialize and monetize new areas of tourism that previously belonged to the sphere of the lifeworld, for example, when social network sites use the emotional and social capital of individual tourists as commercial resources. Social media technologies enable the process of separation in which previously non-tradable areas of the tourism lifeworld become assets in the process of capitalist production and the expansion of instrumental rationality. However, paradoxically these very same technologies are also agents of the expansion of the lifeworld, communicative rationality, and the diminution of commercial spheres in tourism. They create new communities of strangers based on communication practices and provide tourism services and experiences outside of the marketplace. The case of CouchSurfing is an example of social media expansion of communicative rationality and the lifeworld.

This chapter challenges Habermas' division between mass media and steering media. The barrier between these two types is today increasingly blurred. Social media are at the same time tools that expand personal freedom and entail new possibilities for control and monitoring. Web technologies mix commercial and communicative practices. They allow tourists to plan different and transformative tourism experiences but also enable organizations to monitor and control individual choices and behavior. The chapter questions discourses that portray social media platforms as neutral and open communicative scenes. The examination of social media sites such as TripAdvisor or Facebook shows that tourists conform to preestablished communicative limitations. These technologies are not democratic public spaces; they incorporate new rules and frameworks limiting what can be represented and discussed. Tourist-generated content increases the diversity of tourism voices and promotes the voice of the tourist consumer as the new centrality of the touristic cyberworld.

Social media have the power to foreground actors in and to redefine and reframe the tourism phenomenon. The virtual space reproduces the unequal opportunities to initiate and participate in communication about tourism that exist in the material world. E-fluential tourists that can digitize their travel experiences have access to economic, sociocultural, and political capital. The interplay of tourism and technology is tied to political systems and economic growth. Positive discourses on the web do not change the fact that individuals are excluded from tourism by visa restrictions, poverty, sociocultural constraints, lack of personal freedom, and increasingly also poor e-literacy and lack of access to ICT. There is an abundance of materiality in the immaterial world of tourism social media. Exclusion and divisions of the material world are reproduced and reshaped in virtual spaces. Finally, as scholars we should increasingly question the purpose of tourism social media research and ask for whom this research is conducted (Tribe, 2006). An examination of the literature shows that technology research in tourism is mainly dominated by positivistic approaches and technical interests (Bronner & de Hoog, 2011; Huang et al., 2010; O'Connor, 2010; Schmallegger & Carson, 2008; Xiang & Gretzel, 2010) and that critical views on the exploitation of online resources and the study of marginalized voices is rare. The academic community needs to adopt new modes of inquiry and theoretical paths to question the complex interplay between tourism and technology development. Increasingly, it becomes critical to address the interests that dominate technological research and embrace critical perspectives to make sense of digital media and their consequences for the future of tourism.

Chapter 4

Symbolic Convergence and Tourism Social Media

Szilvia Gyimóthy
Aalborg University, Denmark

ABSTRACT

The majority of scholarly contributions in tourism social media have focused on assisting practitioners to optimize online platforms or to describe the digital behavior of prospective individual tourists. These studies are dominated by mechanistic ontological frameworks, which take little notice of the inherently social nature of tourism consumption. Acknowledging the sociality of Web 2.0 communications, this chapter explores the potentials of an alternative analytical framework informed by symbolic convergence theory. The linkages between tourism social media, virtual communities, and symbolic convergence processes are illustrated by examples of postings taking place on the Facebook fan site of Roskilde festival. These examples highlight the significance of symbolic communities in shaping the visitor experience against the backdrop of contemporary consumer culture.

Keywords: Virtual communal marketing; symbolic convergence theory

INTRODUCTION

Social media and virtual communities are becoming significant aspects of tourism consumption, and they may fundamentally change the way people select and consume tourism offerings. Social media platforms present novel

Tourism Social Media: Transformations in Identity, Community and Culture
Tourism Social Science Series, Volume 18, 55–71
Copyright © 2013 by Emerald Group Publishing Limited
All rights of reproduction in any form reserved
ISSN: 1571-5043/doi:10.1108/S1571-5043(2013)0000018006

strategic opportunities for marketers, offering unsolicited, user-driven, and more trustworthy ways to construct images of tourism organizations and destinations (Wang et al., 2002). Unlike conventional promotional channels, social media also have the prospect of establishing long-lasting relationships between potential consumers and brands or products. However, as online dialogue and brand ambassadorship has only recently entered the world of strategic communication, marketers must rethink how to address and build alliances with online communities.

To assist practitioners in finding new ways of engaging tourists on social media sites, researchers have mainly offered prescriptive recommendations. These include provision of networking platforms and talking points, involvement of customers in blogs and multimedia promotional tools, enabling of dialogue and customer feedback, and the illusion of exclusivity (Muñiz & Schau, 2007). Scholars have so far focused on finding optimal design solutions tailored to the online search behavior of prospective customers or on simultaneously enabling and regulating consumer sovereignty. Arguably, the preoccupation with a normative agenda in contemporary research practices has resulted in sluggish theoretical development regarding the deeper understanding of social media communications in tourism. Instead of building upon recent contributions conceptualizing digital communications and online communities in general, tourism scholars still adhere to a narrow ontological approach to Web 2.0 communications. The following sections review how two particular schools of communication theory dominate tourism social media studies and subsequently identify flaws in contemporary research practices.

Information Systems Theory

Information systems theory (IST), derived from the classic mathematical models of Shannon and Weaver (1949) and Berlo (1960), conceptualizes communication at the syntactic level, modeling it as a message flow and feedback system between senders, receiver(s), and a mediating channel. These models are helpful in addressing pragmatic problems of how to optimize the transfer of information in a noisy, dynamic system and ultimately assist managers to choose the right channels and instruments for their campaigns to maximize marketing effects. Scholars studying the affective design of social media platforms import the conceptual frameworks of IST, assuming that by grooming various parameters, the "right" interactive setting can be created for customers. In the past few years, a number of practical, how-to-do-it books have been published, offering social media management recipes within and beyond tourism (Mangold & Faulds, 2009; Sigala, Christou, & Gretzel, 2012).

There are a number of problems involved with treating social media communications as analogous to mechanistic systems, where human communication and decision making are thought to follow rational transaction processes. First, it is assumed that social media communications can be manipulated along a Pavlovian scheme: given the right design and choice architecture (or conditional stimulus), individuals will respond in a predictable way. Second, marketing meanings are conceptualized in an essentialist way, maintaining that they are ultimately captured and defined by marketers' messages. However, marketing scholarship is today more inclined toward the tenets of the value cocreation paradigm (Vargo & Lusch, 2004), suggesting that meanings emerge from the collaborative interaction between providers and consumers. The notion of consumers as active coproducers of marketing messages is particularly important for understanding social media communications, where anyone can create, comment, and add to social media content (Brown, Kozinets, & Sherry, 2003; Schau, Muñiz, & Arnould, 2009; Thompson & Sinha, 2008). This implies not only that communications happen in multimodal networks (many-to-many instead of dyads), but also that meanings are altered while passing from one messenger to another (Kozinets, de Valck, Wojnicki, & Wilner, 2010). Furthermore, as Baym (2010) suggests, the patterns and "reach" of social media communications are unpredictable. Hence static models based on the theoretical underpinnings of IST remain ignorant on the dynamics of such creative and transformative processes.

Uncertainty Reduction Theory

Uncertainty reduction theory (Berger & Calabrese, 1975) focuses on the pragmatics of communication: the motives of information sharing rather than explaining the structure of communication flows. With its roots in behavioral psychology, this school of thought posits that communication is a goal-oriented action steered by tension-reducing tactics. Research on travel planning maintains that tourists undertake an extensive information search and attempt to maximize their knowledge in advance in order to reduce risk and uncertainty (Gitelson & Crompton, 1983; Holloway & Robinson, 1995; Wang et al., 2002). Following this thread, the majority of studies on the online tourism domain are preoccupied with the role of social media in the online tourism information search (Xiang & Gretzel, 2010). Virtual tourism communities are regarded as peer-to-peer review tools, allowing members to search for various functional, socio-psychological, and hedonic benefits (Wang & Fesenmaier, 2004). Consequently, the operationalization of online behavior and satisfaction of prospective tourists revolves around the conditions of convenient and effective information search (Chung & Buhalis, 2008b) or the factors influencing trustworthiness of different types of review sites (Dickinger, 2011).

Chung and Buhalis (2008, p. 79) regard social media review sites as "an information source [...] and attractive virtual market place," which can be turned into appropriate channels for targeted messages, if only marketers succeed in developing "an informative and substantial online community." However, none of these scholars deals with the question of how exactly a substantial online community arises or how to design marketer messages suitable for social media platforms. Facebook is full of autocommunicating walls owned by tourism firms and destinations, mostly featuring inform- ative postings from their own employees or project managers, and a few "external" fans. This implies that people's involvement in virtual commu- nities may go well beyond activities of information search and the facili- tation of travel decisions.

Consumer Tribes and Virtual Communities

By focusing on identifying individual needs and behavioral characteristics of social media users, tourism research to date fails to take the *collective nature* of social media into account. Consumers do not exclusively use new digital platforms to exchange information (and hence, reduce decision-related uncertainties) but also to build clusters of social affiliations with like-minded peers across geographic or temporal divides. Marshall McLuhan's prediction of society being retribalized based on computer-mediated, inclusive forms of communication, seems to be coming true (in Kozinets, 1999, p. 253). Today, there exists a variety of forms of e-tribes converging on social networking sites, online gaming worlds, and collaborative knowledge projects. People sharing (sub)cultural traits are today gathering in virtual communities, and the emergence of these "tribes" is often due to brand fandom or other consumption interests (Cova, Kozinets, & Shankar, 2007). Common for these affiliative groups is that their online interactions "are based upon shared enthusiasm for and knowledge of a specific consumption activity or related activities" (Kozinets, 1999, p. 254). As such, consumption-related interests and social interests often intertwine. Kozinets (1999) introduces a typology of online communities based on two differentiating features of interactivity: social structure (loose vs. strong ties), and interaction focus (information exchange vs. socialization). For instance, chat rooms are characterized by weak social ties where the primary reason to participate is to socialize with each other; members of lists or rings are strongly connected, but their interaction is more focused on discussing specific themes. Each e-tribe has its own social hierarchy, ceremonies, and practices, which are shaped by shared behavioral norms and moral standards.

These differentiating features (social structure and interaction focus) define four ideal member types in virtual consumption communities, such as devotees, insiders, tourists, and minglers (Kozinets, 1999, p. 255). Devotees and insiders are assumed to be more involved with the consumption activity than tourists or minglers, and their relatively higher knowledgeability would ensure them higher ranks in the social hierarchy of the tribe. Marketers are eager to find ways to use these individuals as opinion leaders to market messages and to harness the inherent trustworthiness of peer-to-peer communications. This could, for example, entail giving away free samples of newly released consumer goods to bloggers for community reviews. Kozinets et al. (2010) demonstrate that such managed word-of-mouth endorsements are a result of a delicate balance between promotional messages and the bloggers' credibility among community members. In order to conform to the communicative norms of a forum and to remain loyal to their own virtual identity, bloggers adopt various narrative strategies while transforming commercial information to stories that are relevant to their particular peers (Kozinets et al., 2010).

Shifting the view of social media as e-tribalized communication platforms has several implications. First, as Kozinets (1999, p. 261) puts it, online consumers are "more active, participative, resistant, activist, loquacious, social and communitarian than they have previously been thought to be." Second, depending on the type of the digital platform, interaction among community members often has a social, ludic, and symbolic character. Hence, by posting brand meanings or promotional messages in these environments, marketers must anticipate that these will be creatively altered and transformed to serve communal purposes. Arguably, research on tourism social media must acknowledge the sociality of social media and pursue an understanding of the dynamics of tribal communication, which goes beyond implications for managerial action. How does meaning emerge in coproduced group communications? How does the social hierarchy of a virtual community affect which meanings endure and which perish? How do consumers relate to overt and covert promotional messages on social networks?

THE NARRATIVE PARADIGM AND SYMBOLIC CONVERGENCE THEORY

These issues can be addressed by taking an alternative worldview of communication epitomized by narrative paradigm theory (Fischer, 1984). It offers an understanding of the nature and function of communication as a constitutive force in the forming of social groups, communities, and organizations. It sees human beings as social storytellers (*Homo Narrans*), holding that social reality and human experience are ordered and communicated as stories. Building on the narrative paradigm, rhetorical theorist Ernest Bormann developed symbolic convergence theory (SCT), claiming that sharing common fantasies may transform a collection of individuals into a cohesive group. Voiced fantasies are instruments to share common experiences, meaning, and emotions. Telling and sharing fantasies enable sharing of a common symbolic reality and thus hold the key for building group consciousness:

> Shared fantasies provide group members with comprehensible
> forms for explaining their past and thinking about their
> future—a basis for communication and group consciousness.
> (Bormann, 1985, p. 128)

SCT describes the interactive process through which human beings converge by telling individual fantasies, dreams, hopes, or fears in a shared symbol system (Bormann, 1985, p. 188) and offers a stringent analytical framework to capture the dynamic progression of meaning creation in groups. By accounting for the processes and symbolic ground that create and sustain group consciousness, SCT may also contribute to a new understanding of how virtual communities arise and interact on social media sites. This chapter discusses the potential of SCT as a framework to analyze the dynamics of social media communications and the cocreation of virtual consumer tribes on social media platforms. The theoretical challenge is to establish a framework to understand and critically examine unfolding communication patterns on social media that can eventually explain the collective behavior of bloggers, tweeters, and tripadvisors. The discussion below critically reviews the basic assumptions and elements of SCT and its adaptation to different contexts. This is followed by an examination of the implications of SCT in tourism social media and virtual rhetorical communities, illustrated by an example from a music festival's social network site.

The Tenets of Symbolic Convergence Theory

SCT is a general theory, combining socio-psychological and rhetorical (humanistic) traditions in communication studies, which offers a theoretical and analytical framework to study the process of group formation through communication. It views communication as a hybrid structuring tool, which creatively constructs and is being constrained by reality. In the beginning of the 1970s, small group communication researchers (Bales, 1970; Bormann, 1972) discovered that group consciousness arises from a particular sequence of communication acts and is sustained through the communication and collective creation of recurring fantasy themes. To illustrate the symbolic convergence process, Bormann introduced a conceptual vocabulary entailing: dramatizing message, fantasy theme, fantasy type, and rhetorical vision. The method of revealing the relationships between these concepts is termed fantasy theme analysis, and it focuses on direct observation of communication with either ethnographic, discursive, or quantitative (Q-sort, content analysis) approaches. Conducting a fantasy theme analysis is a hierarchical sorting process, sifting dramatic content into larger abstract categories (similar to the clustered coding approach of grounded theory). Dramatic content may be traced, for example, in conversations, mass media debates, customer responses to marketer messages, or virtual forum postings.

A central term in SCT is *fantasy*, which refers to the creative, imaginative, and shared interpretation of real events. Etymologically, it stems from the Greek work *phantaskikos*, originally meaning "to show or to make visible." As Bormann (1985, p. 130) states:

> Rhetorical fantasies may include fictitious scripts but often relate to things that have actually happened to members of the group or that are reported in authentic accounts of history, the news media, oral history or folklore of other groups of communities.

A fantasy chain always starts with a dramatizing message, which is a narratively crafted comment or statement put on display by one individual. When individuals publicly share their own interpretation of an event (fantasy), they often do it by using rhetorical effects. Dramatizing messages may take various figurative linguistic forms, such as inside jokes, cryptic allusions, word plays, anecdotes, allegories, imaginary fables, or legends, which all have the capacity to catch the attention of the listeners (Bormann & Bormann, 1990). Dramatizing messages may stimulate the other members of the group to respond and participate in the story by expanding or enhancing it. When a group of people is caught up in a fantasy, it can develop into an "explosive communication episode" (Bormann, 1983, p. 73), where several people join in to comment. The tempo of the conversation accelerates and similar emotional expressions (happiness, sadness, anger) are displayed. Not only do they appropriate (go along with) the story, but also creatively modify and add to it. The outcome of such a chain reaction is the shared fantasy theme, which will constitute the common symbolic ground to unite the members of the group (Bormann, Knutson, & Musolf, 1997). In other instances, the listeners may respond with apathy and ignorance or reject the dramatizing message by sneering at or ridiculing the messenger. With the sharing of several fantasy themes, common scripts or scenarios emerge. Eventually these develop into broad and consistent views on social reality, pulling together various symbolic elements and fantasy themes into a rhetorical vision (Bormann, 1983). A rhetorical vision could be defined as a grounding symbolic reality that "glues" the community together; the group of people who participates in it is called a rhetorical community. With the structured approach of fantasy theme analysis, one can identify and quantify fantasy themes and types converging into an ultimate (or sometimes several, opposing) rhetorical vision(s). Opposing rhetorical visions demarcate the rhetorical boundaries within communities and may reveal deep roots for cultural conflict.

SCT has been criticized for some explanatory pitfalls (Mohrmann, 1982). First, it does not clarify why people would share fantasies and start dramatizing reality in the first place, apart from referring to the basic assumption of the narrative paradigm (that humans are predisposed toward skilled storytelling). In an attempt to revitalize Bormann's contribution, Olufwote (2006) suggests bolstering SCT with Karl Weick's sensemaking framework: a process of organizing and structuring the unknown by "bracketing cues from a past experience in order to construct meaning out of them" (Weick, 1995, p. 464). When facing uncertainty or crisis, people use retrospective sensemaking to anticipate and enunciate predictable future scenarios. Viewed through Weick's framework, the human predisposition to dramatize reality is essentially a collective sensemaking activity to understand lived experience and ultimately, oneself. Consequently, rhetorical visions may be divided into three master analogues: pragmatic, social, and righteous rhetorical visions (Cragan & Shields, 1981). A pragmatic rhetorical vision is built on rational and utilitarian arguments and practical ways of dealing with problems. Social rhetorical visions are concerned with developing, repairing, or maintaining alliances and relationships among people or social groupings, while righteous rhetorical visions gather elements symbolizing morals and dedication for a higher cause (Bormann, Cragan, & Shields, 1996).

The second theoretical weakness concerns the convergence ideology itself, which assumes egalitarian group dynamics and conflict-free membership in rhetorical communities (Olufwote, 2006). By focusing on the members subscribing to the rhetorical vision, scholars underemphasize diversity and the potential of conflicting opinions. Achieving a cohesive group and common symbolic ground may be paved with disagreement and negotiations. This tenuous and dynamic process is acknowledged in recent contributions, which are reviewed in the next sections.

Applications of Symbolic Convergence Theory

Despite the weaknesses discussed above, SCT has had a significant impact on communication studies and has been adopted in a wide variety of areas, such as organizational communication, intercultural communication, and mass communication (Bormann, Cragan, & Shields, 1994, 2001; Cragan & Shields, 1995). Its popularity may be attributed to its general applicability to a range of communication phenomena on the individual, collective, and socio-historical levels (Olufwote, 2006). For instance, in an organizational communication context, Cragan and Shields (1992) illuminated how a new corporate symbolic reality may be repositioned by creating new and differentiated fantasy themes addressing distinct rhetorical visions of different market segments. Terry (2001) found that fantasy themes of mass-broadcast political campaigns also work effectively to persuade and engage voters. In the intercultural context, Bormann and Itaba (1992) demonstrated the universality of symbolic convergence processes. By comparing North American and Japanese respondents' reception to four different narrative dimensions, they found that people's predisposition toward sharing fantasies and dramatizing messages is similar across cultures. Last, but not least, SCT may provide explanations for understanding the functioning of groups and member commitment to collective causes.

Coalition researchers have recently identified the potential of the symbolic convergence approach in studying the dynamics of group development and the role of rhetorical visions in constituting, reinforcing, or splitting up a symbolic community (Broom & Avanzino, 2010; Olufwote, 2006; Taylor, 2005). Rhetorical visions are deemed crucial for coalition success as they may guide the actions or serve as ideological underpinnings of individual member's action (Foster-Fishman, Berkowitz, Lounsbury, Jacobson, & Allen, 2001).

However, rhetorical visions are seldom conflict-free. Considering Foster-Fishman et al.'s claim that a coherent vision is essential for maintaining a successful coalition, Broom and Avanzino (2010) studied and classified emergent fantasy themes in a nonprofit community coalition. They found two conflicting rhetorical visions serving complementary roles in maintaining group cohesion: one to keep members committed to the group, the other to create symbolic group boundaries and distinguish the coalition ("we") from other communities ("them"). However, contrasting rhetorical visions may also lead to potential group conflict and fragmentation. Demarcations between insiders and outsiders may marginalize certain groups or interests and, in the long term, destabilize symbolic communities. Paradoxically, particular fantasies that contributed to the emergence of a coalition in the first place may, if they become inflexible, run the risk of obstructing the sustainment and renewal of the group.

Bormann et al. (1996) suggest a life cycle analogy to describe how rhetorical visions emerge, grow, decline, and come to an end. They illustrate the rise and fall of rhetorical visions in a five-stage model through a genealogical analysis of the Cold War concept. The emergence of the rhetorical vision (stage one) can always be traced back to a distinct dramatizing event, in this case the Truman Doctrine speech. If several people dedicate themselves to the rhetorical vision, by weaving fantasy themes further and altering their behavior accordingly, the rhetorical vision enters into its second, consciousness-raising phase. In the third, consciousness-sustaining stage, members of the rhetorical community maintain their commitment to the vision either by reiterating or restating key fantasy themes or by defending it against criticism and counter-rhetoric. In this phase, it is important to notice how rhetorical visions adapt to change, as this affects their long-term survival. If the characters, stages, and plotlines are adjusted to new situations, then it is a flexible vision; if it remains static, it would be termed an inflexible vision. Over time, rhetorical visions may lose their explanatory power and decline, or give way to alternative/competitive visions. Eventually, rhetorical visions become too inflexible to explain changes in its community and often end with a rapid implosion.

The cyclical engagement in a fantasy theme has also been studied and confirmed in a tourism-related context. Lanier and Hampton (2008) studied visitor participation in five renaissance festivals in the United States to understand the relationships between the dynamics of fantasy engagement (exposure, learning, acting, modification) and control over the resources of the festival experience. They found that as visitors move through a fantasy cycle (from passively being exposed to it to actively modifying it), their participation in the experience changes. In the fantasy-creating stage, their involvement in the experience is characterized by utilizing resources provided and controlled by the festival producer. In the consciousness-raising stage, visitors enhance their fantasy engagement by codesigning and coproducing stories together with the producers. Finally, consumers may take entire control over the experience, searching for new ways to produce and engage with the rhetorical vision (for instance, by staging medieval reenactment or role-play with other consumers). Consequently, visitor participation differs significantly in each stage and adopts different resources and strategies to enact renaissance fantasies. This approach may also contribute to a more dynamic reading of the archetypal tribal members described by Kozinets (1999). Rather than imposing a structural confinement and seeing devotees, insiders, tourists, and minglers as distinct individuals, one might argue that they could be the same person at various stages of a tribal career (see also the notion of the versatile tourist, Ooi, 2002b).

Symbolic Convergence and Tourism Social Media

SCT offers a framework that may be appropriate for delving deeper into the social dynamics of tourism social media. By exposing communication strings and online polylogues to fantasy theme analysis, the rhetorical vision of a virtual community may be identified. Such an analysis may also give an indication of the group cohesion and reveal symbolic grounds for group conflicts or fragmentation. For an illustration, this section explores a fraction of the symbolic converging practices of an established Scandinavian rock festival in cyberspace.

Popular cultural events and festivals are typical examples of tribal gatherings where sense of community is as important as the featured artists themselves. Marketers have long acknowledged the collective power of the community in creating, appropriating, and sustaining unique meanings connected with a festival brand. However, such tribal enactments have been so far concentrated within the temporal confines of the event. Social media platforms enable the creation of tribal practices and the negotiation of collective identities throughout the year, thereby offering new marketing opportunities to cater to the existential needs of a tribe.

Roskilde Festival is a Danish music festival established in 1971, currently attracting over 130,000 attendees every year. The essence of Roskilde Festival is labeled "Orange Feeling," referring to the iconic Orange Scene (the largest concert venue of the festival), but connotatively pointing at a range of symbolic meanings that embrace ideologies born and cultivated in the 1970s (solidarity, community, rock and roll, liberal attitudes to sex, and boundary-crossing festivities). These (such as the traditional Naked Run competition or the donation of surplus consumables to marginalized groups) are manifested in tribal rituals during the festival as well as frequently mentioned and debated by the online community. Roskilde Festival's Facebook wall offers a particularly rich gateway to study the symbolic convergence of fans, as the virtual community is substantial, both in terms of number of fans (130,000) and average frequency of postings (67/day), with a 32:1 fan/wall owner posting ratio (Larson & Gyimóthy, 2012). For the purposes of this chapter, a fantasy chaining process is illustrated below, revealing contested rhetorical visions.

The distinct communication event started on July 27, 2011 (the day after the festival ended) with the wall owner posting a recurrent post-event question on Facebook: "Do you have a great idea how we can make Roskilde Festival in 2012 even better?" One dramatic response triggered an exalted discussion. Note the accelerated tempo indicated by the time stamps in brackets:

> Better music less crap…. don't be like everyone else and make Roskilde Festival one big cleaning, organic beer, unknown music, come-together mekka. Thx. (19:20 by S)

> It would be nice if the organization behind Roskilde Festival will use 2012 to decide whether it is a music festival a charity event or a Tivoli. Then the audience have a better opportunity to set their expectations from the type of the arrangement they are participating in. (20:03 by PLH)

> Start by playing some damn good music. (20:08 TJS)
> No, we need EVEN worse bands next year. They must be TOTALLY unknown and REALLY crap. Thanks in advance. (20:12 MT)

> David Bowie….please convince him to come to Roskilde. I would gladly pay more for my ticket to hear one of the real legends. (21:17 AT)

The opening response by the "S" launches a chain reaction of dramatizing comments (Bormann, 1983, p. 73), rich in imaginative language, including allegory ("come-together mekka"), slang ("less crap"), double entendre ("we need even worse bands"), and analogy (referring to Tivoli, a historical amusement park in Copenhagen). Some days later, another symbolic explosion takes place chaining further on the same theme and highlighting a clear disagreement in the fan community:

> How about putting the energy produced by dancing festival guests into good use [link to website]. Join the co-creation of Audience Energy! (11:13 Roskilde Festival)

> Use the money on some music instead :-). (12:29 MBR)

> More rock n' roll, less Greenpeace bullshit. I'm sick and tired of all that stuff. It is not rock n' roll. (12:53 FBF)

These excerpts show different fantasy themes emerging, highlighting contested notions about the *raison d'être* of the Festival. The discussion starts with the reiteration and re-enchantment of the inherited rhetorical vision of a solidaristic and sustainable event (by actualizing it through the cues of organic beer, concerns about the future, charity event, putting dance energy to good use), which is directly disapproved of by a cheeky fan. In his view, pro-environmental activities are developed at the expense of the musical program, even though the festival claims that there is no irreconcilable conflict between the two:

> Rock n' roll doesn't mean being reckless with the environment. (13:28 Roskilde Festival)

> That is PRECISELY what it means. But seriously, it could be nice if RF concentrated more on the people who pay 1800 Kr to go to the festival instead of anything else. I just don't like the fact that Roskilde Festival has become a "Greenpeace Festival" and that everywhere you go you see almost religious signs and messages telling you what is right and wrong. The whole is getting on my nerves, because I see it getting more and more every year and the music is getting worse and worse. (13:39 FBF)

In this particular fantasy chain, "Greenpeace" is symbolically reassigned from meaning rebellious environmental activism practiced by a minority group to signifying actual governmental priorities on sustainable development. Hence, the discussion reflects a contemporary debate in Danish society where green is mainstreamed by the political majority. In contrast to egalitarian group dynamics of rhetorical communities suggested by Bormann (1985), the unfolding dialogue on the virtual forum is not devoid of power negotiations. The fantasy chaining process is abruptly closed by an anonymous member of the festival communication team: "Perhaps you should find another festival to go if that's how you feel" (13:54 Roskilde Festival).

By using the corporate signature of Roskilde Festival rather than his/her own profile, this person gave additional weight to an arbitrary comment penalizing a rank-and-file member. Instead of letting the majority decide upon the boundaries of the rhetorical community and legitimate fantasy themes to be discussed, the representative of the wall owner takes the freedom to single-handedly "exclude" FBF. Within a few minutes, another fan is taking sides, approving of the new elitist line of the festival management:

> The last festival newsletter this year talked about that RF isn't for everyone. They want creative people who care and not just drunk, "use and throwaway" people. I like Roskilde as it is and willing to pay almost 2000 DKK to get a festival who cares about the future of the world and the problems we will face. (14:09 DA)

Explicit statements of appropriate and less desired attendee behavior (not being reckless about the environment, not for "use and throwaway") are interpreted as a sign of orthodoxy, underscored by moral and religious metaphors (telling people what is right and wrong, "get-together mekka"). As the rhetorical vision is fixed into black-and-white value statements, the symbolic coalition begins to disintegrate: there are dedicated, fiercely protective fans, telling off others with an alternative vision. Paradoxically, the counter-rhetoric is also justified by a nostalgic interpretation of Roskilde Festival's cultural heritage (legendary rock music with related negative and provocative attitudes). The fissure within the symbolic community becomes articulated through a trade-off between musical quality and charity:

> Lower the donation of money to humanitarian organizations and up the budget for bands this year. The 2011 budget was definitely weighed more on donations than on bands. And personally, I come for the music. (14 July, 17:53 MBR)

However, as argued above, the claimed trade-off between music versus charity or music versus environmentalism points to a deeper issue, which may indicate a mid-life identity crisis for the festival. The values of the 1970s flower-power generation are being mainstreamed by national political agendas and by the Danish middle-class, hence they have become hegemonic symbols of the neatly streamlined welfare state. Paradoxically, although the rock festival community often defines itself as rebellious, refusing to comply with the rules, the symbolic community is crumbling from within when some members get into conflict over the very ideology that grounded the festival in the first place. Furthermore, the example also shows that despite the international appeal of Roskilde Festival and the potentially global reach of social media platforms, the symbolic meaning creation processes taking place on this Facebook wall are mainly embedded in a local (Danish) sociocultural context.

This case also illustrates the links between sensemaking processes taking place in the physical and virtual fan community, which bear important implications for practitioners. Community dynamics (convergence and disagreement on the dominant ideology and endorsed values of a festival) existed long before the emergence of social media. The decline and terminus of the rhetorical vision and the disintegration of a fan community may be one of the likely causes behind the collapse of festivals with a long tradition. However, such tribal disputes have been so far concentrated within the temporal confines of the event. The online platform extends the temporal dimensions of tribal co-enactment, allowing fans to exchange consumption knowledge, and socialize and simultaneously allows festival managers to tap into tribal discussions and take the "temperature" of the community. As demonstrated above, the online communication behavior of Roskilde Festival representatives may contribute critically to the sustainment of the symbolic community, which may not only include facilitation of virtual tribal gatherings, but also mediation in membership conflicts.

CONCLUSION

This chapter introduces a theoretical framework grounded in a narrative paradigm to inform studies of tourism social media. It is argued that SCT is appropriate for analyzing the constitution of online communities, owing to its capacity to explain the symbolic roots of group communication. It posits that collective consciousness emerges through a discursive process imbued by figurative language and fantasy themes. Fantasy themes grow into a rhetorical vision, encompassing the *raison d'être* of the symbolic community. Over time, rhetorical visions may become altered, mutated, and obsolete or challenged by alternative counter-visions, which can ultimately lead to the disintegration of the community.

As illustrated above, a similar pattern of sensemaking can be traced by studying communication patterns of online communities. The dialogue excerpts from Roskilde Festival's Facebook wall show that single postings with a dramatizing content trigger equally dramatizing responses and may weave into a fantasy chain. The emotional outbursts of individual fans point to recurring fantasies and socially shared narrations, implying that interactions are rarely about information exchange or targeted advertising messages. Rather, social media augments non-digital tribal practices and ceremonies and redefines the communicative practices of traditional communication channels. Instead of focusing on building dyadic relationships between the individual fans and the festival brand, marketers may now provide the festival tribe with a virtual *agora* with many degrees of freedom.

This virtual agora is characterized by a fluid structure and random interaction patterns. Most postings are autocommunicative (status) messages that are not responded to by the rest of the community. Particularly active, self-acclaimed devotees or insiders are likely to be considered "village tossers" or being collectively ignored, which questions a virtual hierarchy based on posting frequency alone. The wall owner itself (Roskilde Festival) is often subject to critical comments, which is sometimes responded to, sometimes not. However, representatives of the wall owner may use their position to settle debates and arbitrarily expel members from the rhetorical community. By letting fans appropriate the social media platform for a variety of comments, Roskilde delegates the communicative task of enacting and re-enchanting the Orange Feeling. On Facebook, the rhetorical vision is constantly evolving: it is confirmed, questioned, redefined, or reflected upon. In other words, it is *kept alive* by the tribe.

The fragmentation of tribal communications on Facebook also has implications for the conceptualization of a virtual social hierarchy. In contrast to Kozinets and his colleagues' approach, it is suggested here that the social hierarchy of the symbolic agora is indistinct. Anyone can enter a debate and no member can be considered as central over time. Power structures are ephemeral, emerging, and disappearing in fleeting alliances (for instance, when two or more fans endorse a retort with a "like" sign). Similar to a marketplace, convergences and divergences among members are temporal and do not fundamentally evolve into a solid hierarchy.

By bringing insights from consumer tribes and the narrative paradigm into market communications on tourism social media, a whole new array of research avenues lie ahead. There is a need for more empirical research that does not adopt, but problematizes, challenges, and extends SCT in a social media setting. Communications in a virtual community are significantly different from those of a group meeting face-to-face. It is then plausible that the technological interface may influence the way rhetorical visions arise online. In contrast to Bormann's (1983) fantasy chain model, there is little consistency in the development of fantasy themes into one grand rhetorical vision. Owing to the chaotic and simultaneous character of Web 2.0 communications, sensemaking is partial, rather than hierarchical, and results in multiple collages or snapshots. However, the demarcation between these rhetorical snapshots is not clear-cut, as the contrasted categories are more interdependent than mutually exclusive.

These conditions raise a number of new issues to address. For instance, how do particular characteristics of online communication (simultaneity and lack of co-spatiality) affect coalition patterns in the fan community? How do ideological conflicts and counter-visions emerge and how are they resolved? Is there an asymmetry between posting frequency and tribal positions and how is this addressed by marketers? How and when do "silent" members of the virtual tribe engage in collective meaning creation? These and related questions may contribute with a renewed agenda to tourism social media studies.

Chapter 5

Social Media Sites in Destination Image Formation

Raslinda Mohd Ghazali
Purdue University, USA

Liping Cai
Purdue University, USA

ABSTRACT

Studies about destination image have been discussed extensively in the literature due to its impact on tourist behavior. Despite the significant number of contributions, existing models are outdated in the context of globalization. This chapter synthesizes relevant literature and evaluates the effects of social media on destination image formation. Built on the seminal work by Gartner and that of Tasci and Gartner, the chapter extends the existing understanding with a conceptual model. The construct posits that, with the social media sites as the agent, an overall conative image of a destination can be formed by the overlap of provision and evaluation of cognitive and affective information by and among suppliers, consumers, and third parties.

Keywords: Destination image formation; globalization; social media sites

INTRODUCTION

From a psychological perspective, image refers to the mental representative of meaning, which involves a process of concrete imagery (Paivio, 1969).

Tourism Social Media: Transformations in Identity, Community and Culture
Tourism Social Science Series, Volume 18, 73–86
ISSN: 1571-5043/doi:10.1108/S1571-5043(2013)0000018007

Pictures, as well as words, often arouse the image people develop in their minds. In the field of tourism, literature on destination branding has reached a consensus about the importance of image and its effects on behavior (Echtner & Ritchie, 1991; Gallarza, Saura, & Garcia, 2002; Hunt, 1975; Pearce, 1982; Pike, 2002).

Pike (2002) and Gallarza et al. (2002) have identified specific themes mentioned by various scholars of destination image. Pike (2002) analyzed 142 destination image papers published between 1973 and 2000. Out of 142 papers, only 2 focused on image formation. Gallarza et al. (2002) analyzed 65 works related to theoretical and conceptual approaches to tourism image published in main tourism journals and books between 1971 and 1999. They concluded that, despite many studies conducted in this area, there was no consensus on the process and nature of destination image formation. Their study recognized the work of Gartner (1993) for developing eight image formation agents and that of Baloglu and McCleary (1999) for explaining in detail the static and dynamic natures of destination image formation. These two extensive reviews by Pike (2002) and Gallarza et al. (2002) have served as important sources for the discussion in this chapter, especially in understanding the historical perspective of research in destination image.

Gunn (1972, in Gunn, 1988) pioneered the topic of destination image and initiated the concepts of organic and induced images. The former is formed through tourists' impressions about the destination without physically visiting the location. The impression normally derives from indirect sources not associated with any marketing activities. On the other hand, the latter refers to an image formed through the result of promotional efforts. Advertisements, for instance, are believed to have significant effects on the induced image that tourists have about a particular destination. Gartner synthesized previous studies and proposed that a destination image is "formed by three distinctly different but hierarchically interrelated components: cognitive, affective and conative" (1993, p. 193). In highlighting the importance of understanding the tourist selection process, Baloglu and McCleary (1999) emphasized image as an attitudinal construct that includes cognitive and affective elements. They believed that other than the stimulus factor, destination image is also formed by tourist characteristics or personal factors such as motivation and sociodemographics.

Different types of information sources have varying degrees of effect on cognitive and affective evaluation of a destination, which in turn affects how its image is formed. These information sources also include those brought about by globalization. Munar (2009) suggested that globalization involves two elements: the expansion of the world market and the use of information and telecommunication technology. The latter, for instance, enables people to communicate with other users from many different locations while changing a vast variety of credible information. Therefore, it increases the flow of information beyond national boundaries and cultures and has changed the life of postmodern society in many aspects. This shift in social life has contributed abundant information from non-commercial sources including electronic word-of-mouth about actual visits to destinations. Hence, information that used to be unidirectional from business-to-customer has changed to customer-to-customer. Further, the emergence of the interactive Web (known as Web 2.0) enables rapid information sharing among users. In her study, Munar (2010a) a explained the phenomenon of Web 2.0 and the typologies of these information-sharing platforms. According to her, one of the main elements of Web 2.0 is the online community (social media web sites). These social media web sites consist of the combination of user-generated content with some simple tools and applications. The communities vary in terms of size, member-ship, and activities involved. There are different types of social media web sites, including content-driven sites, media sharing sites, virtual worlds, blogging sites, social bookmarking and voting sites, and social networking sites.

Many studies have revealed how social media sites are making a tremendous change in modern life. The trends are occurring as a result of globalization, where technological advances act as a medium of information exchange worldwide. Information about destinations, for instance, has become abundant and easy to access through many types of social media sites. As a result, consumers are becoming more active in the search for information. Other than receiving information, they also can use the new platform as a supplier of information. Consequently, the image formation process has becomes more complex. While Ahmed (1991) claimed that induced image can be changed through strategic promotion and positioning efforts, its role in image formation is now becoming more uncontrollable, when people acquire many forms of information from other sources that can shape cognitive and affective images of destinations. Despite many studies about the wide usage of social media sites, limited research address their effects on the formation of destination image. In addition, the field of information communication technology itself lacks theoretical support for empirical research (Sheldon, 1997, p. 32). This chapter attempts to synthesize the literature and conceptualize a model that can explain and evaluate the effects of social media sites on destination image formation.

IMAGE FORMATION REVISITED

Following the introduction of the organic and induced image concept by Gunn in 1972 (in Gunn, 1988), Hunt (1975) examined the phenomenon of destination image as a developmental factor. Pearce (1982) conducted an empirical study to determine differences between pre- and post-travel images among British tourists who traveled to Morocco and Greece. In 1988, Gunn discussed the process of image formation, which included the accumulation of mental images about a destination, their modification by more information, a decision to take a trip, travel to the destination, participation in travel activities, return home, and modification of images based on experience. Such understanding of image formation was supported by Chon (1991), who agreed that significant destination image modification occurs as a result of a tourist's visit to the destination. Recognizing the implication of image formation on destination selection process, Gartner (1993) identified three components of destination image formation and originated the typology of eight image formation agents. The three components are cognitive, affective, and conative, while the eight agents are Overt Induced I, Overt Induced II, Covert Induced I, Covert Induced II, Autonomous, Unsolicited Organic, Solicited Organic, and Organic.

Echtner and Ritchie (1991) argued that most of the destination image studies prior to the 1990s were weak in conceptualization and measurement. The definition of image itself is often vague and incomplete due to the complex nature of the construct. Image is often described as "impressions of a place" or "perception of an area." Some studies use other terms to explain image, such as destination attractiveness, awareness, perception, attributes, and quality. Such a wide spectrum of perspectives has led to difficulties in developing a comprehensive definition that covers all aspects of the image construct. As Echtner and Ritchie focused on literature prior to 1990, Tasci and Gartner (2007) extended the literature by investigating the conceptualization and operationalization of the destination image construct since 1990, including the shift in focus as well as other related issues. They discovered that most research defined and measured destination image based on a particular set of aspects, showing that the theoretical basis remains insignificant.

Theoretical Framework

The main idea of Gartner's (1993) work focused on the three interrelated components of destination image: cognitive, affective, and conative. While cognitive concerns the understanding and evaluation of a known product, affective involves motives and feelings an individual has for destination selection. This is often followed by an action component, known as conative. This action typically depends on the images developed during the cognitive stage and the affective evaluation of the destination. Baloglu and McCleary's (1999) empirical study was consistent with and supported Gartner's three-component proposition. In the second phase of Gartner's (1993) framework, he introduced the eight agents that stimulate the three image components, expanded and modified from Gunn's idea of organic and induced image. The key idea of induced image is that most parts of a physical product cannot be changed, but perceptions or images can be manipulated.

The first agent, called "Overt Induced I," is comprised of traditional advertising. Marketers attempt to construct a favorable image in the mind of the targeted audience. The media used for this purpose are highly visual to create emotional appeals. One example of this agent is advertisements on television. Since affective images of a destination could vary across positive and negative dimensions (Baloglu & Brinberg, 1997), positive emotion among potential tourists through advertising is stimulated. The second agent explained by Gartner is "Overt Induced II." This agent involves inter-mediaries such as travel agents and travel wholesalers who act as gatekeepers of information. Their main function is to create attractive images to their clients. They normally select and portray only favorable images, often unrealistic. Beerli and Martin (2004) recognized the important role of travel agents in influencing induced image compared to other secondary sources, such as brochure-related materials. Though, the levels of interaction involved may vary. Brochure-related materials, for instance, only involve a one-way interaction, information transferred from the materials to potential customers. In contrast, the use of travel agents involves a two-way interaction, whereby customers receive information and have the opportunity to raise questions or concerns. Thus, they believe that two-way interaction is more influential than the unilateral.

The third and fourth agents involve the power of an influential person. For "Covert Induced I," destinations create an agreement with a celebrity to attract the attention of potential customers. One example is Australia's strategy to collaborate with a celebrity such as Paul Hogan (Crocodile Dundee) to promote wildlife tourism to the international market. In addition, in early 2011, Tourism Australia chairman made a public announcement about the partnership between Tourism Australia and a well-known American series, The Oprah Winfrey Show, which has the potential to reach audiences in 145 countries. In the agreement, the television program was required to showcase Australia as a world destination in at least two full episodes during the show's 25th season. Other partners that joined the venture were Qantas Airways, Tourism New South Wales, the Sydney Opera House, Tourism Victoria, Tourism Queensland, R.M. Williams, and Network 10 (Tourism Australia, 2011). Despite the enormous cost, Tourism Australia believed that it was worth the investment, considering the reputation of the program among millions of viewers. "Covert Induced II" utilizes the influence of an individual in the public eye, which includes familiarization tours organized for travel writers. In return, travel writers publish their experience in the destination as a way to promote it. In this case, people are not aware that the writers actually are appointed as promoters for the destination.

The first four agents describe the role of induced image in its total formation process. The next four focus on the influence of organic image. The fifth agent, "Autonomous," consists of independently produced reports, documents, movies, and news articles. These sources are believed to have an impact on cognitive and affective evaluation of a destination. The two categories of Gartner are news and culture. In most cases, these agents are independent and usually out of the immediate control of destination marketers. Tasci and Gartner (2007) viewed these independent sources as semi-dynamic and semi-controllable. Although destinations often have very little control over what appears in the news and culture, they believed that the destination marketers have the ability to adjust and modify their marketing activities depending on the information reflected by these sources. A study by Kim and Richardson (2003), for instance, suggested that a movie could be used as an effective tool to change destination images, due to its ability to affect audiences' interest in visiting a place. The sixth agent, "Unsolicited Organic," consists of unrequested information from various external sources. This information can be gathered through daily conversation with other people. Similar to the previous agent, this information is difficult to control. Although it has the potential to influence other people's intention to travel and the decision-making process, the credibility of the informer is important for the retention level. In contrast to the "Unsolicited Organic" agent, where information comes from unrequested sources, the "Solicited Organic" consists of information from knowledgeable sources, considered more reliable as the information normally originates from those who share a common social class or family life-cycle characteristics with the requestor. The last image formation agent discussed by Gartner is "Organic," sharing a similar source with the seventh agent. This type of information is acquired based on personal experience and sources are often credible.

While the framework by Gartner (1993) focused on the supply-side approach, Tasci and Gartner (2007) added demand-side and independent approaches. In the improved model, they emphasized the two ends of information transmission that involve destination (supplier) and perceiver (demand). The study suggested that a holistic concept of image should include three perspectives that deserve attention: the supply-side approach (projected), the demand-side approach (perceived), and the independent approach (autonomous). Despite the additional perspectives in the model, they still focused on unidirectional information transmission, since the marketing strategies are directed at the consumers and the potential to induce a positive image in their minds. The revised model is shown in Fig. 1. Gartner's (1993) framework and Tasci and Gartner's (2007) improved model provide the groundwork to examine the effects of social media sites on destination image formation. This discourse is necessitated by the dynamic nature of destination image formation and the sociotechnological advances of the past decades.

Effects of Globalization and Social Media Sites

Changes in technology have occurred rapidly in the era of globalization and have had effects on social life (Kozinets, 2008). One of the outcomes is the emergence of various types of social media that have grown tremendously for the past 10 years. This new media, known as Web 2.0, allows people to connect with their networks from many places around the world. The connections include text messages, pictures, and videos posted on the sites. People can easily upload photos and share with their friends and relatives through these social media sites. Presently, there are many types of social media sites used by tourists to fulfill their social needs, including Travelocity, TripAdvisor, Facebook, and Twitter.

Munar (2009) posited that the expansion of the world's market as a result of globalization has substantial effects on tourists' perceptions and feelings toward destinations. Previously, most marketers focused on creating a favorable image in the mind of potential tourists. The information tended to be unidirectional, as described by the first four image formation agents in Gartner's original framework. Even at the time the article was written in 1993, he noted that the credibility of the first four image formation agents range from low to medium, compared to the organic image with higher standing. In looking at the current situation, the vast development of social media sites has brought an even greater challenge to the credibility of these agents. The direction of information has changed significantly. The

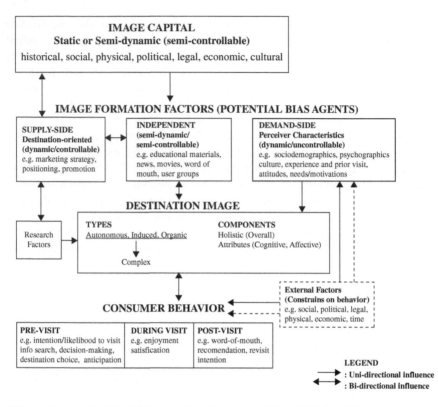

Figure 1. A Model of Destination Image and its Relationships
Source: Tasci and Gartner (2007), reprinted with permission

effectiveness of the four agents that used to stimulate travel is consequently challenged by the information from social media sites. People tend to search for more reliable sources that are not necessarily associated with business. Such is the turning point where the strength of organic image seems to outweigh induced image.

With the development of social media, social network sites appear as one of the typologies of the system, showing a tremendous growth. Twitter, for instance, claimed over 75 million user accounts at the end of 2009 (ePractice Media, 2010). Facebook has more than 500 million active users to date, with the average user having 130 friends. These people spend over 700 billion minutes per month on Facebook and upload about 500 million photos to the site each month (Facebook Press Room, 2011). More than 5 billion pieces of content are included on Web links, news stories, blog posts, notes, photo albums, and much more shared among users each week (ePractice Media, 2010).

The widespread use of social media sites raises issues related to social influence in the global market. Bronner and de Hoog (2011) used the term "e-fluential" to refer to people who post information on a review site. In most cases, peers, as influential groups, tend to affect the attitude and behavior of other individuals (Currie, Wesley, & Sutherland, 2008). The pictures and messages posted on social media sites about past tourism experiences are believed to have influence on destination image and choice. The same study by Currie et al. (2008) revealed the influence of proximal relationships on destination choice. It determined that stories about vacation experiences have a significant influence on peers' travel choice, especially among students. The influences include planning for a trip to the same or to a different destination. Most females stated that they were curious and excited about the stories of the destination. For males, jealousy became a stimulus to travel. The studies by Lam and Hsu (2006) and Currie et al. (2008) strengthened this contention by emphasizing the importance of reference groups in influencing travel behavior intention. Since the users of social media sites often communicate with their existing network regularly, they can be regarded as a reference group by their network. The reference group on the social media sites is an organic source of information that affects the image formation of a destination.

In addition to personal computers, social media sites can be accessed via mobile phone, creating a new culture among youths and adults. According to a study by Murnan (2006), youths between the ages of 18 and 23 reported a high use of mobile phones, followed by adults between the ages of 30 and 40. Furthermore, the use of smartphones continues to rise among these age categories. As current youth become adults, a new pattern of social life will likely be more common (Kwan, 2007). With the increased use of smartphones, many people can now update their status on their social media sites and upload or download pictures from almost anywhere in the world as well as publish them in real time. This trend may have substantial effects on the perceptions or feelings toward destination brands (Munar, 2009).

In studying tourist behavior, Litvin, Crotts, and Hefner (2004) believed that cultural dimensions such as power distance and the dichotomy of individualism and collectivism have a moderating influence on tourists' external search behaviors and travel patterns. This explains the varying communication preferences across cultures. Ishii (2006) presented an example of Japanese people with unique personal relations, who are more likely to avoid direct communication with friends. Instead of face-to-face contact, the Japanese prefer to seek information and communicate with their network using mobile phones. Another study, by Jansen, Zhang, Sobel, and Chowdury (2009) examined microblogging (Twitter) as a form of electronic word-of-mouth for sharing opinions concerning brands and noted that social interpretation is often based on personal and subjective perspectives related to one's background, culture, and other factors. Gursoy and Umbreit (2004) also indicated that culture shapes the delivery and interpretation of verbal and nonverbal messages. Therefore, messages on social media sites may have varying effects on destination image formation among viewers, depending on cultural interpretations. A study by White (2010) investigated how people decode and interpret photos and how these images influence viewers' travel decisions. The study affirmed that the interpretation of meaning is influenced by a reader's sociocultural experiences.

Besides these concerns, another issue that rarely receives attention is how macro social and cultural conditions surrounding technology consumption form into ideologies that influence consumers' thoughts, narratives, and actions regarding social media sites. There are few empirical studies that systematically explore and document how technology ideologies affect interpretation and consumption acts. While electronic word-of-mouth involves consumers sharing attitudes, opinions, or reactions about businesses, products, or services with other people (Jansen et al., 2009), the way consumers express their emotions and satisfaction through social media sites has significant effects on brand awareness and its image among viewers. Doh and Hwang (2009) also found effects from various online messages on attitudes toward products and purchase intentions.

Furthermore, the contents and terms used in a social media site itself are subject to cultural interpretation. For example, Facebook uses the term "friends" to refer to the users' networks. Boyd and Ellison (2008) argued that the term is ambiguous and could be misleading. It could be interpreted as close friends, who always communicate with each other, or as ordinary friends who are in seldom (or never) communication. In addressing this complexity, Facebook has designed categories of friends, such as close friends and acquaintances. Users can group them based on their own interpretation. Since some people in the "friend list" are not necessarily so (they could be siblings, parents, or relatives), users can create other categories for these people. There is also a classification called "restricted friends." The purpose is to limit what people in this category can see without having to "unfriend" them. Based on the previous argument on social influence by Currie et al. (2008) and the influence of sociocultural factors on the interpretation of social media by White (2010), any message or picture posted by an individual could carry different meanings depending on the category of "friends" who posted the message (proximal relationship) and the sociocultural background of the viewer.

Since social media sites are becoming part of daily activities for many people, they affect life in variety of ways. Hedonic elements such as social pleasures and enjoyment may be seen to merely satisfy social needs. However, from the perspective of social psychology, the concept of social influence is relevant as well. According to Hart, Ridley, Taher, Sas, and Dix (2008), curiosity is another element of hedonism in social media sites other than social pleasures and enjoyment. Their study of Facebook has shown that it is common among users to be "nosy" and stalk other friends by checking their status updates, photo albums, applications used, and other aspects of their life. This phenomenon is somewhat related to the concept of "techspressive" by Kozinets (2008). The concept explains how the interaction with technology can lead to technologically mediated pleasure, escape, expression, diversionary, and fleeting. A similar perspective, shared by Munar (2010a), referred to this activity as digital voyeurism. The term explains the pleasures of observing other peoples' private activities without making one's presence known. Consequently, this "nosy" tendency exposes users to different values of individuals. The text messages and pictures people normally post on their personal page represent beliefs and life orientation. This kind of exposure may further lead to social influence as previously discussed by Currie et al. (2008).

Conceptual Model

In an era of networking, many aspects in social life have changed. People are exposed to abundant information in their daily lives, whether they look for the information or the same flows freely to them. In the past, information about destination products reached customers through marketers. However, in this era, almost everyone is able to post destination pictures on social media sites and write reviews about the place, which has an impact on a brand's image and awareness (Jansen et al., 2009). Doh and Hwang (2009) concluded that the direction of electronic word-of-mouth messages (positive or negative) could affect a viewer's response. In the context of globalization, overall technological advance, and social media sites, a conceptual model could be proposed (Fig. 2). This model is built on the framework by Gartner (1993) that focuses on the supply-side of the

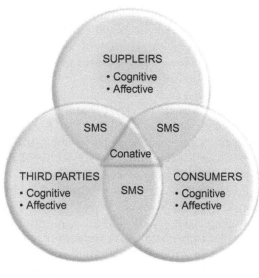

Figure 2. Effects of Social Media Sites on Destination Image Formation

destination image formation and its improved model by Tasci and Gartner (2007), which expanded the model by adding the demand-side and independent approaches.

The conceptual model recognizes the role of social media sites in shaping the three components of destination image: cognitive, affective, and conative. The model posits that social media sites connect suppliers and consumers, suppliers and third parties, and consumers and third parties, and at the same time influence the formation of the three image components through the interaction among suppliers, consumers, and third parties. Suppliers create marketing activities intended to induce positive images to consumers. Gartner (1993) discussed the role of image formation agents in instilling favorable images in consumers' minds. In today's world, an increasing number of suppliers make use of social media sites to convey their messages to consumers. This process involves psychological elements that contain cognitive and affective evaluation of information and reactions by consumers, followed by their actions or inactions, known as conative in Gartner's (1993) term. While destination marketers believe they can control the information provided to consumers, the interpretation of that information is often uncontrollable due to the dynamic nature of consumers and technology. Consumers in the conceptual model exhibit characteristics of both receivers and senders; their interpretation of suppliers' messages and their reactions influence and invoke responses and reactions by suppliers and third parties. Depending on macro social and cultural conditions surrounding technology consumption (Kozinets, 2008), cognitive and affective evaluation of messages on social media sites is now multidirectional, interactive, dynamic, and fluid. It challenges the validity of the first four agents of destination image formation originated by Gartner, and the concept of induced image in general.

Prior to the introduction of the computer network, consumers had very limited access to product information. They were more passive and relied heavily on traditional media such as television and brochures with unidirectional information (Lueg, 2003). As a result, marketers tended to manipulate human cognitive characteristics by creating favorable images, in addition to the consumers' limited organic images that may form false product beliefs in the supply-side approach. Since technology has changed tremendously, the direction of information has started to shift from business-to-consumer and business-to-intermediaries-to-consumer, to consumer-to-consumer. The destination image is increasingly formed by information gathered from consumers' social media and their daily interaction with other members in their social media sites. During such interaction, consumers play dual roles as users and suppliers of information. The borderless world of information has encouraged consumers to become more active in searching for and providing information to others. Thus, the changing role of consumers leads to more uncontrollable information in the market. The effectiveness of traditional advertising in destination image formation is questioned.

Despite the indirect role of third parties, they have a powerful influence on affective and cognitive evaluation of destinations, leading to the formation of organic image. Organic image represents the existing image an individual has about a particular destination based on two important sources: existing knowledge and his/her previous experience at the destination. The former may be derived from daily activities and interactions with other individuals in person or through social media sites. Text messages and pictures posted by third parties on social media sites make new contributions to the organic image of a destination. Considering the ability of peers to influence travel decisions (Currie et al., 2008), this indirect information by third parties either enhances or dilutes the induced image attempted by destination marketers. In the situation where the individual has no intention to travel, the indirect information may not be perceived as intense. However, in another situation, when the individual has a prior intention to travel, the message may entice him or her to pursue further information in enhancing the existing knowledge. One can conclude that third parties via social media sites play important roles in influencing both organic and induced image of a destination, explaining the overlaps between suppliers and third parties and consumers and third parties. The intersection where all three types of active components overlap, which is the conative, represents the action component of a destination image using Gartner's term. It marks the point where the overall image of a destination is formed. Therefore, the conceptual model illustrated in Fig. 2 suggests that mutual exclusivity of organic, induced, and autonomous image is practically nonexistent with the presence of social media sites.

CONCLUSION

The seminal work by Gartner (1993) has been influential in destination image literature. The understanding of how destination image is formed has been advanced by many conceptual and empirical contributions since then, including Tasci and Gartner in 2007. In the context of globalization and advances in information technology, particularly the emergence and popularity of social media sites, this chapter proposes a conceptual model of destination image formation that extends the existing understanding of it. The model consists of three intertwined parts that represent suppliers (destinations), consumers (tourists), and third parties, respectively. The model posits that, with the social media sites as the agent, an overall conative image of a destination is formed by the overlap and intersection of provision and evaluation of cognitive and affective information by and among suppliers, consumers, and third parties. Future studies are warranted to further articulate the conceptual relationships outlined in the model and empirically examine such relationships to advance the study of destination image and to assist the tourism industry in fully utilizing social media sites for image building.

Chapter 6

Sustainability and Tourism Social Media

Adriana Budeanu

Copenhagen Business School, Denmark

ABSTRACT

Sustainable development of tourism depends on the fragile balance between its fast growth and the tendency to "consume" its own life support systems: nature, culture, and communities. Finding equilibrium between the two conflicting aspects requires a shared rule making, which is seldom encountered, especially in tourism-centric approaches. The emergent new technologies, and particularly the evolution of social media, seem to offer a neutral ground that favors open participation and stakeholder dialogue. This chapter explores the employment of social media by individual users of TripAdvisor and by institutional actors (destination organizations) as platforms for initiating stakeholder dialogues that focus on sustainable tourism. The findings show that individual and institutional actors are slow in adopting social media as a means to discuss the sustainability of tourism.

Keywords: Sustainable tourism; social-media; stakeholder dialogue

INTRODUCTION

Tourism has a dualistic nature characterized, on the one hand, by a high resilience and constant growth, and on the other hand, by a short-sighted greed of "consuming" its own support systems: nature, culture, and

Tourism Social Media: Transformations in Identity, Community and Culture
Tourism Social Science Series, Volume 18, 87–103
ISSN: 1571-5043/doi:10.1108/S1571-5043(2013)0000018008

communities (Snepenger, Snepenger, Dalbey, & Wessol, 2007). Both aspects are stimulated by the strong influence of globalization on institutional, organizational, and policy formulation (Hall, 2005). Consequently, the fragile balance required by sustainable tourism development (European Commission, 2003a; Simpson, Gössling, Scott, Hall, & Gladin, 2008) is often at risk from conflicting goals of conservation versus tourism development. In order to cope with challenges or conflict situations caused by scarce resources, tourism governance needs to include shared rule making and agreements among interdependent actors with divergent opinions and goals. In practice, tourism-centric approaches are the dominant paradigms for planning sustainable tourism.

The new social media platforms seem to offer alternative frameworks for negotiation outside of market-based values, based on democratic, open participation that can facilitate consensus regarding sustainable tourism. The arrival of the Internet has connected social, cultural, and economic spheres of tourism, giving a tremendous momentum to its expansion (Buhalis, 2008). The more recent emergence of social media has transformed the individual–organization interaction into an interactive model that combines traditional and web-based media, and consumers are both initiators and receivers of information (Hanna, Rohm, & Crittenden, 2011), enhancing communication to an unprecedented intensity. In essence, the arrival of social media is an evolution back to the roots of the Internet, as it retransformed the World Wide Web into what it was meant to be from the beginning: a platform to facilitate information exchanges among people (Kaplan & Haenlein, 2010). Despite the recognized potential of new technologies to reshape tourism practice (European Commission, 2003b; Novelli, Schmitz, & Spencer, 2006), little is known about how and under what conditions social media are being used in the context of sustainable tourism.

This research represents a first attempt to investigate the extent to which social media are being used in stakeholder dialogues that promote sustainability in tourism. Exploratory in nature, this chapter examines current applications of social media and identifies sustainability-focused dialogues, with the hope of understanding the dynamic of virtual interactions between individual and institutional tourism actors. The investigation examines primarily the types of involvement in tourism planning and raises awareness about sustainability, the conditions and willingness of participations, and whether such interventions can contribute to a sustainable development of tourism.

Using literature accounts, the chapter starts with a look at the polarized involvement of stakeholders in sustainable tourism. This chapter discusses the evolution and characteristics of social media in tourism, as well as a brief account of research explaining some implications of social media for sustainable development in general. Theoretical knowledge is used to filter two streams of data, as explained in the study method, followed by an extensive discussion of the findings. The empirical data are accounts of stakeholder dialogues that have sustainable tourism in focus, as found on the largest tourism public platform, TripAdvisor, and on the web sites affiliated with the top 10 destinations in 2012 (European Consumer Choice, 2012). The answers provided by this research may be insufficient for all questions raised by the use of social media in the context of sustainable tourism; however, the concluding discussion crystallizes a few ideas to stimulate a constructive debate and further research on this topic.

TOURISM, SUSTAINABLE DEVELOPMENT AND SOCIAL MEDIA

Tourism and Sustainable Development

Tourism is growing in symbiosis with the surrounding political, institutional, social, and cultural landscapes (Rotmans & Martens, 2002). Dependent on the good quality of natural and sociocultural assets, tourism has an ambivalent relation with the global culture and economy, which—projected on its future growth—calls for a careful and responsible development of tourism. According to the World Tourism Organization, sustainable means "tourism that meets the needs of present tourists and host regions while protecting and enhancing opportunities for the future" (WTO, 2000). In essence, sustainability is institutionalized as a guiding principle for economic development that does not come at the expense of human and ecological development, crystallized around concepts such as futurity, equity, and holism (Pekkola et al., 2000). In practice, the sustainable development of tourism is the result of a management of resources that fulfills economic, social, and aesthetic needs while maintaining cultural integrity, essential ecological processes, biological diversity, and life support systems (Simpson et al., 2008). Particularly for tourism, sustainable management involves raising efficiency and effectiveness of service provision, through recycling, energy efficiency, the optimization of value creation processes (such as closed loop management), and a redefinition of tourist consumption at levels that create meaningful experiences within the limits of available resources. Addressing environmental, social, and economic aspects of tourism practices, the sustainable development has the ultimate objective to "maintain its viability in an area for an indefinite period of time" (Butler, 1999).

The journey toward a balanced future where humans have an acceptable way of living on Earth, as Giddens (2009) defines sustainability, can be seen as constructed on two diagonal concepts, one emphasizing the involvement of natural, social, and economic capital in the future of humanity (Dyllick & Hockerts, 2002) and a second that outlines intra- and intergenerational differences in ownership of capital (Liu, 2003). As gradient concepts, the two diagonals stretch between positions of abundance and scarcity, inclusion and exclusion, and in between host numerous tensions generated by challenges such as poverty, biodiversity loss, economic and political instability, and corporate greed (Macbeth, 2005). Ideally, solutions to such challenges emerge at the intersections of rational approaches that use regulatory, technical, and management instruments to achieve a balance between the production and consumption of tourism, with ethical app-roaches that call for morality and fairness (Hughes, 1995). In practice, however, tourism-centric approaches dominate, with the needs of the indus-try shaping sustainability goals, while ethical questions remain hidden behind the rhetoric of sustainable tourism (Macbeth, 2005).

Sustainable development of tourism is best reached through democratic governance, where moral, social, and institutional issues can be clarified (Hall, 2011) and the interests of profitability, legitimacy, and sustainability can be reconciled (Treuren & Lane, 2003). However, in tourism-centric approaches, policymaking is highly polarized between dominant powerful players—industry and governmental actors—and stakeholders with (tradi-tionally) weaker economic status, such as locals, tourists, and communities. The marginal involvement of the less powerful stakeholders in policy-making finds justifications in the heterogeneity of knowledge and ability to give input (Liu, 2003), together with a limited responsibility for sustain-able tourism (Budeanu, 2007; Forsyth, 1996). A true democratization of policymaking needs to be accompanied by a decentralization of planning with direct involvement of local communities in decisions about the locations, types, and management of tourism (Hall, 2005) and a relocation of the industry position in decision making (Pekkola et al., 2000). One of the newest developments of information and communication technologies—the emergent social media—seems to provide neutral grounds for interaction outside of market-based contexts where representation and participation are decoupled from the economic status of participants. However, to date, little is known about the opportunities of using such communication platforms for initiating dialogues about sustainable development of tourism and the extent to which they are being used to stimulate the empowerment of locals and tourists.

Tourism Social Media

The social web is an online place where people with mutual interests can share thoughts, opinions, and comments without time or location constraints (Weber, 2009). Better represented as an ecology of new kinds of media (Kietzmann, Hermkens, McCarthy, & Silvestre, 2011), social platforms are structured by the type of relations between users, such as personal interests (e.g., Digg, Photobucket, Flickr, Picasa, YouTube), friendship (MySpace, SixDegrees, Friendster or Facebook), or professional affiliation (LinkedIn). Functioning through the shared input of its users, social media represent one step beyond the one-way communication provided by the Internet. The use of social media has spread like fire fuelled by an insatiable need of people to connect and communicate. From individual users, the platforms were quickly adopted by mass media, manufacturing, and service sectors, and entered the political sphere where public offices are creating eGovernance functions to get closer to citizens and local communities. In a relatively short period of time, the social web, and the social media platforms in particular, have become part of the individual, commercial, and institutional spheres of communication, intensifying and enlarging the spectrum of connectivity to unprecedented levels. The rapid evolution of popular technologies such as Facebook, Twitter, and Flickr shows that the role of social media in shaping contemporary communication is not yet settled (Hagen & Robertson, 2010).

The explosive adoption of social media in tourism is driven by the inspirational value of holidays for content creation, and the intrinsic satisfaction it brings by nourishing individuals' need for "belonging" and "sharing." Enabling the free construction and wide distribution of content (Munar, 2011), social media fall in line with the postmodern interest of tourists in learning and communication (Hughes, 1995) and becomes part of contemporary holiday experiences. The virtual communities created around shared experiences or affinities help build new social interactions through a process of trust and verification (Munar, 2011). Over time, the affirmative power of social interactions leads to a confirmation of identity and empowerment through a status consolidation. In addition, the sharing function of social media erodes institutional monopolies over tourist information by allowing cheap, fast, and relatively equal access for all stakeholders. Wider access to information is leveling the tourism playing field to include actors with lower economic status, and enhances the opportunities for stakeholder dialogue, which may constitute an opportunity to reach democratic agreements on sustainability goals.

Nevertheless, the existence of social media does not immediately lead to its use or necessarily to a successful outcome. The lack of control can easily lead to a frenetic creativity where "anyone armed with a hundred dollar digital camera and a connection to the Internet is a potential Spielberg or Riefenstahl" (Gaines-Ross, 2010). In the absence of a careful balance between policies on sharing and privacy protection, the lack of accountability among users can lead to cyberbullying (Kietzmann et al., 2011) and wide misinterpretation of facts and images. Burdened by numerous green-washing attempts, negotiation of sustainable goals depends on a trusting background and can be vulnerable to manipulation in open dialogues. Without a culture of use, responsible gatekeepers, and protective rules for access, the open social dialogues on virtual communities can be easily discredited. To understand to what extent social media can offer a democratic platform for negotiating sustainability objectives, it is necessary to examine the style and content of stakeholder conversations that take place on social media platforms.

Social Media and Sustainable Development

Enhanced connectivity through social media platforms can have multiple implications for sustainable development, by facilitating numerous approaches to social, environmental, and economic aspects of human activities. Virtual connectivity allows reductions of transportation and energy use, while the production, operation, and maintenance of necessary technology and software applications create new opportunities for investment and employment (OECD, 2007). At the same time, social media opens up possibilities for organizations to prove their responsible presence in the community, adopt transparent policies in relation to their activities, engage local communities, and encourage an informed and aware customer demand. Bilateral dialogues enabled by social media offer possibilities for organizations to operate in a transparent way and create ties with local communities in support of regional development (Rasche, 2010).

As a tool primarily for individuals (Fournier & Avery, 2011), social media are a good channel to encourage a socially and environmentally aware demand (Reisch, 2001; Zapico, Brandt, & Turpeinen, 2010) through sharing of experiences among people and fostering a culture of sufficiency. Besides experiences, debates over values that lead to unsustainable actions may outline societal changes as illustrated by the Occupy Wall Street movement. The multiple formats used on social media enable the transmission of powerful messages about abuses of human rights, trafficking, economic exploitation, and ecological irresponsibility, creating opportunities for emotional responses across geographic and cultural borders. Such support is invoked by nongovernmental organizations that lobby against social or environmental *faux pas* and organizations involved in sustainable development initiatives such as the United Nations Environment Program.

By allowing individuals to have access that is not conditioned by affiliation to bureaucratic organizations (public or private), social media may give a voice to those who previously were less heard in the public space (Reisch, 2001). Furthermore, with sufficient awareness and responsibility, people can exercise their roles as global citizens and realize one of the most important goals of sustainable development—of becoming part of the decision making process and increasing the chances for a fair distribution of resources and responsibilities. While the subject of social media gains momentum in research, there is almost no information about its use and implications for a sustainable development of tourism. Therefore, important questions are still pending: How are social media used to enhance the involvement of locals and tourists in sustainability? What benefits and risks can the use of social media tools bring to governance for sustainable tourism? A possible way of providing answers to these questions is by examining virtual conversations around the topic of sustainable tourism. To capture dialogues initiated by individuals and institutional actors, this chapter examines posts on TripAdvisor, considered the platform with the widest input of user-generated content by tourists, and the web sites affiliated with the top 10 destinations as ranked in European Consumer Choice in 2012 (European Consumer Choice, 2012). The chapter also discusses the study findings to give a better understanding of the usefulness of social media for promoting consensus and sustainability in tourism.

Study Method

Taking a constructivist perspective, the chapter posits technology to be an enabler for the creation of social relations. Particularly, the intent is to map the virtual conversations involving local communities, which were found to be less represented in tourism governance (Hall, 2011), and the organizations that coordinate tourism and secure the well-being of the community.

This exploratory research is concerned particularly with the use of social media tools to enhance the connectivity among tourism stakeholders, under the assumption that this can have consequences for sustainable tourism governance. In the broader sense of stakeholder research, connectivity includes passive provision of information as well as stakeholder dialogues. Therefore, this investigation takes as the building blocks for discussion the virtual presence of individuals (locals or tourists) and public organizations (governmental or destination management organizations) as found on social media platforms and on online interfaces of public tourism authorities. Of all posts, only dialogues with subjects pertaining to sustainable tourism were selected and their content examined together with the eventual response triggered from the audience. The process had two steps. First, it identified the dialogues concerning decision making and planning and then it expanded to include the subjects of awareness and marketing.

The concept of local community is not restricted to the residents of a destination, but it includes both residents and tourists, to capture a large variety of possible interventions. For example, the community in a destination will be very interested in debating the location of a new waste treatment facility, first because nobody wants to have it in their backyard and, second, because the resources necessary for such a development is withdrawn from the total budget of the community and its allocation concerns all citizens. Indirectly the debate is also relevant for tourists, as their waste justifies the development in the first place. Their input is relevant yet very different, and to the best extent possible, it is treated as such in this analysis. However, further examinations into the role of social media for sustainable development would require closer attention to the background differences of various actors providing input.

As research on sustainability and social media is in incipient stages, this discussion follows in the footsteps of traditional web research, using observation and content categorization as the principal method of investigation. For the sake of a constructive simplification, the examination is narrowed to two streams of data. The first one includes the review of online information from public tourism organizations of the top 10 city destinations in 2012, according to European Consumer Choice: Porto, Vienna, Dubrovnik, Prague, Brussels, Berlin, Budapest, Lisbon, Florence, and Edinburgh (European Consumer Choice, 2012). The investigation reviews of the marketing organizations and the national ministries in charge of tourism development, searching for the employment of social media tools in decision making. As data collected was insufficient, a second round of reviews included the local municipalities, looking for information related to sustainable tourism and for the use of social media to involve locals in consultations related to environmental or tourism issues. A total of 33 web sites were reviewed for this study. Due to language barriers, some information was not accessible to the English-speaking researcher, a fact that limits the generalization of results.

A second stream of data comes from the review of individual posts on TripAdvisor, the single biggest social media platform used in tourism planning (Conrad Advertising, 2011). Founded in 2000, at the start of 2012 it had more than 50 million monthly visitors, 20 million members, and over 60 million reviews and opinions (TripAdvisor, 2012a). The open access encourages its frequent utilization by individuals as well as organizations keen on being visible throughout the process of tourism planning. As sustainability is not yet a frequent subject in tourism, the large sample of TripAdvisor users is likely to offer more possibilities for observation. The investigation started with a search using "sustainable tourism" and "sustainability" as criteria. Later the search was enlarged by including "sustainable destination" and "sustainable holidays" as criteria. The posts reviewed here represent the perceptions of tourists about sustainable aspects related to their travel, tourism providers, or authorities. The searches were repeated once a month between February and April 2012, but no major differences were noticed in the number or types of postings. As this chapter has as the main objective mapping out and categorizing social media content in relation to sustainable tourism, no detailed textual analysis was performed on these posts, and the author has selected a few samples to illustrate the discussion.

Sustainability on Tourism Social Media

One argument that promotes social media is its ability to transform communication and expand access to decision making (Kietzmann et al., 2011), and particularly to democratize political communication (Tambini, 1999) by mediating the interaction of civil society with decision makers (destination management organizations, industry, trade associations, etc.). As democratic inclusion of all stakeholders in governance processes is an element of utmost importance for successful sustainable development (Dahlberg, 2001), it is pertinent to claim that by empowering individuals and local communities to become more assertive (Johnston & Tyrrell, 2005), social media create opportunities for the sustainable development of tourism. The claim relies on the assumption that if local communities get involved in policy making debates, they will be in a better position to expect a fair share in the allocation of local resources, benefits, and responsibilities associated to sustainable tourism (Johnston & Tyrrell, 2005). However, it is not clear whether the alleged new roles of individuals are indeed capable of changing institutional processes. In addition, a meaningful input implies that participants have sufficient skills, knowledge, and understanding of the sustainability concepts and conditions required for implementation. In order to investigate the potential capabilities offered by social media, two types of interactions between individuals and tourism organizations are examined.

Inclusion. A review of web sites of the top 10 city tourism destinations in 2012 illustrates that many tourism organizations use social media to augment their traditional roles in tourism planning (ministries and local authorities) and marketing (destination management organizations). Typically, governmental agencies excel at promoting their efforts to mitigate global impacts such as climate change by reducing emissions from accommodation and offering the possibility to offset their air travel using primarily, but not exclusively, Web 1.0 strategies (Zeppel, 2010). The same is evident for the 10 destinations investigated here, with seven municipalities providing information about waste management, green spaces, water and infrastructure management, renewable energy, and environmental permitting procedures, and contributing to raising awareness about the link between the success of tourism and the quality of environmental conditions. Most of the organizations surveyed provide downloadable information for tourists (such as guides, maps) and locals (including permit applications, activity reports), accompanied by e-mail contacts for further clarification. However, specific information about sustainable tourism is rather difficult to find on the web sites of tourism ministries and municipalities and absent from the destination management organizations. Exceptions are the city of Dubrovnik and the German Ministry of Tourism, which acknowledge their commitment to the United Nations World Tourism Organization's Global Code of Ethics and provide links to more information about sustainable tourism.

The use of Web 2.0 technology and social media is not yet common practice among tourism organizations. Only 2 municipalities encourage people to participate in forums debating tourism plans and none of the 10 organizations had any open public consultation. However, considering that public consultations are common practice and often a legal requirement in environmental permitting procedures, their absence from the results of this investigation may be due to the holiday time period when the data was collected (June 2012). The use of media tools (e-mails, online information, forums) makes voting on development plans easier for citizens and cheaper for authorities (Viborg Andersen, Henriksen, Secher, & Medaglia, 2007) and not using these functions is an administrative oversight.

In contrast to the subtle attempts to involve people in tourism policy, marketing strategies of destinations are being visibly reshaped to take full advantage of new media applications. Without exception, all organizations reviewed had links to Facebook and Twitter accounts, and about half of them use blogs and links to accounts on LinkedIn, YouTube, Tuenti, Flickr, or Foursquare. Each type of platform uses different media formats (photo, video, chat), but they are all used in an integrated way, complementing each other and functioning as virtual appetizers for the main marketing web site of the destination. Taking advantage of the high importance that people give to feedback from peers (the third most trusted source after family and friends), destinations stimulate the sharing of testimonials (Conrad Advertising, 2011), and nearly one third of organizations examined include photo, audio, and video testimonies in the marketing materials, with one calling for blogger contributions with personal stories.

Finding interactive opportunities to engage people in tourism provision (planning, delivery, etc.) seems to be a creative challenge for governmental organizations. The one exception found among the 10 examined is the marketing organization of Brussels, Visit Brussels, where user involvement is a central feature of the web site. In addition to the tourism information shared on Facebook, Google +, and Twitter, the upcoming Web 2.0 version of the site "will place greater focus on dialogue with its visitors (surveys, quality questionnaire, Wiki space) and will even allow them to personalize it (photos, direct access pages and favorites)" (Visit Brussels, 2012). The call for contributing with content is direct and optimistic:

> This website is yours. We hope it will convince you to digitise your administrative tasks and will help you to navigate the abundance of services at your disposal. Enjoy your tour of Digital Brussels! (Visit Brussels, 2012)

Although the web site does not explicitly promote sustainable tourism, it has features that reflect ethical concerns: an open access policy through an e-portal available to everyone and a commitment to reduce the digital divide by providing automatic translations and securing access to information for disabled people. At the same time, calls for creative input illustrate how—in the absence of clearly defined rules—the voluntary work of users can be exploited for others' profit (Ritzer & Jurgenson, 2010). Despite its flaws, this example shows how tourists and locals can be included in activities that were, until recently, the subject and responsibility of the state or industry organizations.

As illustrated by the examples reviewed, tourism organizations continue to prefer the one-way communicative function of Web 1.0, and have little use for the interactive functions of dialogue and cocreation. This trend coincides with the industry's attitude, where one in three hotels does not have a social media strategy and one in eight uses it for marketing (Travel Mole, 2012b) Justification may be the desire to minimize the risk from excessive exposure or the absence of necessary skills to use advanced functions of social media (Hanna et al., 2011). Furthermore, the predominance of a one-way supply of information and the narrow opportunities for providing input within prescribed frameworks may indicate a paternalistic attitude of tourism authorities toward individuals, inhibiting their involvement in policy and planning for sustainable development. In the absence of direct involvement of locals in policy and planning, using only one-way communication is likely to perpetuate the gap between public offices and locals.

Intervention.   Outside of institutionalized channels, input from individuals relevant to the sustainable development of tourism is reduced and more difficult to capture. Searches on TripAdvisor show that posts about sustainable tourism are rare and address predominantly tourism products rather than destinations, with no mentions of policy. Frequent subjects are hotels and restaurants labeled as "sustainable," while sustainable transport, tour operators, and attractions are less popular. Opinions about "sustainable destinations" refer to sociocultural aspects encountered during holidays. Voluntary reviews and comments react to claims made via eco-labels, environmental awards, or sustainable policies. Not often encouraging or positive, commentaries validate or contradict industry claims, acting as feedback on quality issues rather than input on decision making.

> This is an interesting little place in the old downtown area. It's a "socially conscious" establishment that serves sustainable seafood. That also means pricey. The lunch menu was simple. The she-crab soup was very good. ... My wife's oysters were very small. ... But we'll try this place again. (Review by RoswellDad on TripAdvisor, 29 September 2010)

This spontaneous feedback indicates that people feel comfortable using concepts related to sustainable development of tourism, contesting industry fears that tourists are disturbed by issues related to "responsibility" or "sustainability" (Forsyth, 1996). Less encouraging is the fact that the majority of TripAdvisor reviews reproduce eco-claims made by tourism organizations, without questioning them, and eventual exchanges of opinions die off after 3–4 messages (on average). This indicates a low inquisitive spirit among tourists and that the topic of sustainable tourism is not enticing enough to sustain critical debates. This result is not surprising considering that previous research suggests that people do not connect abstract subjects, such as sustainable development, to their own tourism, a barrier that also hinders sustainable tourist behaviors (Budeanu, 2007).

Scarce and rather unfocused, individual interventions potentially relevant to sustainable development of tourism can get lost among the multitude of tourism comments. Sometimes they gather sufficient critical mass to make a difference in tourism policy, as shown by a recent Twitter campaign promoting the Maldives in July 2012. This effort backfired with a splash of public protests that revealed the hypocrisy of the campaign, mentioning the social realities of the country, human rights violations, corruption, and social unrest. Touching a nerve with "ordinary citizens," the campaign received harsh replies from around the world, accompanied by disturbing stories and audio-visual material, displaying a reflexive and inquisitive character of online debates that challenges values and initiates shifts in attitudes (Travel Mole, 2012a). In the face of abstract and complex subjects, such as the sustainable development of tourism, individuals may feel overwhelmed and confused regarding the choices and opportunities to intervene, and benefit from the encouragement and guidance of opinion leaders or specialized nongovernmental organizations such as Travel World or Tourism Concern. One example is the Greenpeace campaign against a tourism project in Baja California Sur (Mexico) that received over 200,000 supporters online and led to the insertion of special conditions for environmental protection in the development plans (*Latin American Herald Tribune*, 2012).

The Dynamics of Status and Power. The examination of interactions between institutional and individual tourism actors reveals two situations characterized by distinct power relations. On the one hand, the provision of input is controlled by powerful institutional actors and democratic access is doubtful. On the other hand, the equal status among participants cultivated on social media platforms helps level the conditions for representation in public debates.

On formalized spaces of dialogue (such as web sites of official tourism organizations), institutional entities have the role of gatekeepers: deciding who can participate, setting the rules, the agenda, and specific modes of input (voting, consultation, etc.). Such duties are certainly among the responsibilities of tourism organizations, but their objectivity may be challenged by the temptation to promote specific political goals, even at the expense of the long-term sustainability. Furthermore, the proven possibility to influence online interactions through the design of interactive platforms (Hagen & Robertson, 2010) casts a shadow over the objectivity of official use of social media. As a result, skeptics warn that social media are likely to reinforce existing power structures in destinations instead of balancing them (Peters & Pierre, 2001), offering few chances to intervene and shift the paradigm of tourism operations toward democratic participatory models. The versatile possibilities of social media to facilitate the involvement of individuals or local communities are still in their exploration phase and tourism institutions—destination management organizations, local munici-palities, and tourism ministries—have a great opportunity to restore institutional trust in tourism by taking the facilitator role in an independent process of agenda setting where all partners have equal positions.

Circumventing and contrasting institutional channels of interaction, social media regimes offer open spaces for dialogue where status and participation are not granted according to market values but according to social capital as negotiated with others. Shared values and the degree of "likeability" among users award status on social media platforms, leading to a repositioning of institutions versus individuals on a more equal basis. As a result, individuals become able to exercise new functions as producers of content, coproducers of experiences, or participants in debates of public agendas. Encouraged by users with similar values or concerns, people provide feedback at different (unpredictable sometimes) stages in the tourism planning. At the same time, institutions no longer have dominance over some of their traditional skills of accumulating value—creation, marketing, distribution—as they are now accessible also to individuals through social media. In contrast to the controlled inclusion extended by tourism organizations, users of social media have the opportunity to experiment with their social roles in a virtually equal climate, a fact that gives people sufficient knowledge to challenge the values, policies, and actions of institutional actors (Dahlberg, 2001).

Equal status with institutional actors and the opportunity for free expression on social media platforms empower individuals and reduce organizational power. Specialists say that social media have shifted institutional power to individuals (Dahlberg, 2001). Perhaps it is more accurate to say that social media have created a new type of power, based on sentiments and characterized by high subjectivity. In the true spirit of the expression "no man is an island," relationships spurred by social media are constructed on emotional values and "likeability," while power is acquired from the support of others (friends, family, or unknown people with similar values). In contrast with the pragmatic market values of economic systems, relations based on social power work parallel with market systems and change quickly with the evolution of social media (Hagen & Robertson, 2010). Although not elucidated yet, intersections between the two fields of power become visible in the way market benefits are being extracted from the voluntary work of social media users.

Awareness and Responsibility. The interactive capacity of online tools has institutionalized the right of citizens to communicate directly with their representatives, to ask questions, and provide replies to issues of concern, democratizing political communication (Tambini, 1999). The data collected from TripAdvisor reveal an undeveloped sense of responsibility among tourists who are reacting to industry claims but seem uninterested in other issues than the ones prompted via marketing campaigns. The fact that a large majority of user reviews refer to quality aspects when validating eco-claims, indicates an assimilation of sustainability with quality, a possible result of the translation of abstract concerns into personal concerns. Rather unfocused, individual comments found on social media platforms about sustainable tourism add up to a cloud of fractioned opinions, much in line with other studies on tourist behavior (Budeanu, 2007). While the low demand for sustainable tourism cannot be denied, it is clearly a direct consequence of the scarce promotion of this concept by tourism organizations.

However, a democratic approach in socioecologic management and decision making does not immediately translate into active participation (Stringer, Dougill, Fraser, Hubacek, Prell, & Reed, 2006). A positive contribution by individuals and local communities to the sustainable development of tourism relies on a sufficient understanding of the tourism system and its dynamics, and a critical spirit that enables a constructive debate on the goals and means for consensus (Moscardo, 2008). The data studied for this intervention show that critical approaches are still dormant with regards to sustainable tourism, but some initiatives may wake up the responsible spirit of communities, as shown by the Greenpeace campaign in Mexico. Reflexive capabilities of individuals can be elevated through group learning, which social media foster through communication, dialogue, and sharing experiences (Munar, 2010b). Moreover, reassurance provided through group cohesion can elevate passive possessors of knowledge to an active level of engagement, triggering the citizenship role of individuals.

Using interactive techniques such as workshops, focus groups, or scenario building exercises, tourism organizations can foster social learning and community skills by channeling multidirectional information toward multiple stakeholders and fostering participatory processes (Stringer et al., 2006). The successful collaboration of tourism agencies and local groups on community-relevant projects (Jamal, Hartl, & Lohmer, 2010) can be initiated or intensified through the virtual dialogue between locals and elected governments. This potential is used by a large number of reputable nongovernmental organizations (e.g., Rainforest Alliance), activist groups, and international organizations (International Union for Conservation of Nature, United Nations Environment Program, and World Tourism Organization), which are opening up new discussions about sustainable tourism on Facebook. Their scope is often multifaceted, providing information, encouraging the sharing of experiences and opinions, while also stimulating people to evaluate and distinguish what "good" or "bad" tourism might be. In the long run, such complex engagements have the highest potential of creating a demand for sustainable tourism, which in turn would stimulate and encourage its institutionalization as part of tourism production and consumption.

CONCLUSION

Extensive and diverse, tourism is bound to strive under constant uncertainty. In 2008, tourism was one of the six sectors in "the danger zone" due to regulatory, physical, and reputational risks related to climate change (Cohen, 2010). Resilient governance structures are essential to enable social justice in situations where conflicts over resource distribution occur. However, governance structures for sustainable tourism are challenged by the power imbalance between multinational companies and hierarchic tourism structures, which risk a subordination of sustainability goals to private interests. Emerging communication technologies offer a few possibilities for restoring power imbalances and managing the new relations that have emerged on social media platforms.

Without a doubt, social media have opened up opportunities for participation in tourism decisions by enabling individuals to provide their input to tourism decision making and planning (through inclusion and intervention) and by creating opportunities for new patterns of interactions among individuals, giving them confidence to scrutinize institutional actors and empowering collective action. Despite the vast opportunities to generate dialogue outside of institutional channels, commercial organizations, and authorities are unassertive on social media platforms (Hanna et al., 2011). Partly due to lack of understanding of social media tools, and partly with the hope of maintaining control over the image they portray through traditional marketing, these they remain reluctant or unable to engage effectively with social media. Their limited understanding of the challenges and the need to adapt to the requirements of the newly enlarged mass of listeners gives enormous power to those who "ride the wave of social media." However, at the moment, tourism organizations are more comfortable providing information and less accustomed to managing abundant feedback and the scrutiny of millions.

Although individuals have a dominant presence on social media, their presence may not represent a sufficient input base for a sustainable tourism. Much like their attitude in practice, the virtual interest of individuals in the sustainability of tourism provision or consumption is in its infancy. Although trust is scarce and interactions are cautious, the fragile virtual friendships between tourism organizations and local communities may in the future reshape institutional relations in tourism. While the presence of individuals remains valuable from a democratic perspective, it is the challenge of tourism authorities to identify how to make best use of their input and to design suitable incentives to capture the benevolent support of the crowds for sustainable tourism goals.

To the claim that social media cause a power shift from institutional to individual actors, this research responds with the suggestion that it adds a new regime of social power in tourism. Recommendations provided by industry specialists who monitor the virtual space have an encouraging yet final tone, such as "say goodbye to domination" and "follow the theory of acceptance," suggesting the dramatic changes that are expected in terms of interactions between individuals and organizations. Whether they would translate into a transformation of marketing or create a new business function able to exploit the opportunities offered by the virtual world, including the possibility to enhance individual input to sustainable tourism development, remains to be seen.

PART II

PRACTICES AND EMPIRICAL DIMENSIONS

Chapter 7

Inspiring Design: Social Media from the Beach

Mads Bødker
Copenhagen Business School, Denmark

David Browning
Polytechnic of Namibia, Namibia

ABSTRACT

This chapter outlines opportunities for designing place-based or localized social media services and technologies for tourist settings. Following an exploration of how ephemeral, collaborative social networks emerge, consideration is given to understanding tourist places in terms of networking and socialization. In the field of information technology design, there are many examples of experimental mobile, location-based services that provide informational overplays for tourism sites and generally seem to merely replicate the functions of guidebooks or online information services. However, viewing the performance of tourism through a lens that emphasizes place-making as a social practice could inspire the innovation and design of new mobile social technologies to enrich tourist places and interactions.

Keywords: Tourism; design; place; fieldstudy

INTRODUCTION

There is a growing realization that tourist sites are inherently social (Pearce, 2005). There are places constructed as much from social relations, as from

Tourism Social Media: Transformations in Identity, Community and Culture
Tourism Social Science Series, Volume 18, 107–131
ISSN: 1571-5043/doi:10.1108/S1571-5043(2013)0000018009

the material performances afforded by the destination's topography. This should prompt a turn to the social as an important source of inspiration for the design of technologies and services that enable and stimulate new forms of interaction. Yet, much of the current design of digital technologies and services to support tourism remains centered on the production for and passive consumption of information by tourists. In this chapter a number of design sensibilities are proposed that might inform and inspire the design of innovative *in situ* tourist social media: mobile, social, and locative technologies designed to enhance onsite experiences. The chapter considers how digital technologies designed *for* places might be constructed in a manner sensitive to the social relations and interactions that are so crucial to the performance and experiential context of tourism.

Much contemporary design of mobile digital technologies intended for tourists (such as mobile information systems, mobile guides, or social media applications running on mobile devices) rests on a tacit assumption that tourism practices are predominantly guided sightseeing activities that require timely information procurement to be satisfying and rich (Benckendorff, Moscardo, & Murphy, 2005). Information technology design for tourists typically draws on a particular trope of tourism which supposedly is driven by an urge to "master space," a notion that privileges an organizing (and orderly) gaze (Hollinshead, 1999; Urry, 1990). An alternative view holds that tourism is considerably more complex and diverse than sightseeing or similar canonical practices (Selstad, 2007). The argument pursued in this chapter is that such reconceptualizations of the domain can be fruitfully employed in tourist technology design efforts. In his seminal work on design thinking, Buchanan (1992) describes placements as the repositioning of a design problem, shifting the underlying hypothesis about the nature of the problem a design solves. Since practical design interventions typically adhere to a (conscious or unconscious) set of ideas about the nature and category of the problems to be solved and the solution to be provided, such a reframing of the problem space can fuel innovation efforts. Here it is argued that, rather than accepting the tourist-as-*sightseer*, the tourist-as-*networker* and *place-maker* can be valuable labels for informing design work that focuses on social and location-based mobile tourist technologies.

The point of departure for arguments advanced in this chapter is that place making is central to being a tourist. Together tourists themselves *create* places through numerous and varied pretravel and onsite activities. Acknowledgment of this notion of performativity leads to a rejection of perceptions of tourist locations as strategically manufactured, static "sites" implicit in typical designs for mobile and location-based technologies.

Instead, tourist places should be seen as the product of the tourists' performances, performances that are replete with dialogical meaning making, appropriation, and transformational interactions. Further, while the furniture of a place works to afford certain performances—as do previous experiences, place-images, the assumptions that tourists carry with them from home, and perhaps a particular sociability that is part and parcel of being removed from one's mundane location, to say nothing of later reflections—tourist places are inherently ambiguous and open ended (Craik, 1997). Their situated construction, as experiential loci or sensibilities, might thus be considered foundational when designing for tourist socialities through technology.

Empirical work to support such designerly sensibilities should aim to elicit the diversity and richness in tourists' interaction with, and participation in, local material, social, and cultural topologies by being attendant to the indexical, contextual, social, and ultimately place-based nature of tourist performances (McCarthy, Wright, Wallace, & Dearden, 2006). Drawing on participant observations on Magnetic Island (North Queensland, Australia), this chapter supports a very literal network "placement" to inform future design of innovative, digital mobile, social, and location-based tourist technologies. Analysis of such observations provides a vehicle for read-dressing and reimagining tourists as networkers and thus offers a basis for using what (some) tourists do to influence design. Specifically, a tourist–tourist encounter at a beach, viewed through the lens of a networking placement, is used as a springboard to formulate five sensibilities that might shape an appropriate design space.

The empirical research carried out was framed as design ethnography (Salvador, Bell, & Anderson, 1999), aimed at inspiring and informing design work and methodology within the area of tourism social media innovation. Egocentric point of view (egoPOV) video data was collected using a form of visual ethnography (Bødker & Browning, 2012; Browning, Benckendorff, & Bidwell, 2009). The video was recorded on small cameras attached to participating tourists' hats. This was enhanced by "accompanied tourism," a variant on "accompanied shopping" traditionally used in retail experience ethnographies (Healy, Beverland, Oppewal, & Sands, 2007). From a methodological perspective, the egoPOV video and analysis method is discussed in relation to the conceptual and technology design-oriented work. The method employed shows how collection and analysis of the egoPOV data produces artifacts that can be used to shape the design of social and locative information technologies in keeping with the networker model.

SOCIAL MEDIA FROM THE BEACH

The Internet, the World Wide Web, and the current offspring of the many social media platforms that support cross-geographical collaboration and virtual communities (Rheingold, 1993) have been seen as technologies that facilitate new and hitherto unattainable kinds of community. Similarly, the increasing access to ubiquitous mobile devices (Weiser, 1991), such as smartphones (Barkhuus & Polichar, 2010), tablets, and location-specific networking services (Lane, 2003), have the potential to change the ways in which people interact with local topologies and resources. These new possibilities seem to urge researchers, designers, and practitioners to ask how, why, when, and where tourists might make use of opportunities to interact locally, using mobile social media platforms, in addition to their interactions with friends and family that tend to be distributed over geographical distance. A further relevant question is what effect this would have for the practices in and experiences of place (Dourish, Anderson, & Nafus, 2007; Wellman & Haythornthwaite, 2002).

A prominent notion in the social media discourse is that the Internet is increasingly becoming a "platform for participation" as opposed to a static presentation space for so-called "brochure-ware," static web sites that, so the canonical story goes, feature little more than logos, corporate information, and images. Research on social media technologies has focused extensively on participation in the form of user- or customer-generated content and the patent change in power relations between producers and consumers (Cook, 2008). Scholars such as Tapscott and Williams (2007) have popu-larized the idea of social media as facilitating new models for business in which user participation features as a driver for economic exploitation. Some proponents of social media and tourism research (Wang & Fesenmaier, 2004) emphasize participation through social media as a community-building feature of large travel community memberships (Wang & Fesenmaier, 2004), typically involving people who are widely geographically distributed. Another strand of research discusses the consequences of genre-typical social media for tourists in the form of travel-related web sites such as hotels.com, tripadvisor.com, and various travel blogs. Hotels.com and tripadvisor.com in particular facilitate "crowdsourcing" of user-generated recommendations to help decision making around what to do, where to stay, and what to see. Travel blogs facilitate peer sharing of experiences, as well as connectivity and trust-based virtual communities around destinations (Yoo & Gretzel, 2008), fundamentally changing consumer access to, and engagement with, information about sites and services.

One of the particular and frequently stated values of social media is the opportunity to aggregate and make available past visitors' and locals' insights about destinations (Bronner & de Hoog, 2011; Volo, 2010). Thus, tourists looking for suggestions to aid their decisions on travel are presented not only with the idiosyncratic beliefs of a single stranger or an organization wanting to promote its interests, but also aggregate data collected from a large number of reviewers. Arsal, Woosnam, Baldwin, and Backman's (2010) discussion of the perceived usefulness of such aggregated contributions provides an informative example of this research strand. Their study found that travel blogs and traveler online communities are highly influential resources for the pretrip stages of travel planning (and to some degree for maintenance of connections and community). Their research on how residents' knowledge of a destination is used by tourists focuses almost exclusively on residents and locals as information sources for tourists in the pretrip planning phase.

There is a tendency in commercially available mobile social media apps and services to give relatively high priority to features that are place-related and, in various ways, sensitive to geographical location. Place-related social media are seen as digital platforms for collaboration and participation explicitly concerned with consumers being colocated rather than being geographically dispersed. Along with the increasing accessibility of high-bandwidth mobile data infrastructures, a range of smartphone apps that support smaller community-based and localized knowledge sharing have emerged. In 2011, alongside high-profile location-based media platforms (such as Facebook Places, Gowalla, and Foursquare), mobile applications (LOCQL, Localmind.com, Yahoo!Local, Google Places, and Aloqa) are some of the contestants involved in providing knowledge relevant to geographical locations, often those with considerable opportunities for social interaction, and making it useful and searchable on a mobile platform when users or customers are on location.

Although the technological potential and social incentives seem clear, the commercial interest in location-based social media, however, has yet to demonstrate a comprehensive engagement with tourism as a complex and multifaceted concept. Such an understanding is vital to understand how to respond technologically to tourist locations becoming increasingly eligible for local, here-and-now interactions through the increasing mobilization of computers and data infrastructures. Both this type of research and the commercial application of it have many interesting opportunities to involve tourists and locals alike in the provision of content. This extension can and should be grounded in more direct access to the experience of the practice of tourism, if its potential is to be more deeply explored.

Though this chapter draws on the sociotechnical sensibilities essential to the general understanding of social media, a type of technological media that can enhance and extend collaborative efforts, it is further suggested that the social in tourism can be usefully understood as small-scale, intimate interactions. It is accepted that increasingly mobile media devices provide a plausible medium for facilitating and extending such interactions. To this end, issues of network size, critical mass, and other firmly established interest areas within social media, such as the tendency to focus on the centrifugal powers of social media, are excluded in the current study. Further, mainstream lines of inquiry inspired by Tapscott and Williams' (2007) suggestion of social software as "platforms for participation" and their ability to foster radically different business opportunities that also signify larger cultural and economic shifts (2007, p. 183) are not considered in the present chapter.

In contrast to research based on social media as user- or customer-aggregated information sources, this chapter draws on a study of fine-grained aspects of participation as it takes place within the local social context of a typical tourist location, a beach, with a view to eliciting interpretations of social interactions that might inspire designs of place-related social media. It shows how appropriate technological responses to the new mobility of digital tools and the ubiquity of data infrastructures can be based on engaging with tourists and their activities in place, taking inspiration from a profoundly situated understanding of human social behavior to inspire the design of IT.

Design Sensibilities

One of the original aims of introducing ethnographic practices into information technology research was to make findings from the domain of the practice to be engaged with available for technical interventions. This has often consigned much ethnographic work in design to requirements gathering, a tool for prescribing "what should be done" in terms of designing for the domain in question or for providing a simple bridge across the gap between social worlds and technical worlds. This instrumental view of ethnography in design has been criticized by Dourish (2006), who argues that the analytical commitment in ethnographic work is lost when the sole output is simple implications for technical work, since this entails an insistence on solving discrete, observable sociotechnical problems rather than more broadly understanding how actors participate in a particular system of practice and what new perspectives and new ways of thinking might be helpful in understanding the practice under scrutiny.

The fine-grained engagement with tourists covered in this chapter affords the grounding of sensibilities in the interaction under study (McCarthy, Wright, & Dearden, 2006), with a view to using such grounded sensibilities to support or inspire the design of social and experiential aspects of tourist technologies. So what is meant by design sensibilities and how are sensibilities related to design? Design sensibilities should be understood as tools that

> underpin an empathic design process...[stressing] sensual and emotional aspects of the relationship between designer, user, and artifact. Sensibilities are embodied in people as ways of knowing, seeing, and acting. They are not external representations or rules to follow blindly. (Wright & McCarthy, 2008, p. 10)

For this case study, the sensibilities are grounded in what Button calls "scenic field work" (2000), fieldwork that is descriptive rather than analytic of the domain under scrutiny, but derive from a particular theoretic position and a reflexive engagement with the process of walking within a "touristic" world, what it means to be a tourist, and what is at stake in the form of touristic sociality performed in the case.

In this sense, design sensibilities are not presented as "implications for design," at least not in the sense that they are traditionally reported in corporate ethnographies or in the academic research on human–computer interaction (Dourish, 2006). Nor are they "principles or guidelines for designing enchanting experiences (Sengers, Boehner, Mateas, & Gay, 2008), [since such] traditional approaches seem too formulaic and too removed from the particulars of felt life" (Wright, Wallace, & McCarthy, 2008, p. 10). In focusing on design sensibilities, according to the latter study, the emphasis is on a particular perspective of design practice which argues that successful designs (from practical, social, political, or cultural perspectives) hinge on empathy. Empathy, in this case, is meant to connote the ability of a designer to transcend one's personal experience to engage in the other as an object of concern. In other words, empathy is a specific kind of knowledge of and care for "the other," who, in Information technology design, is most often referred to as the user. Design sensibility, as the term suggests, aims to sensitize designers toward experiential qualities that might underpin an emergent design space. Rather than outlining scenic findings, artifacts yielded that can be used to open up a design space to intuitive, empathetic, and creative processes.

The practical approach outlined in this chapter is two tiered. First, since the argument that inspiring design for social technologies in tourist places requires sensibilities acquired through exploration and interpretation of tourist social interaction, a case of a tourist–tourist encounter is used to exemplify the networking and place making performed in and through a tourist place. However, environments such as those engendered by tourist networking and place making are fragile, itinerant, and dynamic and thus pose numerous practical and methodological challenges. In order to provoke the desired design sensibilities, designers of social media technologies (that facilitate and enrich tourist socialities and place making) require a set of low-impact and actionable methods to understand when, where, and how often very mobile tourists interact by using social networking in order to support their particular needs, wishes, and sensibilities. The second tier suggests and outlines a method of gathering data to support design in tourist environments in which mobile social media are typically used.

Mobile and Location-Based Media for Tourists

Often explored within proof-of-concept frameworks, research has focused on validation and evaluation of mobile information systems prototypes for different kinds of tourism (Park, Nam, & Shi, 2006). Inspired by the seminal Cyberguide project (Abowd et al., 1997) and the GUIDE project (Davies, Mitchell, & Cheverst, 1998), a project that utilized mobile computers in a variety of settings to design localized and context-sensitive information systems functioning as guides or visitor resources, several projects have focused on mobile information systems and guides for tourism. The mobiDENK project (Krosche, Baldzer, & Boll, 2004) shows how historical monuments, an archetypical feature of a tourist site, can be embedded with smartphone-accessible information, thus enriching the informational environment of a site. Technology acceptance research, assessment of end-user acceptability, and the adoption potential of digital technologies for tourists are also strongly represented in the tourism technology literature (Evjemo, Akselsen, & Schürmann, 2007; Schmidt-Belz, Laamanen, Poslad, & Zipf, 2003). Benkendorff et al. have researched tourist attitudes to the inclusion of digital technologies in the tourist experience itself to suggest drivers and moderators of technology acceptance (2005, 2006).

The work of Brown and Chalmers (2003), Tussyadiah and Fesenmaier (2008), and Axup, Viller, MacColl, and Cooper (2006) constitute three notable exceptions to the predominant focus on information and guide technologies, purely technical issues, and technology acceptance challenges in a tourism context. Brown and Chalmers use an ethnographic study to draw out implications for designing mobile technologies for tourists. Tussyadiah and Fesenmaier use "netnography" to analyze and understand spatial patterns of the tourist experience. Both studies emphasize the need to approach tourism as a practice that takes place in the interaction with a particular setting. Brown and Chalmers focus on the improvised and collaborative problem solving in which tourists typically engage when at a destination, typically problems associated with planning and navigating while onsite. Tussyadiah and Fesenmaier examine what they tentatively call the "tourist experience." Both studies emphasize how tourist experiences and practices are mediated or brokered by mobile technologies, and point toward implications for design. In a somewhat similar fashion, Axup et al. propose low fidelity prototyping interventions to explore social practices among backpacker tourists. Focusing particularly on mobile devices, Axup et al. investigate how ubiquitous computing service prototypes that offer matchmaking and information sharing for tourists can reveal the problem-space of tourist socializing practices to ultimately inform design.

Excluding such different approaches mentioned above, location-sensitive and location-dependent technologies in tourism are often designed around an incomplete notion of the tourist as a knowledge-deprived actor who needs timely and relevant provision of information to make order and sense of her or his surroundings (Bødker & Browning, 2012). Tourists are cast as informational detectives, using mobile technology to stitch together a meaningful story about a location. As an alternative to this, it is proposed that, in the age of ubiquitous and mobile computing technologies capable of facilitating co-localized collaboration and community, supporting a wider set of design objectives grounded in tourist performances, in the very experience of being a tourist, would be refreshing, stimulating, and valuable.

The EgoPOV Method

As Scarles notes, visual methods in tourism studies can be a "potential route to accessing the embodied, sensual and emotional experiences of tourists' encounters with place" (Scarles, 2010, p. 1). Sharing the pace and rhythm of walking with tourists, creates a space for a certain closeness and bonding not attainable by typical (usually sedentary) interviews with participants (Lee & Ingold, 2006; Pink, 2009). For this research project, a series of field studies to explore tourists' interaction with local topologies, including the social environment, were conducted. The field studies provided inputs for a design ethnography intended to widen the design space for place-based and social technologies. EgoPOV (egocentric point of view) videos (collected from hat-mounted cameras) for gathering data and accompanying tourists on their walks were used to generate rich and relevant contextual data on the performance of tourism. The collection of data and the subsequent grounded theory-based analysis process is treated as a technological site of interaction in and of itself. Generating inspirational artifacts becomes a process of repeated interactions with the recordings and field notes collected onsite (Browning, Bidwell, Hardy, & Standley, 2008). This process yields artifacts grounded in the original activity, which can then be used to shape a design space. Compared to simplistic notions of the tourist-as-flâneur or tourist-as-sightseer, this method of shaping better aligns the design space with the notion of tourist-as-networker and tourist-as-place-maker.

The strength of the egoPOV approach lies in the way it provides a relatively unobtrusive means of capturing situations, interactions, and orientations. Mounted on the underside of the peak of a cap, the unobtrusive and lightweight camera quickly disappears from view, being absorbed into the garment, and does not hinder head movement or interactions. EgoPOV video is relatively undirected compared to other video methods. The researcher can accompany the tourist and does not have to aim a camera at the participants. By being grounded in the shared process of walking, the method also serves to produce useful artifacts for contextualizing and understanding the sensory and embodied environment of the participants (Browning et al., 2008).

An example of this involvement in the sensory world of the participants can be seen in a case where one of the authors is walking along the beach with Christiane and Paula, a young Danish and German tourist couple, on Magnetic Island. They are walking with their feet in the shallow water, Christiane wearing the hat with the camera on this hot, calm, and intensely sunny day. The participant researcher is conducting a think aloud and, as the respondents are quiet, feels the need to prompt the participants:

> Researcher: Ah, …could you talk a little about, about what you are thinking about?
>
> Christiane: Yes, we…I actually don't think that much right now (Laughs). Just enjoying.
>
> Researcher: So, when you are thinking something…
>
> Christiane: …yes…(walks, looking down at her feet in the water)

[9 seconds elapse]

Christiane: Again, I think it is strange why there isn't [sic] any people on the beach here, when they have these summerhouses…

This example shows how Christiane's immediate embodied interaction with her surroundings, her feet in the shallow water and the hot sand (which she later mentions) is disturbed by the researcher's prompt for "thoughts" or some representation of what she is experiencing. Quite a substantial interval elapses after the researcher's prompt, and her response seems somewhat unnatural and strained. Researchers are taught to probe, to ask, to interview, and to engage with quiet respondents to create rapport. However, here, at the beach, at this precise moment, Christiane is simply too immersed, fascinated with her own activity, caught up in the pleasure of simply moving her feet through the water, feeling, enjoying. Reviewing egoPOV sequences facilitates seeing and recalling such moments. It allows the researcher to notice how the participant's attention is engaged, to see that while she strolls down the beach, Christiane's attention is fixed on her feet, walking in a slow, contemplative, and peaceful pace without saying a word. Such interactions with an environment can be very hard to appreciate from, for example, interview data alone, and even from third-person (researcher) video recorded accompanied trips, as the actual posture, kinesthesia and head orientation can be difficult to capture (Browning et al., 2008). Thus, egoPOV lends itself to furnishing an ethnographic intervention with a richer and more embodied and sensory perspective that supports the kinds of sensory ethnographies (Pink, 2009) crucial for understanding and representing experiences.

Magnetic Island. Tourist participants were recruited at a local hostel on Magnetic Island with the cooperation of its operator, who conferred with the researchers before recruitment decisions were made. Magnetic Island is a 52-km^2 island, 20 minutes by boat from the city of Townsville. The main attractions on the island include the semisecluded swimming beaches and some water sports activities (kayaking, sailing, jet skiing), historical shipwrecks that ring the island, World War II remnants, and koalas and other wildlife to spot on the numerous island walks. The participants, who were either friends/cotravelers or couples, were given a free night's stay at the lodge and access to a 4 × 4 vehicle as an incentive. They had the freedom to choose to visit one or more locations that invited some interaction or pleasurable traversing (e.g., beaches, forest areas, villages) during an approximately 4–5 hour trip. The researcher, who accompanied the tourists, engaged in casual conversation to create and retain rapport as well as to facilitate "thinking aloud" while moving around in the landscape. During the visit, one of the tourist participants wore a small camera mounted on the hat, while the researcher carried a standard handheld video camera and an audio recorder.

"Coconut" Beach.   On this occasion, a young French couple in their mid-20s (Guy and Isa) and the researcher traveled by 4 × 4 vehicle down a winding gravel road toward one of Magnetic Island's southern beaches. The researcher struggled with a notepad, an audio recorder, and a small video camera in the back seat of the car as the young French chauffeur parked in an overgrown parking lot. After getting out of the car, the car key-fob camera was mounted on Guy's hat. Guy's English is something of a parody: the "h" is not pronounced, so that the oft-talked-about weather in North Queensland was described as "ot," as in, "It was 'ot yesterday." (In the following conversations, some francophone mannerisms are maintained, but edited so as to be readable.) The group walked down a narrow, overgrown path toward the beach, semienclosed by cliffs, while conversing. The foreshore has mixed vegetation, prominently featuring tall, swept coconut palms. Fig. 1 shows the beach area and the surroundings of what came to be called "Coconut Beach."

Upon arrival at the beach, Guy first noticed a van. They quickly notice another couple, possibly also tourists, whom they identify as the owners of the van, and begin fantasizing about life on the beach. He promptly stated, "Oh, I am jealous," and a little later, " [h]ow did they get the van [h]ere?" Guy and Isa were clearly attracted to the idea of the "traveler-style" van. They commented on the beauty of the place, noting the water and the bounding rocks that make the place look like something out of a tourism brochure. Fig. 2 shows the foreshore and the typical access way to the beach. An abandoned metal chair also prompted several comments that related to a fantasy of living or making a temporary home on the beach. Guy for instance, said, looking at the chair, "You see the chair? You sit, take your coffee…no one 'ere'."

Guy and Isa soon began to pay attention to the van owners' efforts trying to catch a coconut with string and a piece of wood. The head-mounted camera showed Guy looking back toward the other couple several times. Isa unsuccessfully tried climbing a smaller palm tree, approximately

Figure 1. The Florence Bay Area on Magnetic Island (© 2011 Google/Tele Atlas)

Figure 2. First View of the Beach and the Other Tourists.

30 meters from the other couple, while Guy threw a stick to get a coconut from the same tree. At some point, he overthrew the stick and just missed hitting the van. The other couple (referred to by the researchers as Bob and Alice, who appear to be an Australian couple in their late 20s) promptly moved the car 10 meters back from Guy and Isa's tree. Guy moved gradually closer to the other couple, while looking up toward the coconuts they wanted to harvest. The other couple had clearly noticed Guy and Isa now, and they laughed a bit at their own efforts to get the coconut from the tree. Guy then went back to the other tree, and tried more vigorously to dislodge a coconut. He then again returned to the area occupied by the other couple who had now progressed in their effort. Referring to the coconut, Bob said:

> "S' coming."
>
> Guy: "Ah, it's very hard."
>
> Bob: "Yeah, it's strong."
>
> A coconut falls from the tree.
>
> Isa: "Yay!"
>
> Bob, (smiling, shrugs): "Only took two hours but…"
>
> Guy and Isa laugh, Guy: "Two hours for one coconut…"
>
> Bob: "Yeah, it's more energy than you get from it."
>
> Isa: "And… you drink it, after?"
>
> Bob: "Yeah, it tastes alright."
>
> Guy: "It's good?"
>
> Bob: "Not good enough for the work, but…" [Shrugs]
>
> Now Alice, Bob's partner, takes a knife from the van and starts stabbing at the end of the coconut. She walks towards Isa and Guy.
>
> Guy: "It's not too 'ard to open the coconut."
>
> Alice walks towards Guy and Isa and places the coconut on the ground, picks it up and continues to knife it.
>
> Isa: "You want some help, maybe Guy can try."
>
> Alice: "Yeah, you can give it a try if you want…"

Figure 3. Success!

Fig. 3, Bob shows the result of the struggle to Guy and Isa—a freshly caught coconut.

The couples took turns trying to pry open the coconut, and after a few futile attempts, the conversation turned toward accommodation. Isa asked whether they stayed on the beach (in the van), but, as it happened, both couples stayed at the same hostel. As Bob and Alice prepared to depart, Guy said:

> Guy: Oh, maybe we come back tomorrow [looks up at the palm tree], we have to think of a new technique, to get the coconut... [Bob and Alice laugh] ...ok, [Guy turns], maybe see you tomorrow.
>
> Alice: Yeah, maybe
>
> Guy: In the same place...
>
> Alice: Have a good afternoon
>
> Guy: Enjoy! [Laughter]

Guy and Isa decided to leave and started to walk away from the beach. Guy explains how "these are the best moments." As they walked, they talked about how great it is that suddenly, on a secluded beach, you could find yourself engaged in a kind of meaningless situation:

> Isa: What did you do today, "Oh, we tried to take a coconut"...(laughs) but it is good to say that, you know...

> Guy: I think, if we come here with some picnic, we can try *all* the day to take one coconut.

The whole sequence at the beach lasted approximately 16 minutes.

Study Analysis

The Coconut Beach instance was chosen as it provided numerous design sensibilities, some of which are reported here. The particular success of this encounter, in terms of the yield of inspirational insights, is perhaps due to the particularly good rapport developed with the participants, that led to engaging and rich interactions between both the researcher and the participants and the between the participants and the other couple on the beach. Although the sequence could be seen as being initiated by the researcher's presence and a possible tacit expectation of having something extraordinary happen during the walk on the beach, the interaction in and of itself does not seem "unusual" or strange in a tourist setting. Even when encumbered with the trappings of a research agenda, tourists go about their business of being tourists, of making place, and connecting with various sociomaterial networks.

Strathern (1996) notes that the network is "an apt image for describing the way one can link or enumerate disparate entities without making assumptions about level or hierarchy" (Strathern quoted in Burrell, 2009, p. 189). Through the lens of the network, the aim of the analysis was to identify and describe how disparate entities are enrolled into the performance on the beach. The interaction took place in a relatively bounded space (a beach and the foreshore). It is, of course, acknowledged that tourist networks extend way beyond the immediate experience and activity. However, since the objective here is to inspire designs of mobile and locative social media, providing an account of the immediate network of interaction, as a property that reflectively structures and shapes interactions, is useful. It is this interaction that plays a considerable role in Coconut Beach's evolution into a place.

The Coconut Beach case has some similarity with White and White's (2008) description of tourist–tourist social interactions at a campground in the Australian outback. Both entailed "the possibility of sociability that was bounded, transitory, nonintimate, brief, and focused on functional issues, rather than engendering relationships requiring maintenance and nurturing" (White & White, 2008, p. 46). At Coconut Beach, the place making is not performed around a pre-given unit (a family, a group of friends, a group of fellow travelers) but around a transitory "chance encounter" and the incidental collaboration among strangers.

Similar to Bærenholdt, Haldrup, Larsen, and Urry's (2004) observations of tourists temporarily taming the beachside to make it inhabitable and pleasurable, it is noticeable how Coconut Beach is transformed from its beginnings as a natural, attractive sight to a site of collaboration and performance through a transient network. Guy/Isa and Bob/Alice transformed the beach and foreshore from what is described in tourism brochures as a "natural" space into a performed place, where the social performance, afforded by the furniture of the space, gave rise to a new perspective. Coconut Beach promptly became a social place, a temporary small world wherein the tourists interacted. The coconut palm trees become physical nodes around which collaboration was carried out and fantasies of playfulness invoked. The palm trees were additively transformed from being part of the furniture of the location to practical challenges that required work to overcome. They became temporary *boundary objects* (Star & Griesemer, 1989) that provided flexible bridging between the two groups, allowing them to perform a short-lived, small-world network in the pursuit of their touristic and hedonic interests. Most of the activities during the actual encounter were carried out with references to the palm or the coconut, from which the couples derive a multitude of different meanings. From the beginning of the encounter, as Guy and Isa begin imitating Bob and Alice's activity, to the final sequence where they cheer and lend a helping hand in opening the coconut, the setting worked as a catalyst for the collaborative activities. This process can be described as a process of domesticating the beach, the practice of making a location one's own place despite the fact that most tourist places are public and easily accessible (Bærenholdt et al., 2004).

Larsen (2008) quotes Ingold to say that, "Just as the landscape is an array of related features so—by analogy—the taskscape is an array of related activities" (Ingold, 2010, p. 195). Larsen continues,

> Taskscape highlights how tourists enact corporally and multi-sensually, routinely and creatively with landscapes. They step into the "landscape picture," and engage bodily, sensuously,

and expressively with their materiality and "affordances."
And throughout this engagement they *build* landscapes and
things, such as sandcastles. (Larsen, 2008, p. 28)

At Coconut Beach, the *i situ* network enabled the change from the beach as
a "beautiful vista" to a playful, collaborative activity, as evidenced by the
frequent comments during the interaction. The couples built and shared in a
fantasy of leisure and agreed on a particular engagement in place,
fundamentally unconcerned and free from the involuntary itineraries of the
everyday. This is highlighted in Bob's comment that the effort of getting the
coconut from the tree was not really worth it, suggesting that the interaction
was not to be taken too seriously. In interacting with the landscape and each
other as part of it, the couples where engaged in a sociality founded on their
voluntarily entering into a collaborative form of play.

In this setting, the interaction was performed with a particular touristic
sensibility, the two parties constantly and jokingly referring to the fact that,
for all practical purposes, the work they were doing was irrational and
meaningless, devoid of any rational, practical purpose and quite different
from their everyday lives. The assumption built up seemed to be that the
activity was a form of play that occurred only within the boundaries of the
beach and lacked any sort of plan or assumption of an end goal as would
typically be required by collaborative work. This was supported by Guy's
reference to the van and to the chair as they came to represent situations of
being somehow isolated from the real, everyday world. Yet this interaction is
never monolithic but always interspersed, albeit occasionally, by more
ordinary tasks. Guy's statement, "I think, if we come here with some picnic,
we can try *all* the day to take one coconut," indicated that the research
itinerary he was committed to, and the fact that time was limited, put some
constraints on the activities. This was further demonstrated when, after the
encounter, Guy and Isa were asked whether they are hungry. They not only
nodded in unison, but Guy mentioned that they had completely forgotten
about that. The participants and the researcher visited Horseshoe Bay to get
some food. The bodily and mundane fact of hunger had intersected with the
more playful activities.

Little verbal accounting seemed to occur during the encounter and no
formal introductions were ever made between the tourists and the couple on
the beach. Rather than spoken language, body orientation and movement
become the primary devices for acquiring and maintaining contact. Guy and
Isa seemed to gain initial recognition from Bob and Alice by imitating the
"coconut catchers" at a distance, the latter couple laughing and cheering as

they came closer, so as to acknowledge the first couple's presence. Goffman (1967) in his essays on face work and interaction rituals argues that social interchange entails keeping up *face*, that is, a situationally constructed and embodied appearance of self that must be maintained. *Face* rests on social and interactional conventions, and actors in a social interchange work to maintain both their own integrity of *face* as well as the integrity of the others *face*. Bob and Alice's acknowledgement by way of body and verbal interjections such as "whoa" or "yay" as Guy and Isa come closer intimate an openness to extending the social interaction and eventually lead to Guy and Isa being included in their activity. That this is done carefully and nonverbally, rather than by explicit invitation suggests work, was performed to avoid the possibility of a rejection by the other couple.

Video has often been used as a supplemental data-recording tool in qualitative research contexts where human interaction is the main focus (Goldman-Segall, 1989, pp. 118–119). However, video data has a number of limitations, quite apart from the large data sets being awkward to work with (Buur & Soendergaard, 2000). Video cannot be considered as an objective document, and people's interaction cannot be recorded undisturbed. As Pink puts it, "people in a video are always 'people in a video'" (2007, p. 98). Not only is the footage always constructed in some way, it would be unethical to film the activity without the participants knowing. Further, knowledge that designers might be interested in does not necessarily exist as observable, delineable facts. Some of the most pertinent designerly information emerges from interaction with the technology used to capture the data and in the subsequent interaction with the artifacts that are the products of analysis of that data (Browning et al., 2009).

Rather than to contribute to a comprehensive ethnography of tourists' place making, the researchers' concern in this study was to produce a subjective, designerly account aimed at inspiring design. This is never an impartial project, but rather is produced by an iterative process that, in turn, uses and is reflexively informed by the bodily collaboration of the participants and the relationships staged between the researcher and the participants. The key idea is that the video of the participants' traversals is not simply a supplemental recording that helps in the production of weak ethnographic knowledge, something to be transformed into a written account of the interactions at Coconut Beach, but rather a way of providing a site for further interactions around interpretations of the activities depicted in the video representation (Browning et al., 2008). It is this intervention that affords the shaping of a design space, grounded in the interactions that occurred at Coconut Beach. By the researchers repeatedly "revisiting" Coconut Beach in the video sequences, a number of themes emerged that hinted at particular qualities of the interaction, which helped to open up the design space. Even such a partial analysis of the short sequence on Coconut Beach presented above raises valuable insights for inspiring and informing technical design.

The Tourist-as-Networker

If the intention were traditional ethnographic inquiry, the data collected might be considered sparse and not empirically generalizable, such as would be required if the intention was a broad, ostensibly objective understanding of tourists' behavior. Rather, the experiential data, and, importantly, the products of interaction with it, should be viewed as artifacts for inspiring design interventions, affording the innovation of mobile and *in situ* social media technologies for tourists. Five design sensibilities are highlighted that suggest new points of departure for the design of social media technologies aimed at tourists.

Tourist Sites Are Places.   Following Harrison and Dourish (1996), a *place* can be understood as a *space* that is practiced in a particular manner. Tourist locations are not simply transient or nomadic spaces. The gaze does not master them: the distance and difference seemingly afforded by the tourist gaze collapses in the face of the bodily and social performances that engage tourists as active participants in the (re)construction of meaningful and significant places. Thus, designing mobile and *in situ* social media for tourists entails understanding place making as a necessary, dynamic, embodied engagement that draws on networks between the furniture of a space and social activities. In the Coconut Beach case, the people, context, palm trees, coconuts, Bob and Alice's van, and the derelict chair, as well as the playful activity of catching coconuts, constitute some of the central nodes used for place making. The transformation of Coconut Beach, from a beautiful vista, narrated as a fantasy place of leisure, into a place of collaboration and play, demonstrates how tourist performances are inherently unpredictable. Places are unfinished. Meaning, as it relates to place, although necessarily indexical to the location, derives from the situation that evolves during the processual social interaction that takes place. In considering the theme of social media, it follows that innovative technologies, as tools for extending or making possible onsite tourist social interactions, should be designed with a sensibility for their capacity to shape place, and to give rise to particular networks-in-place and situated performances. Social media, in this sense, are productive of place, rather than merely an informational overlay for the tourist/consumer.

The Tourist in Place. If Urry's notion of the tourist gaze (1990) has been an influential way of understanding how tourism tends to subsume locations under a predominantly visual regime, the metaphor of the tourist-as-networker emphasizes the assemblage of the active tourist body through material, cultural, and social constituents. To be a tourist is to be *in place*, immersed in networks of things, people, information, discourses, and interactions. A sensibility to networked performances by tourists, such as those presented above, spawns a richer repertoire for the early problem-setting stages of design, since it fundamentally questions received notions of tourism as pure leisure, a primarily visual, colonizing endeavour or as a quest for authenticity. For instance, designing and innovating social media could utilize an understanding of tourist practices as the construction of a series of networks that allows for embodied play and provide means to connect to itinerant and brief forms of place making as drivers or motifs in the design process. In terms of the design of social media, the trope of the tourist-as-networker again emphasizes how media are not incidental to, but *productive* of place. Networks gives rise to the creation of new nodes, new constellations of interaction in the social environments performed in place.

The Importance of the Body in Place-based Interaction. Social networks facilitated in and through digital networks are typically seen as tools to transcend colocation and geographical distance. With colocated social networking facilitated by digital media, the body (which has been left rather inconsequential in "virtual" networks) becomes a piece of "consequential equipment," according to Goffman. If the body facilitates "activities that are consequential, problematic, and undertaken for what is felt to be their own sake" (Goffman, 1967, p. 185), the design of colocated social networks needs to be sensitive to the ways in which the body is used appropriately in a locale, and how the (social, communicative) body demarcates and arranges space. In the case of *in situ* tourist social media, observing liminalities and the shifting boundaries between public and private locales affords understanding of how to represent availability and openness to social interaction or the types of social interaction in which users are prepared to be involved. This sensitizes designers to the often tacit signals in embodied interactions, and reminds designers how bodily cues such as proximity, gestures, and other signals might be made available to understand how places are negotiated in the continuum of the private and the public.

Shifting Tempos and Rituals.   Associated with the body as a medium for negotiating availability and openness, the intensity of the social interaction on a tourist site fluctuates. In the Coconut Beach example, Guy and Isa walk to-and-fro, not immediately deciding whether to begin a conversation with the other couple. The ritualistic component embodied in the interaction is evident in the way Guy and Isa imitate Bob and Alice, thus suggesting that they find their coconut catching "game" interesting. At times, Guy and Isa's movements back and forth seemed defensive and hesitant, as if preparing for a loss of *face* and potential rejection from the other couple. At other times, their advancements seemed probing and direct, aimed explicitly at establishing contact. The other couple reacts to Guy and Isa's phatic advancements with laughter and interjections, acknowledging their presence and opening themselves to further interaction. This advancement and withdrawal of engagement is characteristic of the mutual recognition and negotiation of interaction (Goffman, 1967) Designing for such encounters requires a sensibility toward the social minutiae that define pleasurable social interactions from confrontational or adverse interactions.

Ephemerality and Memory.   The social networks performed in the Coconut Beach example entail no formal introductions and neither party makes any lasting commitments. Formalities or lasting commitments were apparently not prerequisites for the collaboration. Subtle cues to the status of other tourists perhaps became more appropriate when entering into a conversation and collaboration, such as when Guy noticed the van while walking to the beach, and when Isa subsequently fantasized about Bob and Alice staying the night on the beach. These cues, indicating Bob and Alice's status as tourists of a particular kind, worked as prompts for interaction, as Guy and Isa became curious about (and somewhat envious of) the other couple. Even though the encounter was short and uncommitted, Guy and Isa seemed to linger on the subject of the meeting during the walk back to the car. They mentioned the Australian hospitality and what they perceived to be the national laid-back nature. This later brought to mind other stories from their travels around the country. In this way, they linked their recent encounter with Bob and Alice to other experiences of the same kinds of sociability they had experienced during their travels in Australia. This emphasizes the need to understand how, in practice, a design of place-based social media for tourists should begin to mediate the social landscape, how connections formed might require a "phatic," connective, and ongoing component, but also how interactions facilitated by technologies might fade over time or become connected to other ephemeral-yet-memorable interactions.

In sum, the design sensibilities developed from the encounter give rise to new ways of understanding the tourist site as a social place. They suggest new perspectives from which to intervene technologically in tourist experiences. Localized or place-based tourist social media that productively utilize the often concentrated-yet-ephemeral social encounters give rise to opportunities for creating services to enrich travel experiences and to support the temporary sociality and network building that can arise during tourist activities. Shifting the emphasis away from the interpretational situations that mobile tourist technologies have typically been designed to intervene in, such as providing objective information about places or sights or aiding in way-finding, opens up possibilities for designing with a more holistic notion of the tourist experience. It allows designers to address a wider range of concerns in tourism: interpretation, emotional experiences, and the embodied, social, and affective components of being a tourist.

CONCLUSION

The encounter related and analyzed above is a type of experience that can be used to demonstrate a plausible vision of the aesthetics and affective components of a particular kind of tourist experience. Harrison (2001) argues that the aesthetics of tourism experiences are to be discovered in both monumental encounters (of the canonical type), as well as in the mundane things *in situ*, that, despite their everydayness, are pleasingly sensual, such as the smell of the ocean, the feel of the sand between one's toes, the taste of a cold beer, and so on. Relating Porteous' notion of environmental aesthetics, Harrison argues that more often, striking and gratifying aesthetic moments occur in a liminal engagement with place, by being connected as well as disconnected to a place, or by being tentatively and ephemerally connected. In the case related above, these occurred when the couple set off on a potentially (socially) risky encounter, "bumping into" practices where the social and collaborative experiences mattered rather than interpretational work or information work. Their "work," in terms of attention, bodily exertion, and social skills, in facilitating the interaction was not simply a set of problems to be overcome, but part of the hedonic and pleasurable landscape.

This chapter shows how a performative view of tourism can give rise to design sensibilities that transcend the typical (techno-centric) understanding of tourist practices as distanced and informational. The Coconut Beach case demonstrates how a location can take on a particular kind of meaning through social activities performed there. Attending to this performative notion of tourism will enable designers and developers of place-based social media to look beyond the information-seeking tourist, and to focus on the socializing activities that tourists carry out as they perform the making of meaning *in situ*. Crucially, in meaning making at a particular location, tourists are engaged in constructing or reconstructing their sense of a place that is indexed to a location. They are enriching their understanding of that place by interacting in place in a dialogical and processual manner. This process does not begin or end with their interaction in a specific location. In all probability, it began before they arrived and will almost certainly continue after they leave. But it is their engaged interaction in *place* that puts the meat on the bones.

This chapter has argued that tourist sites are fluid places made up of social, technical, and natural things, and that technological media that facilitate or aid social interactions in place can become means by which places are temporarily and dynamically made by tourists. Seeing the tourist-as-networker provides designers with the opportunity to reconsider tourist practices and enables new ways to think about social technologies and services for tourism. Social media in place need not be solely about aiding the formation of collaborative interpretational situations where technology is used, for example, in an effort to aggregate data and information from large numbers of users. Instead, in this chapter, it is suggested that social media in place might purposefully be built around enabling or enriching situations of place-based sense-making, extending the possibilities for engaging in social performances and play when visiting tourist sites. This requires a turn toward an ontology that foregrounds performative and emergent aspects of being a tourist. Being a tourist or experiencing in a touristic manner requires an effort, and resulting experiences may arise out of seemingly serendipitous encounters and situations. Similarly it requires an engaged and deep engagement in tourists' actual practices of place making in the effort of supplying inspiring research artifacts that can aid designers of place-based social media.

Such an effort might give rise to technologies that, for example, support pleasurable experiences by enabling short-lived and ephemeral connections among tourists, allowing them to get in touch with strangers and thus support the collaborative staging of place (e.g., in purposeful, if somewhat irrational, activities) that make sites pleasurable and memorable. New services and technologies could be part of the appropriation of sites and the relating of places in terms of "our sense of self, our personal history, and our anticipated future" (McCarthy et al., 2006, p. 126). Although such services support social meetings and networked activities, they might equally augment the reflection on embodied, sensory experiences and narratives of place and bring enriched and even new aspects to the full experience of being a tourist.

Chapter 8

The Virtual Fan(G) Community: Social Media and Pop Culture Tourism

Maria Lexhagen
Mid Sweden University/ETOUR, Sweden

Mia Larson
Lund University, Sweden

Christine Lundberg
Mid Sweden University/ETOUR, Sweden

ABSTRACT

This chapter focuses on the importance of social media for pop culture fans. A web survey for fans of the *Twilight Saga* is implemented, using the concepts of cognitive, affective, and evaluative social identity and personal, product, and situational involvement. The purpose is to examine to what degree social identity and involvement can explain pop culture fans' future intention to travel, make recommendations to others, and use social media. Findings show that pop culture fans use social media to a large extent and that these means are important for making decisions about traveling and event participation. Moreover, the chapter shows that involvement dimensions are more important than social identity dimensions to explain future intention to travel, to recommend to others, and to use social media.

Keywords: Pop culture tourism; virtual community; social identity; involvement

Tourism Social Media: Transformations in Identity, Community and Culture
Tourism Social Science Series, Volume 18, 133–157
Copyright © 2013 by Emerald Group Publishing Limited
All rights of reproduction in any form reserved
ISSN: 1571-5043/doi:10.1108/S1571-5043(2013)0000018010

INTRODUCTION

Pop culture can be defined as a culture liked by many, something other than "fine culture," situated in the context of mass production and consumption, culture by the people for the people, accessible, and commercial (Lindgren, 2005; Strinati, 2004). The term "pop culture tourism" refers to tourism induced by pop culture. The tourists that engage in this type of tourism can be characterized as fans. This form of tourism is becoming increasingly popular (Beeton, 2008). It is highly demand driven (Müller, 2006), and since tourists associate the destination with dramatic events or dramatic characters portrayed in literature, on TV, or in a film (Kim & Richardson, 2003), it tends to create strong emotional ties to the destination visited. Tourists are mainly attracted to the mythology of a destination, not the "real" place (MacCannell, 1999; Selwyn, 1996). Perhaps this is an even more important aspect for pop culture tourists (Connell, 2005) since their motives are far more complex than what the traditional push–pull model suggests (Beeton, 2005).

The majority of published research within the field of pop culture tourism has been focused on film tourism. According to Beeton's (2010) review, scholars have moved from estimating tourist flows (Riley, Baker, & Van Doren, 1998; Riley & Van Doren, 1992; Tooke & Baker, 1996), to exploring tourism motives (Beeton, 2005; Riley & Van Doren, 1992), and management issues and effects on destinations (Beeton, 2005; Mordue, 2001), to postmodern interpretations of the phenomenon. To date, the literature is dominated by case-based research, in which specific destinations and/or films/TV-series have been in focus. One of the most investigated cases is the film series *Lord of the Rings*, shot in New Zealand (Buchmann, 2010; Buchmann, Moore, & Fisher, 2010; Croy, 2010; Jones & Smith, 2005; Tzanelli, 2004). Another popular research case within the field is Dracula tourism in Romania (Huebner, 2011; Light, 2007, 2009; Shandley, Hamal, & Tanase, 2006; Tǎnǎsescu, 2006). This research has to a large extent focused on the recreation of a destination's image as a result of a popular book/film character. Furthermore, regional effects of film and TV-series tourism have been documented in a number of studies on the British Isles (Brereton, 2006; Meaney & Robb, 2006; Young & Young, 2008). For example, *Harry Potter* (Iwashita, 2006; Mintel Group, 2003) and *Braveheart* (Scottish Enterprise Forth Valley, 2000) have been under study. Australia is another example where the effects of film tourism have been documented. High-profile cases are Ned Kelly (Frost, 2006) and the Australian outback (Frost, 2009). Hence, research on this form of tourism is not new. However, the explosive growth of the creative industries of film and TV in recent decades, offering consumers an enormous number of choices and hence fierce competition among businesses, combined with the increased use of Internet and social media making popular culture products more accessible, calls for additional perspectives on research in this field. Fans of pop culture do not exist in isolation. They communicate with each other, facilitated by various Web 2.0 applications, and access new information on the phenomenon in question from the constant flow of updates and sources available on the Internet. The contribution of the research in this chapter is thus to introduce technology mediation into the study of pop culture tourism.

It is by now a widely established fact that consumers' use of social media applications such as Facebook and Twitter reached enormous proportions by the end of the first decade of the 21st century. Also, the number of blogs on the Internet is now counted in the hundreds of millions (Pingdom, 2012; Tumbler, 2012). Social media are very much the essence of Web 2.0 and the applications on the Internet are characteristically customer-centric, user-generated, interactive and dynamic, foster community participation, and build on collective community intelligence (O'Reilly, 2005). Social media have become increasingly important for tourism. PhoCusWright (2010) reported on social media in travel and states that travelers' reviews, photos, trip planning and sharing, and blogging are all influencing how these people connect to and interact with suppliers and products. Results from Xiang and Gretzel (2010) support this view. They found that social media constitute a substantial part in the search engine results of travel searches. PhoCusWright (2010) also noted that there was a 34% increase between 2008 and 2009 in number of visitors per month to social travel websites.

The possibility of using the Internet to diffuse information and share opinions at the "speed of light" is an important factor that influences the proliferation of pop culture phenomena and hence potentially also the development of pop culture tourism. As Guex states, "the Web has become for many a travel companion who gives good advice and has an attentive ear" (2010, p. 426). The study reported on in this chapter investigates whether various forms of social media use are important for pop culture fans in terms of planning and choosing to travel and participate in events. The purpose is to examine to what degree social identity and involvement can explain pop culture fans' future intention to travel, to make recommendations to others, and use social media. The study explains to what extent fans use social media to make travel decisions, and what characterizes these fans in terms of involvement and social identity. These are important factors both for developing marketing strategies and for destination planning and development.

SOCIAL MEDIA AND POP CULTURE TOURISM

Literature on social media in a tourism context is limited but rapidly increasing. Importantly for marketing management, use of social media has been researched from the perspective of how a destination or a tourism company is portrayed in social media (Jeong & Jang, 2010; Schmallegger & Carson, 2009; Wenger, 2008; Ye, Law, & Gu, 2009; Zhang, Ye, Law, & Li, 2010). Further knowledge is found in the majority of tourism-related research, which is focused on user behavior from various aspects. Research on why consumers use social media can be exemplified by research on triggers of electronic word-of-mouth (Jeong & Jang, 2010), motivations to write online travel reviews (Yoo & Gretzel, 2008), and using online reviews and recommendations (Zhang, Pan, Smith, & Li, 2009). Further, research on satisfaction (Jiang, Mills, & Stepchenkova, 2008), perceived usefulness (Zehrer et al., 2011), consumers' response and source credibility (Xie, Miao, Kuo, & Lee, 2010), and the complementary role of online reviews for holiday decision making (Papathanassis & Knolle, 2010) contribute to understanding the value and impact of social media for tourists. Literature specifically focusing on member participation, involvement, and identification can also be found (Arsal, Baldwin, & Backman, 2009; Casaló, Flavián, & Guinalíu, 2010; Huang et al., 2010; Qu & Lee, 2011; Sanchez-Franco & Rondan-Cataluña, 2010).

Research focusing on participation, involvement, and identification points to a relevant feature of social media: the formation of virtual communities where users share content and communicate. The forming of these social communities seems particularly relevant for pop culture communities due to the often high levels of involvement of users.

Formation of Consumer Tribes and Virtual Communities

Highly involved pop culture consumers are often referred to as fans. It has been suggested that fan tourists to a large extent are motivated by sociocultural and social belongingness needs such as cultural and tribal connections (Chen, 2007; Kim & Chalip, 2004; Smith & Stewart, 2007). From a marketing perspective, Cova and Cova (2002) suggest that citizens in the 21st century are more interested in social links and the identities that come with them, than in the pure consumption of objects. Cova et al. (2007) argue that these new types of consumers, consumer tribes, are active and enthusiastic in their consumption, sometimes to the extreme, and produce a range of identities, practices, rituals, meanings, and even material culture. Maffesoli (1996) defines a consumer tribe as "A group that is loosely connected, inherently unstable, and is held together essentially through emotion and passion" (Maffesoli cited in Otnes & Maclaran, 2007, p. 52).

Unruh's (1980) concept of the social world can be seen as an early conceptualization of the phenomenon of consumer tribes, noting that common "worldviews" are often created that unite social actors in terms of practices, procedures, and perspectives. Four features of involvement are typical for social worlds: voluntary identification (the entry into and departure from the social world is relatively free, accessible, and occasionally unnoticed); partial involvement (any social actor can only be involved in a portion of the total "goings-on" in any social world); multiple identification (all actors, organizations, events, and practices are probably involved in, or function to support, multiple social worlds); and mediated interaction (reliance on channels of communication rather than spatial, kinship, or "formal" ties necessarily implies the importance of mediated interaction in forming and maintaining social organization in social worlds). Unruh (1980) discusses communication centers as vital to the coordination of activities, production, and interrelationships among those involved in the social world. Whatever formalization occurs in social worlds (Unruh, 1980) arises out of these centers of communication. They are generally the "hub" of debates concerning authenticity, procedural matters, the extension or contraction of boundaries, and decisions revolving around the organizational focus.

Social media can be seen as a form of communication center in Unruh's (1980) conceptualization of social worlds. In the early 1990s, following the rise of online discussion groups, the concept of a virtual community was introduced. In 1993, Reingold defined a virtual community as "social aggregations that emerge from the Net when enough people carry on ... public discussions long enough, with sufficient human feeling, to form webs of personal relationships in cyberspace" (quoted in Parks, 2011, p. 105). Parks refines this definition as

> ... a group might qualify as a virtual community if its members engaged in collective action, shared in rituals, had a variety of relational linkages, and were emotionally bonded

to others in a way that conferred a sense of belonging and group identification. (2011, p. 177)

In virtual communities, such as Second Life, people are motivated by entertainment and getting away from real life, as well as to meet and interact with people from around the world, to communicate and maintain relationships (Zhou, Jin, Vogel, Fang, & Chen, 2011). Similar motivations are found in research on participating in online social networks. Chung and Buhalis (2008a) found that information acquisition (such as finding information, sharing experiences), social-psychological (seeking identity, belongingness), and hedonic benefits (having fun) influence level of participation and attitude toward an online travel community. Parra-López et al. (2011) confirmed this and also found that there is a series of conditioning factors that can act as incentives for tourists' social media use: availability of the technology, altruism, the environment, individual predispositions, and trust of the users' information exchanged and written online. They also found that the users' perceived costs (related to possible loss of privacy, the effort required, and/or the difficulty of using the technologies), have no significant impact on the predisposition to use social media.

People are further motivated to contribute to content in social media. Yoo and Gretzel (2008) found that those who write online reviews are motivated by the sense of helping travel service providers, concerns for other consumers, and needs for enjoyment and a desire for positive recognition from others. Bronner and de Hoog (2011) confirm this in their study of tourists who post onsites. They found the following motivations: being self-directed, helping other vacationers, getting social benefits, empowering consumers, and helping companies. They also found that the main discriminating factor for why a tourist chooses a particular site is the factor that sets tourists with a primarily self-directed motivation apart from those with a more other-directed help motivation. Jepsen (2006) found that an information search in virtual communities to some extent replaces information from marketer-dominated sources.

Based on these literature insights and the fact that pop culture fans are also tourists and part of a community, a number of hypotheses emerge:

H1: Online pop culture fans are intensive users of social media.

H2: Social media are important for pop culture fans when planning and making decisions about travel and event participation.

Social Identity and Online Community Participation

Social identity and a sense of belonging are important for understanding any social community. Social identity is widely used to explain group and collective behavior (Bagozzi & Lee, 2002). Research on social identity and virtual communities (groups of people who interact online for the sake of achieving personal as well as shared goals) is part of a more general theme of research that tries to understand the nature and role of the social influence exerted by the community on its members. Bagozzi and Dholakia (2002) and Dholakia, Bagozzi, and Klein Pearo (2004) use the concept of social identity to understand virtual community participation. They state that social identity "captures the main aspects of the individual's identification with the group in the sense that the person comes to view himself or herself as a member of the community, as belonging to it" (Dholakia et al., 2004, p. 245). In their research, social identity is conceptualized as having cognitive, affective, and evaluative components. The cognitive component concerns how the individual forms a self-awareness of virtual community member-ship, the affective component implies that social identity includes a sense of emotional involvement with the group, and evaluative social identity is focused on the evaluation of self-worth on the basis of belonging to the community. Dholakia et al.'s conceptualization of social identity was later used by Cheung and Lee (2010) to study intentional social action in online social networks. The importance of all three dimensions of social identity was confirmed, and their results show the importance of social identity in the development of a virtual community.

Similarly, the real value of online travel communities lies in the extent to which members can identify with the group through interaction (Casaló et al., 2010). Highly interactive travel community members are more likely to share and promote the community with others (Qu & Lee, 2011). According to social exchange theory, people interact in virtual communities because they expect that it will be rewarding both in terms of tangibles such as goods or money and in terms of social benefits such as friendship. Further, the outcomes of interaction as well as the interaction itself can offer benefits. Interaction is about how to interact, with whom, and what should be exchanged (Füller, 2010). Research on consumer interactions in virtual communities shows that the stronger the social ties and the more enjoyment experienced in interactions, the more likely the member is to display reciprocal behavior (Chan & Li, 2010). Hence, consumers not only focus on utilitarian values but also value hedonic social relationships and enjoyment when determining their engagement in virtual communities.

However, virtual communities are found to consist of both "lurkers" (persons who read but never post) and "posters"; lurkers are the more common role (Baym, 2010). Welser, Gleave, Fisher, and Smith (cited in Baym, 2010, p. 87) identified two different kinds of posters: "answer people" (frequently respond yet never initiate) and "discussion people" (both initiate and respond). Discussion people could be considered "e-fluentials," who are opinion leaders who spread information via the Internet (Burson-Marsteller cited in Sun, Youn, Wu, & Kuntaraporn, 2006, p. 1105).

As noted above, a sense of belonging is important in online communities. Although research shows that members of a travel community with a high degree of identification with the group take an active role by sharing knowledge, they may not be influenced in their product-related behaviors. Nevertheless, this is moderated if members of a community are highly interactive (Qu & Lee, 2011). Furthermore, in blogs people share detailed accounts of experiences. These blog posts later influence readers and potentially impact purchase decisions. Research has shown that blog users find multiple evaluations that are concordant to be helpful, irrespective of whether they are positive or negative. Negative postings are not always a bad thing if they are followed by a positive counter-reaction (Zehrer et al., 2011). Attempting to influence behavior and retain customers for their online services, websites such as Virtual Tourist and Lonely Planet have integrated community functionalities to build a sense of belonging and trust (Sanchez-Franco & Rondan-Cataluña, 2009). Consequently, three additional hypotheses about online communities are proposed:

H3: A high level of perceived social identity increases pop culture fans' future intention to travel and participate at events.

H4: A high level of perceived social identity increases pop culture fans' future intention to recommend to others to travel or participate in events.

H5: A high level of perceived social identity increases pop culture fans' average use of websites/blogs/communities.

Concept and Practice of Involvement

The extent of consumers' involvement with an object is said to impact behavioral decisions (Zaichkowsky, 1985, 1986). According to Andrews, Durvasula, and Akhter (1990), the level of intensity in involvement varies by product types, situations, and individual conditions. Involvement is defined by Park, Lee, and Han as "the perceived personal relevance of a product based on the individual consumer's needs, interests, and values" (2007, p. 129). In order to explain bloggers' intention to purchase travel products, Huang et al. (2010) propose modeling involvement at three levels: personal, product, and situation. The first is related to consumers' inner needs, interests, and values. The second is focused on the consumers' perceptions about the product such as the risk involved, price, symbolic meaning, endurance, pleasure, importance, brand, and purchase duration. The third is defined as the situations that consumers face when interacting with product communication, purchasing the product, using the product, and risk perceptions. High-involvement travel bloggers are more likely to form a favorable impression toward marketing communication in blogs (Huang et al., 2010). Sanchez-Franco and Rondan-Cataluña (2010) find that level of purchase involvement has a strong moderating effect on consumers' willingness to engage in online service relationships and that virtual communities should be designed according to the customers' involvement levels. Furthermore, Cai, Feng, and Breiter (2004) conclude that consumers who have high levels of purchase involvement are more likely than others to use the Internet to search for destination information. These studies clearly show the effect of involvement on consumer perceptions and behavioral intentions.

Hence, different personal perceptions, product characteristics, and situations will lead to various levels of involvement. In this study, Huang et al.'s (2010) model of involvement (personal, product, and situation) is used to understand pop culture fans and their use of social media. Level of involvement is explored, both in the pop culture phenomenon itself and involvement in the online community. The effect of involvement on future travel intent and intention to recommend is also investigated. Therefore, still three more hypotheses about online communities are proposed:

H6: A high level of perceived involvement increases pop culture fans' future intention to travel and participate in events.

H7: A high level of perceived involvement increases pop culture fans' future intention to recommend to others to travel or participate in events.

H8: A high level of perceived involvement increases pop culture fans' average use of websites/blogs/communities.

The Twilight Saga Fans, Tourists, and Web Users

The empirical case for the role of social media in tourism discussed in this chapter is focused on the pop culture phenomenon and international blockbuster movies and bestselling books known as the *Twilight Saga*. This is a story about the teenager Bella Swan and her impossible romance with vampire boyfriend Edward Cullen. It is primarily set in the small town Forks (Washington) which is the rainiest town in the continental United States. She also befriends a young man called Jacob Black who turns out to be a werewolf. The story has a strong romantic element with a touch of fantasy (http://www.stepheniemeyer.com). The four books included in the series have sold a total of 116 million copies worldwide (http://www.publishersweekly.com/pw/by-topic/childrens/childrens-book-news/article/44733-little-brown-to-publish-official-twilight-guide.html). The five films in the series that have been released on the big screen and on DVD/BlueRay have grossed more than US$ 4 billion worldwide (The-numbers.com, 2012a–2012d).

Contrary to the media-perpetuated image of Twilight fans as young, screaming, obsessive girls, the *Twilight Saga* attracts a wide range of fans, mostly females between the ages of 8 and 80 (Wilson, 2011). Twilight's main attraction can be found, according to scholars, in its vacillation between contradictory messages: "a series that presents neither a subversive nor a conservative view of larger social contexts but is an ambiguous mixture of both" (Wilson, 2011, p. 8).

The *Twilight Saga* fan community includes many websites, blogs, forums, and online networks that are dedicated to this phenomenon. These fans discuss their own constructed meaning of Twilight: "In both the virtual world and the real world, love, romance, and desire are held up as the meaning behind Twilight." In addition, their online behavior includes more superficial elements, at least among the more mature female fan-base, which focuses on the romantic message of the saga: "albeit in a more 'sexed-up' form … a sort of Playgirl for Twilight fans (sans the full-frontal nudity but with plenty of bare chests and bulging muscles)" (Wilson, 2011, p. 44).

Furthermore, fans use Twilight websites, blogs, and forums when searching for and communicating information before, during, and after their Twilight-related travel. Many of them include various types of explicit tourist information (Fig. 1), often provided by other users. For example, a user-generated slide show with voice-over and music can be found on one website. The slide show includes screen dumps from films compared to real

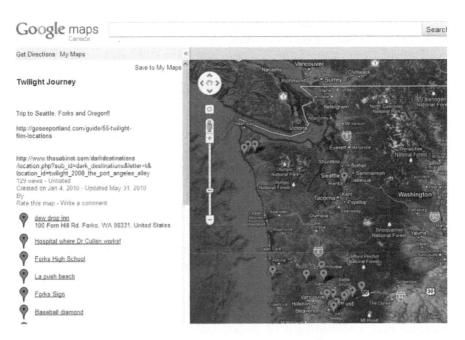

Figure 1. Google Map with Places Linked to Twilight

life photos taken by a fan traveling to Italy where there are several locations connected to the books and films. These "online spaces" constitute a platform for fans to interact, search for, and share information related to their interest in this pop culture phenomenon and hence potentially influences the behavior of these fans, including their tourism behavior. The fandom can be described as very organized, not least when it comes to tourism. There is an abundance of examples of online Twilight fandom: organized trips to the locations where the films have been shot, to the destinations where the books are set (Twatwaffels on Twitarded.blogspot. com), and Twilight events, conventions, and get-togethers (TwiMOMs Conventions and Get-Togethers on Twilightmoms.com). The principal destinations for Twilight tourism in terms of setting (where story is set, Frost 2006, 2009) are two small towns in the United States and in Italy: Forks (Washington) and Volterra (Tuscany). Regarding the locations where the films have been shot, the main attractions are Portland (USA), British Columbia (Canada), and Montepulciano (Italy). In addition, in major cities all over the world, official and unofficial Twilight events or conventions are held with thousands of visitors several times a year by event companies such as Twilight Convention Tour, Twicon, and Eternal Twilight.

Study Methods

An international web survey was implemented as a link on websites for Twilight fans offering Web 2.0 applications in September 2010 to measure the activities of the *Twilight Saga* online community and their tourism behavior. Forty websites dedicated to the *Twilight Saga* were identified through a search for websites/blogs/communities with a large number of visitors/users (based on the number of visitors/users published by the site or through their position as nodes in the online community, meaning that they were frequently linked to by other sites or frequently found as links/ mentions in Twitter flows or in online communities). When a site was identified, it was searched for affiliation with, mentions of, and links to other sites, which were then added to the list of websites that could be used for sampling. This can be described as a form of snowball sampling. Attention was also paid to the geographical location of websites to achieve an international representation of respondents. Only sites using the English language were included. But based on country of origin of the fans contributing with content, as seen in comments by fans, an attempt was made to include as many countries as possible. The owners/administrators of the websites were contacted and invited to publish the link to the web survey, and six of them published the link. The link was also picked up by Twitter users and was both tweeted and re-tweeted, generating additional respondents from the online Twilight community.

The questionnaire was developed based on literature reviews for the research themes included in the survey and pilot tests were conducted using friends and colleagues as test respondents. The survey measured behavior related to Twilight tourism and participation in events, motivation, perceived value, future behavioral intention, as well as use of the Internet, including the use of websites. Thirty-eight questions were included and items were measured using a Likert-type scale from 1 to 7 as well as categorical, dichotomous, and open-ended questions. The total number of respondents was 967.

Table 1 shows the descriptive distribution of the sample. However, due to the positioning of the background questions at the end of the survey, the number of respondents to these questions is lower than that of other parts of the questionnaire.

Table 1. Sample Descriptives

Sample Descriptive	% of $n = 407$–433
Gender	
Men	1
Women	99
Age	
Between 12 and 67	Median: 20
Country of origin	
Sweden	64
North America	19
Other (South America, Asia, Europe, Australia)	17
Family status	
Single	48
Single with children under 18	3
Married/common law	8
Married/common law with children under 18	12
Other	29
Education	
Less than high school	27
High school	24
Undergraduate	41
Post graduate	8

Measurement items on the average use of Twilight-related websites, experience of Twilight-related content on the Internet, purpose of this use, type of use, and Twilight-related tourism behavior were developed by the authors (Table 2). Furthermore, from the literature review it is assumed that future intention to participate or recommend as well as average use depend on two variables: social identity and involvement. Six items adapted from Dholakia et al. (2004) and Cheung and Lee (2010) were used to measure social identity. Based on Huang et al. (2010), 13 items that measure involvement were adapted (Table 3).

The dataset was prepared for further analysis and cases considered as outliers were removed. The total number of respondents retained for further analysis was 881. Reliability tests of the scales used in the regression analysis

Table 2. Measurement Items

Items	Scale	Construct
How often on average do you visit a Twilight-related website/blog/community?	Time scale	Web usage
When did you first start searching for Twilight-related content on the Internet?	Time scale	
When searching for Twilight-related content on the Internet, which are the three main purposes?	Multiple response options	
Have you participated at a Twilight-related event/trip (e.g., convention, visit to movie locations or places portrayed in the books, movie premier, DVD release, get-together, party)?	Dichotomous	Behavior
Please evaluate the following statements regarding your use of social media and your participation at Twilight-related events/trips.	1 = Not at all, 7 = to a large extent	

- I have used information in blogs/communities to plan my participation.
- Information in blogs/communities influenced my decision to participate.
- Information in blogs/communities influenced my decision NOT to participate.
- Information in blogs/communities was helpful while I participated.
- After I participate, I have shared my experiences on blogs/communities

Items	Scale	Construct
How many Twilight-related events/trips have you participated in where Twilight was the primary motive for your participation?	Numeric	

Table 2. (Continued)

Items	Scale	Construct
How many Twilight-related events/trips have you participated in where Twilight was the secondary motive for your participation?	Numeric	
How many Twilight-related events/trips have you participated in where Twilight was the secondary motive for your participation?	Dichotomous	
Regarding your most recent trip/event: What was your primary source of information when planning your event/trip?	Response options	
To what extent is it likely that you would do the following? – Participate at a Twilight-related event/ trip – Recommend to others to participate at a Twilight-related event/trip	1 = Not likely, 7 = extremely likely	Loyalty

showed acceptable levels of Cronbach alpha coefficients (Nunnally, 1978), cognitive social identity (0.88), affective social identity (0.93), evaluative social identity (0.96), personal involvement (0.83), product involvement (0.75), and situation involvement (0.86). The dataset was also evaluated in terms of normality, linearity, and homoscedasticity.

Twilight Fan Behavior and Internet Use

The majority of the respondents (66%, $n = 772$) state that they have traveled to Twilight-related destinations or events. Further, 63% ($n = 517$) report that their interest in Twilight was the primary motive for traveling. The most important source of information ($n = 326$) is Twilight websites (62%), other

Table 3. Operational Measures for Social Identity and Involvement

Items	Scale	Construct
Please evaluate the following statements as regards to your use of Twilight blogs/communities	1 = Strongly disagree, 7 = strongly agree	Social identity (Cheung et al., 2010). Items 1 and 2: cognitive social identity, items 3 and 4: affective social identity, items 5 and 6: evaluative social identity.
1. My self-image overlaps with the identity of the user group as I perceive it		
2. When I'm interacting with other users on blogs/communities I feel there is an overlap between my personal identity and the identity of the group		
3. I am very attached to the user group		
4. I have a strong feeling of belongingness toward the user group		
5. I am a valuable member of the group		
6. I am an important member of the group		
Please evaluate the following statements in relation to your involvement in Twilight.	1 = strongly disagree, 7 = strongly agree	Involvement (Huang et al., 2010). Items 1–4: personal involvement, items 5–8: product involvement, items 9–13: situation involvement.
1. I'm interested in reading blogs about Twilight information and photos, etc.		
2. When reading information in blogs I feel the information is appealing		

Table 3. (Continued)

Items	Scale	Construct
3. When reading information in blogs I feel that Twilight is relevant in my life		
4. When reading information in blogs I feel that Twilight means a lot to me		
5. I'm interested in Twilight		
6. Twilight is essential to me, thus it is difficult to choose between Twilight and my other hobbies		
7. Purchasing Twilight products is a ways of rewarding myself		
8. The Twilight products I purchase symbolize my personality and character		
9. I think Twilight blogs provide good efficiency in information searching		
10. I think Twilight blogs provide sufficient information		
11. I think what is written in Twilight blogs is reliable		
12. I think the communication in Twilight blogs is free from being interfered by sales-persons		
13. I think the communication in Twilight blogs is free from being interfered by friends outside the Twilight community		

websites (16.5%), and social media (10.5%). Specifically, respondents use information in blogs and communities to plan trips and events ($M = 5.64$, $n = 464$) and during their participation in events ($M = 5.59$, $n = 459$). They also state that they share these experiences on blogs and communities ($M = 5.19$, $n = 461$) and that it had influenced their decision ($M = 5.19$, $n = 462$) to travel.

Future travel intentions to Twilight-related destinations are indicated by the fact that 61% ($n = 500$) of the respondents state that it is likely or extremely likely that they will participate in a Twilight-related event or trip. Among respondents, 60% ($n = 498$) also state that it is likely or extremely likely that they will recommend to others to participate at a Twilight-related event/trip.

Twilight fans are avid users of the Internet: 92% ($n = 881$) visit a Twilight-related website, blog, or community from several times a day to a few times every week. They are also experienced users: 50% of respondents ($n = 868$) started to search for Twilight-related content on the Internet between one and two years ago, 30% more than two years ago, and a minority, 20%, did so more recently (up until a year ago). The most important reasons for searching for Twilight-related content on the Internet is to find information in general, to find information on the actors/characters, to read or watch Twilight-related content, to find exclusive Twilight content, and to interact with other fans.

Social Identity, Involvement, and Effects on Use and Future Intention

The variables used for analyzing the effects of social identity and involvement are: future intention to participate in a Twilight-related event/trip (F1), future intention to recommend to others to participate in a Twilight-related event/trip (F2), average use of Twilight-related websites (AU), cognitive social identity (CSI), affective social identity (ASI), evaluative social identity (ESI), personal involvement (PI), product involvement (PRI), and situation involvement (SI).

As shown by the mean values in Table 4, the majority of respondents perceive strong links between the virtual community and themselves, with the highest mean occurring for affective social identity indicating that emotional ties are most important. Involvement variables, on the other hand, show much higher means. The high mean of personal involvement shows how respondents perceive that what is available on Twilight websites, blogs, and communities is very much linked to their inner needs, interests,

Table 4. Descriptive Statistics of the Dependent and Explanatory Variables

Variable	n	Mean	Standard Deviation
F1	500	4.99	2.158
F2	498	4.83	2.156
AU	881	2.06[a]	1.148
CSI	396	3.0051	1.780
ASI	394	3.1256	2.029
ESI	400	2.9438	2.040
PI	439	5.8759	1.140
PRI	433	4.4307	1.496
SI	417	5.0293	1.323

[a]The scale is reversed and 1 represents several times a day and 8 less than every six months.

Table 5. Pearson's Correlations

Scale	1	2	3	4	5	6	7	8	9
F1	–	.813[b]	−.350[b]	.361[b]	.425[b]	.389[b]	.483[b]	.473[b]	.393[b]
F2		–	−.245[b]	.273[b]	.345[b]	.311[b]	.415[b]	.402[b]	.353[b]
AU*			–	−.215[a,b]	−.334[a,b]	−.328[a,b]	−.433[a,b]	−.381[a,b]	−.357[a,b]
CSI				–	.638[b]	.527[b]	.409[b]	.466[b]	.376[b]
ASI					–	.800[b]	.409[b]	.475[b]	.349[b]
ESI						–	.361[b]	.429[b]	.361[b]
PI							–	.542[b]	.580[b]
PRI								–	.498[b]
SI									–

*The scale is reversed and 1 represents several times a day and 8 less than every six months.
[a]The scale is reversed so that 1 indicates high frequency of use.
[b]$p < 0.001$ (Sig. 2-tailed, pairwise exclusion of cases).

and values. Situation involvement also has a high mean score, indicating how valuable the respondents perceive the use of these online websites, blogs, and communities.

In order to test the direction and strength of the linear relationship among the concepts of social identity, involvement, and Twilight fans' future intentions to participate in a Twilight-related event/trip or to recommend this to others, Pearson's correlation was used. Results of correlations between measures of future intention, average use of websites/blogs/communities, social identity, and involvement are shown in Table 5. The interpretation of the results follows the criteria established by Cohen (1988). Between the dependent variables (F1 and F2), the correlation effect is considered large. Large effects are also found between CSI and ASI, CSI and ESI, ASI and ESI, PI and PRI, and PI and SI. All other correlations are considered moderate except between F2 and AU, F2 and CSI, and AU and CSI, which have small effects.

Three models were tested with multiple regression analysis conducted on the three independent variables separately. The independent variables for all the models were cognitive social identity, affective social identity, evaluative social identity, personal involvement, product involvement, and situation involvement. The dependent variable for Model 1 was future intention to participate in a Twilight-related event/trip. For Model 2, the dependent variable was future intention to recommend to others to participate in a Twilight-related event/trip, and for Model 3 it was average use of Twilight-related websites/blogs/communities.

High correlations between dependent and independent variables are first indicators of causal relationships within the overall construct. No multicollinearity problems are shown in the correlations or the tolerance or VIF statistics when compared to established thresholds (Hair, Anderson, Tatham, & Black, 1998; Leech, Barrett, & Morgan, 2005).

As seen in Table 6, in Models 1 and 2 the largest significant contributions to explaining future intention to participate and future intention to recommend to others to participate in a Twilight-related event/trip was found with the personal involvement and product involvement variables. However, in Model 3, apart from large significant contributions to explain average use of Twilight-related websites by the personal and product involvement variables, cognitive social identity also makes a significant contribution to explain this behavior.

The combination of variables that entered the regression explain 33% of the variance in Twilight tourists' future intentions and 24% of their future intention to recommend, as well as 25% of average use of Twilight-related websites/blogs/communities. The effect size (f^2) for Model 1 was .05, for Model 2 it was 0.32, and for Model 3, 0.34. Using Cohen's (1988) conventions for effect size, these are all large effects.

Table 6. Regression Analysis of Social Identity/Involvement on Future Intention/Average Use

Model 1[a]

Dependent Variable	F1 (Future intention to participate at Twilight-related event/trip)					
Variable	Standardized coefficients		Collinearity statistics		*t*-Statistic	Sig.
	Beta	Std. Error	Tolerance	VIF		
CSI	.014	.070	.546	1.832	0.251	.802
ASI	.133	.084	.289	3.463	1.683	.093
ESI	.078	.076	.356	2.806	1.088	.277
PI	.241	.108	.561	1.783	4.237	.000
PRI	.200	.081	.579	1.727	3.569	.000
SI	.077	.089	.608	1.644	1.416	.157

Model 2[b]

Dependent Variable	F2 (Future intention to recommend others to participate at a Twilight-related event)					
CSI	−.040	.075	.546	1.832	−.642	.521
ASI	.133	.090	.289	3.463	1.572	.117
ESI	.043	.081	.356	2.806	.560	.576
PI	.208	.115	.516	1.783	3.430	.001
PRI	.176	.086	.579	1.727	2.939	.003
SI	.100	.095	.608	1.644	1.713	.088

Model 3[c]

Dependent Variable	AU (Average use of Twilight-related website/blog/community)					
CSI	.133		.546	1.832	2.180	.030
ASI	−.112		.289	3.463	−1.331	.184
ESI	−.119		.356	2.806	−1.571	.117
PI	−.257		.516	1.783	−4.262	.000
PRI	−.146		.579	1.727	−2.466	.014
SI	−.108		.608	1.644	−1.875	.062

[a]Model fit: $R^2 = .334$, *F*-value $= 30.616$, $p = 0.000$.
[b]Model fit: $R^2 = .241$, *F*-value $= 19.396$, $p = 0.000$.
[c]Model fit: $R^2 = .253$, *F*-value $= 20.743$, $p = 0.000$.

CONCLUSION

The proliferation of social media use in customers' online activities raises questions as to the effects of this for marketing in general as well as consumer behavior. Based on previous research and available statistics it is clear that social media influence the behavior of tourists in their planning, purchasing, and post-consumption activities. In social media communities, tourists are motivated by entertainment, communication, interaction, and maintaining relationships (Chung & Buhalis, 2008b; Jepsen, 2006; Yoo & Gretzel, 2008; Zhou et al., 2011). Social identity and a sense of belonging are important for the development and success of online communities (Casaló et al., 2010; Chan & Li, 2010) and tourists' level of involvement can explain the formation of certain behaviors (Cai et al., 2004; Huang, 2010; Sanchez-Franco & Rondan-Cataluña, 2010).

Highly involved pop culture consumers can be characterized as fans and they are often motivated by sociocultural and social belongingness needs (Chen, 2007; Kim & Chalip, 2004; Smith & Stewart, 2007). They are also engaged in traveling to places in connection with their interest and they use and meet on various website forums, blogs, and communities. The results of this study show that pop culture fans use social media to a large extent and that they are important for making decisions about travel and event participation. Similar to earlier research on virtual communities in general, and travel communities in particular (Chung & Buhalis, 2008a, b; Jepsen, 2006), the results show that information acquisition is an important user motive, as is contributing content through sharing. The high level of sharing among the fans indicates that this pop culture virtual community, contrary to the findings of Baym (2010), consists of active posters to a high degree. Moreover, the high levels of average use of Twilight-related websites and that affective social identity was found to be the most important dimension of social identity, indicate that indeed these online pop culture fans resemble what Parks (2011) suggests and define a virtual community.

Earlier study findings indicate that all three dimensions—cognitive, affective, and evaluative social identity—were important for the development of a virtual community (Cheung & Lee, 2010). The results reported in this chapter do not support this finding since the mean scores for social identity are much lower than those for involvement dimensions. A possible explanation could be the measurement items *per se*. For instance, the social identity scale used lacks items more closely related to emotion and passion, which are proposed to be important dimensions of a consumer tribe

(Maffesoli, 1996). Personal involvement and product involvement were found to be the most important factors explaining use of social media, future intention to travel and participate in events, and to recommend to others. This implies that fans' inner needs, interests, and values, as well as perceptions about the product, are most important to explain tourism behavior and use of websites and blogs. Cai et al. (2004) specifically found that high levels of purchase involvement increase the likelihood of using the Internet for an information search. This result is consistent with the present study where product involvement, including purchase, was found to significantly increase average use of Twilight-related websites and blogs. Emotional ties and self-awareness are also somewhat valuable explanatory factors as seen by significant or near significant effects on the dependent variables from affective and cognitive social identity. Perceptions of self-worth seem to be less important, implying that fans do not feel that it is important to be valued by the community.

Interactivity has in previous research been found to affect community-related behavior as well as product-related behavior (Qu & Lee, 2011). Although this study did not specifically measure the effect of interactivity on future intention to participate and recommend or on average use, the results indicate the relevance of interactivity with the community. The most important motives for use as well as the relative importance of cognitive social identity, including the interaction aspect of overlap between self- and group identity, are indicators of the influence of interactivity.

This chapter contributes to the understanding of social media use in tourism, particularly, how social media connect to future tourism behavior is better understood. The results also indicate the importance of the cultural dimensions in the virtual community under study. The tribal characteristics of pop culture fans—the common identities, practices, rituals, meanings, and culture that they have produced (Cova et al., 2007)—explain their high involvement in the virtual community. Therefore, the cultural dimensions in a virtual community influence the fans' motives to travel. Hence, the study shows that it is evident that social media are important in shaping tourism behavior. The online travel-related activities do have an influence on the actual physical travel, thus an integration of the virtual and physical can be seen. Therefore, social media are an important part of tourism studies.

The chapter also indicates that the industry connected to pop culture tourism should be aware of the opportunity to use social media in distinguishing the pop culture tourists' inner needs, interests, and values and that their marketing strategies can be formulated accordingly. Furthermore, the findings indicate that fans' perceptions about the product are important for their use of social media and tourism-related behavior. This can be seen as an implication that not all types of tourism products can expect the same benefits from social media marketing. Pop culture tourists can be characterized by their strong involvement in a specific phenomenon (in this case, the *Twilight Saga*) and this drives their use of social media and consequently their intention to travel. This in turn supports the idea that social media use is an important link between pop culture fans and their tourism-related behavior.

Several topics for future research can be drawn from this study. First, the reasons for the weak contribution of social identity toward future intention to travel, recommend, and use social media need to be further explored. Second, if in fact pop culture fans' disposition to be highly involved and show high levels of social media use actually mean that they are somehow different from other tourists, this needs to be validated by comparing them to other types of tourists. Third, since social identity and involvement only partly explain the variance in future intentions and use of websites, blogs, and communities, other concepts need to be explored to complement these findings.

Regarding methods to study social media use in tourism, it is proposed that tourists with high levels of social media use need to be further studied from as many aspects as possible, especially in terms of concepts that can explain the motives behind their use. On the other hand, further knowledge on areas of tourism-related behavior where social media use is not so widespread is needed. For the study reported in this chapter, an online survey was used and the sample was users of websites, blogs, and communities connected to the *Twilight Saga*. A type of snowball sampling was used to frame a sample which, as much as possible, represents the online community of Twilight fans. The generalizability of the results from a sample where the population, to a large extent, is unknown in terms of size and general characteristics, is always a potential limitation. Therefore, a mixed methods approach using triangulation is proposed for future research to increase both reliability and validity. For instance, focus group interviews or in-depth interviews with tourists who use social media for various purposes could be complemented with online surveys and experimental designs.

In this case study, the sample is almost entirely based on female respondents. Although this is in line with the population of Twilight fans, it remains to be explored how the results compare to studies with a more equally distributed sample in terms of gender or a sample dominated by men. For example, would the results be similar for other pop culture fans in terms of social media use? This is important future research since it would clarify whether the results are attributable to a gender aspect or a specific pop culture phenomenon, or whether they could be generalized to a larger population.

Acknowledgments—The authors would like to thank Stavroula Wallström at University of Borås for creative and insightful ideas in the development of the survey instrument. Thanks are also extended to Mid Sweden University and the European Union Structural Funds for their contribution to the funding of this study through the projects "PopCulTour" and *Kunskapsbaserad turismutveckling* (Knowledge-based tourism development).

Chapter 9

Digital Social Construction of a Tourist Site: Ground Zero

Can-Seng Ooi
Copenhagen Business School, Denmark

Ana María Munar
Copenhagen Business School, Denmark

ABSTRACT

Reviews of Ground Zero, New York on TripAdvisor show a diversity of interpretations. Amidst the cacophony of voices, there is communication and a semblance of community. This sense of community—despite the lack of strong coherent and consistent views, a plethora of diverse topics, and heterogeneous perspectives—is brought together and built on chronotopic (time–space) structures. Drawing inspiration from Bakhtin's chronotopes, this chapter shows how spatial and temporal structures are negotiated. The negotiation processes demonstrate that tourists now have a global platform to communicate and are able to stake claims of legitimacy to interpreting foreign heritage. Thus tourists are layering new meanings on historical sites and are contributing to the rewriting of local histories, all as part of glocalization.

Keywords: Chronotopes; glocalization; tourist communication; heritage interpretation; emerging authenticity

Tourism Social Media: Transformations in Identity, Community and Culture
Tourism Social Science Series, Volume 18, 159–175
Copyright © 2013 by Emerald Group Publishing Limited
All rights of reproduction in any form reserved
ISSN: 1571-5043/doi:10.1108/S1571-5043(2013)0000018011

INTRODUCTION

Social media are transforming the tourism industry. With millions of persons commenting, complaining, and complimenting on social media platforms, an era of active public participation in the appreciation and interpretation of attractions and destinations has been initiated. These media have supposedly increased the transparency and empowered the customer base (Israel, 2009; Tapscott, 2009). For instance, the popular tourism website TripAdvisor, which is used as a case in this chapter, allows travelers to evaluate and express their thoughts and feelings toward tourism products. This development has not only created a cacophony of voices in social media but also in the tourism industry as a whole. Different contributors have different approaches and perceptions, giving rise to very diverse types of meanings and perspectives. The spectrum of views ranges from the playful to the serious, the celebratory to the disapproving. Regardless, the sum of different views creates a myriad of voices and opinions and a virtually linked group emerges and evolves. These groups, arguably communities, are constituted by seemingly helpful strangers and fleeting "friends" (Adkins & Grant, 2007).

This chapter shows that Web 2.0-based tourist communities not only reveal how visitors interpret places, inform of the range of different tourist interests, these so-called communities also document and subsequently recreate and enrich the attractions. Drawing on Bakhtin's concept of the chronotope, the recreation of the attraction entails three interrelated processes: re-temporalization, re-spatialization, and re-culturalization. These processes are part of "glocalization" (Robertson, 1995).

Tourism Social Media, Glocalization, and Chronotopes

Globalization does not just entail cultural homogeneity, but also dynamic and conflicting processes of "glocalization," with the local–global nexus playing a crucial role in the way places are consumed, imagined, and changed (Robertson, 1995). International tourism contributes much to glocalization. Local societies host foreign tourists, increasingly aiding the convergence of tourist behavior and subsequently the emergence of the tourist-way-of-doing-things or tourism cultures (Ooi, 2002a). Similarly, the pervasive use of social media has glocalizing patterns. On one hand, online communities, social networks, and interactive forums share a common set of rules and features, constituting a semblance of global culture (Castells, 2001). On the other hand, the interaction in virtual forums is also embedded in localized sociocultural practices and circumstances. Social media are affecting the global tourism industry; a comparison between traditional and social media interaction would help in understanding the process.

First, when compared to other traditional mass media such as newspapers or television broadcasts, social media encourage high levels of interactivity and participation among users (Cook, 2008). This is a potential that has been realized in Web 2.0 platforms like TripAdvisor and Facebook. But at the same time, not all users contribute to the discussions. Second, tourist-generated content can spread widely in an out-of-control manner. One dominant metaphor describing social media is "a virus." Virtual content can spread quickly and globally, like viral diseases. These media bring massive reach in an instant allowing communication with large numbers of people in different locations and at different times (Baym, 2010). At the same time, many stories do not spread.

Third, social media allow for multiple temporal structures as tourists may use online communities to engage in synchronous and asynchronous communication (Litvin et al., 2008). While face-to-face conversations are gone as soon as they have taken place, tourist-generated digital content can easily be stored and replicated. At the same time, online content is also ephemeral and what was posted one day can be modified or gone the next. This way, online content may remain for "eternity" or be modified or deleted instantly. Fourth, the use of these media is becoming increasingly mobile with tourists uploading and accessing user-generated content through mobile technologies (such as posting on Twitter from a mobile phone). The contribution to content has been democratized, in the sense that almost anyone with the appropriate equipment and with Internet access has the possibility to express her or his views, perspectives, and reflections. Contributors do not usually encounter content gatekeepers at the first instance.

Finally, as a consequence of the last point, these media also change what is communicated. Because of the invisibility of the content gatekeepers at the outset, tourists increasingly communicate emotions and feelings, for example, through immediate exclamations of pleasure or displeasure, use of smileys, like-button signs, and the like (Munar & Ooi, 2012). Such expressions also communicate an emotional sense of honesty. Generally, tourists' online conversations and electronic word-of-mouth can change the credibility of different information sources (Litvin et al., 2008), the perception of specific advertisements (Huang et al., 2010; Mack et al., 2008), and affect online information search patterns (Huang et al., 2010).

Despite the uncertainty and fluidity in social media platforms, user-generated content plays an increasingly major role in traditional marketers' strategies (Xiang & Gretzel, 2010). But the use of social media is not universal. Social media practices—as well as media adoption, Internet use, and levels of e-literacy—vary greatly across the globe (Gursoy & McCleary, 2004). Technology adoption and use depend on demographic characteristics (Hsu, Ju, Yen, & Chang, 2007) and national travel markets (Gretzel et al., 2008). Furthermore, the stability and strength of social media communities are questionable. Scholars have argued that traditional late-modern communities are based on reflexivity and individual choice (Beck & Beck-Gernsheim, 2002; Giddens, 1987; Lash, 2002). Castells (2001) suggests the relevance of individual choice and self-connectivity in the era of the Internet. Virtual tourism communities made up of review makers and storytellers appear in an unpredictable gray zone between both the local and the global and the personal and the public. Relationships are instantly created and dismantled. While traditional communities rely on personal identities, anonymous reviewers decouple their identities from their reviews. Fake reviews or misinformation do not necessarily entail penalties for the contributors or the administrators of the sites. In user-generated reviews, the richness of social and personal cues is poor.

In making sense of this complexity in the so-called "virtual world"— the blending of the local and global, communication among strangers and fleeting friends and asynchronized exchanges—meaningful dialogues and discussions still take place. The many diverse narratives are built on chronotopic structures (Bakhtin, 1981). Chronotope literally means "time–space" (Bakhtin, 1981, p. 84). The concept of chronotope asserts the primacy of space and time in the human experience (Bakhtin, 1981; Ooi, 2001; van Loon, 1997; Vice, 1997). Even in cyberspace, messages and stories have temporal and spatial dimensions. This study demonstrates how time, space, and meanings are reconstituted in the cacophony of voices and messages on social media platforms. To Bakhtin, time and space form an intricate matrix that gives body and organizes narratives in the text. A chronotope is a "primary means for materialising time in space, [and it] emerges as a centre for concretising representation, as a force giving body to the entire novel" (1981, p. 250). The narratives in social media, even if they are built mainly on experiences and memory, as will be shown later, offer the authority of solidity because of their temporal and spatial anchors.

Chronotopes heuristically separate time and space, and organize texts "according to the ratio and nature of the temporal and spatial categories represented" (Holquist, 1981, pp. 425–426). One can theoretically frame time and space as separate and distill them from the attached emotions and values in human experiences, but Bakhtin observed that

> [*L*]*iving* artistic perception ... makes no such divisions and permits no such segmentation. It seizes on the chronotope in all its wholeness and fullness. Art and literature are shot through with *chronotopic values* of varying degree and scope. Each motif, each separate aspect of artistic work bears value. (Bakhtin, 1981, p. 243, emphasis in original)

The articulations in social media are not mediated by one single author but by many people and constrained through the channels of communication. As a result, the cacophony of different voices can be confusing. There are different styles of writing, bringing together diverse genres of communication. The mishmash of articulations in social media does not offer a clear flow, but time–space structures remain embedded. As this chapter exemplifies in the case on Ground Zero in New York, the actual physical space and the fateful day (September 11, 2001) have become the spatial and temporal focal points for users of TripAdvisor to connect, communicate, and exchange. Those focal points, however, eventually evolve into a tumbleweed-like time–space structure that leads to the re-spatialization, re-temporalization, and re-culturalization of the site.

This chapter examines the consequences of the pervasive use of social media in the tourism industry and it does so by analyzing the representation of a tourist site—Ground Zero in New York City—in TripAdvisor. In the age of globalization, many objects and places are now part of a global awareness (Held, McGrew, Goldblatt, & Perraton, 1999). Ground Zero in New York is one of them. It is a site that is meaningful and even sacred to people around the world. It is a magnet for Web 2.0 discussions on the Internet. Social media are platforms that bring together people with different backgrounds, experiences, memories, and agendas. With the cacophony of voices and the absence of a "master story weaver," the exchanges have led to the new narratives on Ground Zero.

RECONSTRUCTING GROUND ZERO

The *re-temporalization* process accentuates how the linear chronological flow of time is subverted, as memories, thoughts, and feelings are expressed and presented in Web 2.0. Tourism scholars often divide up a trip into pre-visit,

visit, and post-visit phases (Jafari, 1987). This partition is also replicated in social media research (Fotis et al., 2012). This traditional division, however, becomes ambiguous and fluid in digitized communication, because a person uses the Web 2.0 before, during, and after the trip; on this medium, communication is often asynchronous (Baym, 2010). Comments and reviews are piled up without respect to whether entries were made during different stages of the tourism experience. They are based largely on personal experiences, perceptions, and memories. The fuzziness of temporal references in user-generated contents has consequences. For instance, visitors may be unaware of changes in the destination over time or have dated, preconceived ideas, all of which could lead to pleasant or unpleasant experiences when they evaluate their visits. Past memories, preconceptions, and expectations are blended with the newer site visit experiences in the reviews. With different individuals expressing their own personal reflections, and articulating their own mental construction of time and history of a site, a tourism social media platform offers a carnivalesque mesh of temporal layers. At the same time, the fateful day of September 11 in this case, is the focal point that gives readers and visitors the foundation to jointly articulate their (own diverse) versions of history.

Re-spatialization highlights how the physical boundary of a destination or attraction is mentally constructed in social media. Destinations and attractions often have a well-delimited physical presence, but as discussed later, people's memories and experiences of a place are not necessarily tied to fixed boundaries. Instead, people make mental, experiential, and imagined linkages to other places and selectively describe the place based on their own experiences, thus creating multiple spatial boundaries of an attraction or destination. The physical aspect of place is exerted in the narrative but it is actually being reimagined, leading to a re-spatialized destination. In spite of the fact that different people refer to the same place and the same event (such as Ground Zero and September 11), history gets constructed through narrations and images, as stories are layered one after another, especially when people make comparisons and links to other places. As these layers of stories travel through social media, readers around the world create their own perceived spatial boundaries for the attraction or destination.

The *re-culturalization* of destinations and attractions is inextricably tied to the processes of re-temporalization and re-spatialization, because meanings and interpretations are embedded with temporal and spatial dimensions. Social expressions of time and space carry cultural meanings. With the creation of new temporal and spatial interpretations, so do new social and cultural meanings. Tourists lack the local knowledge of residents, instead they imbue new meanings, as mentioned earlier. The tourist perspective has gained currency in the context of the Web 2.0 platform. For example, online travel reviews and user-generated content are often perceived as more likely to provide reliable information than content posted by tourism organizations (Yoo & Gretzel, 2008). What is perceived as authentic by tourists, however, can be perceived differently by residents. Social media sites have created a parallel virtual existence for the destination and attraction that sidelines local residents by giving primary attention to tourists. But there is no coherence in constituting the tourist-centered story. Instead, contrasting tales and interpretations melt together, constituting new aspects of the site, as will be shown later. What pulls the diverse interpretations together is the chronotopic concreteness of the physical space and September 11. From these starting points, a tumbleweed of temporal and spatial structures develop; together histories are rewritten and invented.

In sum, Web 2.0 tourism platforms are crucibles for the emergence of virtual destinations and touristic spaces, which are filled with tourism stories and imagery. History is literally being written, but not in a coherent manner, as more and more persons join in the discussion and add multiple layers of different views and information. In this way, the idea of what is to be a community is also being transformed. There is diversity and disagreement, and consensus and joint-affirmation (Munar, 2010a; Munar & Ooi, 2012). Despite the semblance of a community, online communities most often do not entail recurrent communication, strong familiarity or the establishment of deeper interdependent relationships (Kozinets, 2002, 2008). The cacophony of views makes for a thriving, fluid community of sporadic connections. Members come and go; many are strangers to one another. Some have the intention of being helpful while others enjoy the possibilities of self-expression, self-enhancement, and prestige (Bronner & de Hoog, 2011). The local cultural context that defines the physical destination has been represented by tourist-oriented perspectives, as tourists themselves create their own destination in ways that they themselves can enjoy, criticize, and feel for. This carnivalesque situation is also orderly if one is to understand it as the re-temporalization, re-spatialization, and re-culturalization of the attraction or destination.

Study Methods

As already stated, this chapter studies TripAdvisor, with Ground Zero in New York as the focal point of discussion and review. It examines the multiple and contrasting meanings and interpretations coming together on a common platform (TripAdvisor) in order to conceive cyber "realities." The inherent ontological frame adopted for this study is the constructive approach (Markham, 2004). In no way the intent is to provide a coherent picture of a virtual community in TripAdvisor; instead, it aims to highlight the heterogeneity and chronotopic fluidity in the articulations of Ground Zero. At the same time, it is important to acknowledge that it is possible for researchers to make sense of this diversity; somewhat coherent stories, interpretations, and histories emerge.

The study method consists of participative observation and it has been used by social scientists in conducting web research (Munar, 2010b; O'Reilly, Rahinel, Foster, & Patterson, 2007). Kozinets (2002, 2008) describes this method as an online evolution of ethnography and defines it as an application of methods of cultural anthropology to online cyber culture. Bronner and de Hoog (2011) suggest that analyses of tourists' contributions can adopt either site-centered or topic-centered approaches. This research adopts a site-centered and genre-focused approach and analyzes one social media site and its reviews. The platform is TripAdvisor, which is the largest networking site focusing on travel and tourism. The main type of content in TripAdvisor is the review of tourism products and offerings. TripAdvisor has over 20 million members; in May 2012 it claimed to have more than 60 million tourism product reviews (TripAdvisor, 2012a). Contrary to other social media sites, such as Facebook, TripAdvisor is an open network. It is not necessary to register or become a member to access the published content. However, it is necessary to create a virtual identity to upload content onto the site.

This study has two different streams of data analysis. The first investigates the structure and possibilities of TripAdvisor to map how tourists make use of this website to present their travel experiences. The analysis was conducted by making several visits to the website between February 2011 and January 2012 with the aim of examining the evolving stories. The second stream involves an extensive documentary analysis of a sample of travelers' reviews of Ground Zero in New York. The sample was established using TripAdvisor's search engine and classifying the reviews of these heritage sites by date and language (English). The search specification was "Ground Zero." The quotes used in this chapter are extracted from the search results of TripAdvisor. More than 80 posted reviews were analyzed.

Following the classical anthropological tradition of ethnographic field-work, the researchers observed, interpreted, internalized, reflected, and made sense of the happenings. This chapter does not offer a single authoritative interpretation of the so-called community. On the contrary, the study inquired what constitutes this community when there are so many different contrasting voices and messages. The simple answer is that TripAdvisor and Ground Zero are the focal points of the group. However, the researchers attempted to delve deeper. Most of the entries are not atomized and unrelated to others. If users are having exchanges, one wonders, what they are saying and how they are bonding. It was only at a later stage of the study that it was decided to use Bakhtin's chronotope to help present the muddy situation without trying to marginalize the diversity. The researchers recognized that they were ordering a narrative onto the heterogeneous narratives they had encountered, internalized, and reflected on.

The Social Digital Construction of Ground Zero

September 11 has been one of the most fateful days in recent history. The sight of two airplanes crashing into the Twin Towers of the World Trade Center in New York has been etched into the collective memory. Official memorial services are held every year to mark the incident. The site where the twin towers once stood soon was dubbed Ground Zero. The redevelopment of Ground Zero has, however, been fraught with debates and controversies. These include the redevelopment of the site, having a Muslim community center close by, and the placement of the memorial. The attacks have also transformed air travel, with security checks at airports tightened all over the world. Ground Zero has become a tourism attraction. It is also a focal point in TripAdvisor, as foreigners and locals come together to tell their perspectives on this site.

Re-temporalization: The Mental Gaps and Leaps

September 11 offers a plethora of memories to people around the world. The memory remains vivid for many and is thus temporally "frozen" in people's minds. In contrast to the memories they hold, many reviewers were disappointed when they visited the site. For instance, StephP09 (January 30, 2010) of Medicine Hat, AB declared "Nothing to see" and wrote: "It is really just a construction site so there is absolutely nothing to see." Similarly, Gary488 of Leeds, UK (August 16, 2011) repeated: "Not worth a visit until the development is done. There is nothing to see but a building site."

To StephP09 and Gary488, a construction site is a non-sight. They have decoupled the massive construction project from its tragic history in their statements, revealing what is interesting and what is not to them. On the other hand, at about the same time, Robo34 of Iowa City commented with the headline, "Must see, but not much to see yet":

> It was surreal to visit this site, especially the fire department across the street from the construction. There were a couple small memorials there along with a poster showing all the brave men and women that gave and lost their lives on 9-11. It was emotional. After spending the first 2 days seeing all the other sites of NYC, I felt this experience cut through all the phonies and advertising and pomp that makes this city what it is. It was sobering, and I'm glad I did it. (April 29, 2010)

Larkie25 of Gainesville, Florida succinctly headlined his contribution, "Things to see is what you can't see anymore" (April 17, 2010). The disenchantment in what is to be seen by some of the reviewers and this last quote bring to mind the greater sensitivity that tourists put on visual elements (Urry, 1990). The site has already been previously imagined and visually objectified and the unfinished, chaotic, and unpredictable view of a construction site does not always live up to the expectation of the tourists' fantasy. Inherent in these contrasting views is that memories and expectations are essential in experiencing and evaluating Ground Zero as a tourist site. A historical site like Ground Zero, by definition, is meaningful because of its past and its stories. Tourists' anticipation regarding this tragic site has been nurtured by massive non-touristic information. One may then argue, these individuals may recall images of devastation broadcast by global media, but in the reviews these recollections are not considered part of the site they have come to visit. This disappointment by some visitors arises from unfulfilled (and incorrect) expectations. Prentice and other researchers show that tourists have preconceptions and they want to reinforce them through their tourism experiences (McIntosh & Prentice, 1999; Prentice, 2004; Prentice & Andersen, 2007). During their trips, these tourists will intentionally seek to affirm their own notions of the sites. These tourists find their heritage experiences richer when they confirm their expectations and see familiar aspects of the heritage sites they visit.

Regardless, in the context of how memories are expressed on TripAdvisor, the temporal dimension in the historical product has become an evaluative criterion of the site. Two opposing views are highlighted. The first is that memories are in the past, and Ground Zero does not have anything to show relating to September 11 because it has been cleaned up and rebuilt. For these tourists, their visits are not worthwhile because their memories of the fateful day will remain as memories, which are not reified, from their perspective. The second view is that those memories are what make Ground Zero the site it is. The world has moved on but being there, armed with one's memory, makes the visit meaningful. But if the memories are what really matter, is visiting the physical site necessary? There will always be an inherent temporal gap between the past and the present. In the case of the discussion on TripAdvisor, different people package Ground Zero along diverse, selective, temporal elements. As a whole, the TripAdvisor community has created a set of "packaged pasts" (Ooi, 2001) that gives Ground Zero several temporal links between the past and present, allowing individuals diverse ways of appreciating, criticizing, remembering, and experiencing the site.

Re-spatialization: Place Linkages

Ground Zero is a site for tourists even though it is based on a tragic event. Different people have different relationships to it. The Bakhtinian chronotopic perspective suggests that time and place are always embedded in any articulations, and so September 11 is a temporal marker in people's memories; the subsequent images of the disaster have come to define the spatial spot of that memory. The disaster area may be where the attacks took place, but the search for meanings to experience the disaster site led to people redefining the boundaries of Ground Zero—that is, re-spatializing the site.

Many tourists see Ground Zero as a pilgrimage site, a must-visit stop in their itinerary of New York. To people around the world, Ground Zero carries emotional meanings. Hertfords, from Hertfordshire, United Kingdom, however, lamented emotionally that they could not visit the new memorial after traveling "five thousand miles":

> If you are planning to visit ground zero and would like to visit the new memorial, then for gods sake get your passes as flying half way round the world and [practically begging] to be let in does not work! (October 10, 2011)

While people around the world remember Ground Zero as September 11, the physical place is now managed and regulations are used to control visitor numbers. Tourists do not necessarily know that. Without the local knowledge, travel can bring about physical and emotional anxiety related to feelings of uncertainty and unfamiliarity in foreign places (Ooi, 2005).

User-generated content fills in the needed local knowledge to save other visitors from disappointment, as Hertfords attempted to do. Tourists contributing to social media sites reveal altruistic behavior and a wish to help fellow tourists (Chang & Chuang, 2011). Essentially, the space has acquired new contexts that require the management of public access. Distant tourists are unaware of administrative changes and carry only iconic images of the place from September 11.

Ground Zero is also re-spatialized by association. For instance, an anonymous contributor from Chicago, Illinois (April 14, 2005) visited Pearl Harbor before and declared that Ground Zero is "our second pearl harbor." A reviewer from Muroia, Spain, said:

> So, you go there, you see all those pictures of the minutes before and after, you see the name of the people who died ... you remember that day when you were watching TV and didn't believe what your eyes were seeing, you remember 4 bombs in 4 trains a year ago in your own country ... well, just to see that my stomach turn upside down, and my eyes start watering ... I don't think that's at all a place to go, as if you'll going to the central park. (July 20, 2005)

What happened in Pearl Harbor and in Madrid were terrible tragedies. Comparisons made to Ground Zero were drawn on the horrors of the events. These are examples of tourists' contemplative views on the sites and also of the centrality of emotions in making spatial connections. These places are coupled together based on their emotional responses (or these places are "twinned"). Inadvertently, a map emerges containing tourism sites that are supposedly similar and emotionally laden.

Such an emotion-related map may have a different shape at a much smaller scale. The following examples show how Ground Zero is associated to nearby places that carry stories. Mental spaces are much more fluid than physical ones. On TripAdvisor, many reviewers provide emotional maps and tips to appreciate the site better, effectively redrawing the boundaries of Ground Zero. SueMunn of Luton, Beds suggested:

> Just stumbled across this Irish Bar after having been to Ground Zero. The place is wonderful. Paul (owner's son) was fabulous. He has a photo album of the aftermath of the tragedy and the rebuilding of the bar which was so moving. His stories were amazing and he has the most fabulous

outlook on life. [...] Met the most amazing people who all shared their own experiences of that terrible event. To really understand the enormity of how this shook the local people, O'Hara's is a must see. (September 26, 2006)

This bar is presented as an authentic space that offers non-staged interpretations, moving the emotional contents of the actual physical site to the bar that carries the stories. With it, Ground Zero as a pilgrimage site has been spatially enlarged. Similarly, TABWisconsin recommended going to the St. Paul's Chapel:

When I was at Ground Zero, there were tarps along all the fences so you couldn't see anything on the ground ... but you could see the rebuilding. I also went across the street to the St. Paul's Chapel. The Chapel tells and shows so much. I am struggling to explain what this experience meant to me. I was so touched by the stories and the artifacts [...] A very very worthwhile place to visit. (September 10, 2011)

In these cases, tourists draw personal emotional maps. In the context of TripAdvisor, the dialogue between mental and physical spaces are cast out, indicating that Ground Zero is only a focal point; September 11 as a space is limited only by people's mental mapping. Ground Zero as a place is spatialized through people's memories and experiences, and TripAdvisor is digitizing the creation of a folklore.

Re-culturalization: Indignation and Change

One may argue that the re-temporalization and re-spatialization of Ground Zero is also about the re-culturalization of the site because new meanings are introduced to the site. Through the sharing of their analysis and opinions, tourists help construct new signs and meanings. One of the issues dealt with by the virtual tourist community is the touristification of Ground Zero. A reviewer from Toronto voiced concerns about touristification, with the heading: "Ground Zero unfortunately now a tourist money trap!"

Last weekend I visited the WTC and was truly disgusted that the area around this site has become home to hoards of people selling twin towers pictures, t-shirts, statues, trinkets, flags, including conspiracy theory wackos giving speeches how this was an inside! A street musician was actually playing a solemn version of the Battle Hymn of the republic with his violin case open for tips. [...] I never thought New York would allow this cemetery to be disrespected after 9/11! (September 23, 2008)

Tourism is seen as having a corrupting influence. To many, there seems to be tacit "do's and don'ts" for a memorial site like Ground Zero. What is acceptable and unacceptable is negotiated online. For instance, StickyNic, from the United Kingdom, declared, "Not a tourist attraction":

It's a very chilling and surreal experience, I had never been to New York before so I can't actually imagine the towers being there [...] People were taking pictures but I didn't feel right doing that as I kept thinking that the remains of people's bodies have evaporated on that site.

It made me put my life in perspective. People should go to pay their respects but not to take pictures or treat it like a tourist attraction. (July 8, 2005)

Earlier in 2004, a fierce debate had ensued. A New Yorker stated:

It is somewhat understandable that tourists may be interested in seeing the World Trade Center site, but please do not treat it as an "attraction". It is not an attraction so please do not go if you are going to be taking lots of pictures and act as though you are visiting a museum or something. New Yorkers do not really appreciate that because we actually were there or near there on 9/11. There is also not really anything to see there, so I don't suggest you go unless you are very respectful about it. I have seen many tourists happily taking pictures of the site like it is just another attraction, but it is not. (August 9, 2004)

Some reviewers "step-out" of the tourist role and claim to represent the "voice" of the locals. Bealll95 from Kansas agreed with the above comment:

I was in NYC this summer and went to the WTC site. To pay my respects. I am a Firefighter and I lost friends in the attack. I can understand if you're going here to pay your respects, but this is a grave site. Not a photo opp. I was extremely saddened by how many people were taking family photos here. I shoot shots for our fire department and I didn't even take my camera out of it's bag. Should you go? Well, think about why you're going. If you're going to pay respect and to help you get the reality of this terrible day ... ABSOLUTELY. If you're going to shoot photos or just to stare at the hole. ABSO-LUTELY NOT. Just realize over 2000 people died there and 343 were firemen saving others' lives. (November 23, 2004)

A contributor from England would not visit the site after reading Realll95's posting:

After reading the comments from the fireman, although strongly put, I am not sure now whether I can bring myself to visit Ground Zero, because as he so rightly put it, it is not and never will be a tourist attraction and yet in me visiting the site, that is what its becoming. I think I'll now pay my respects at a distance. (November 28, 2004)

Responding to these concerns, local New Yorker stevewesb encouraged tourists to visit and take pictures, with the headline "Living across WTC—why you should visit/take pictures":

Consider that each time a family views their pictures from the WTC site they remember: those that lost their lives; the 4+ story, NYC-block grave; the black "shroud" that encapsulates the Deutsche Bank building.

But in addition to this, the family photos hopefully bring about memories of enjoying NYC, the friendliness (thanks to 9-11) of New Yorkers, and thank those that still continue to protect us.

Visiting, taking pictures, seeing WTC is a healing process. If tourists STOP coming to visit this area then the area will continue to be economically damaged ... . (April 2, 2005)

The contributor then suggested that visitors remain respectful during their visit, reflecting on the tragedy and the sacrifices made by the fire and security services. Taking pictures is not to be seen as disrespectful. The discussion of Ground Zero as a tourism site shows that tourists are concerned with touristification. There is no definitive conclusion on how tourists should behave; they now constitute a significant stakeholder to the site. The concerns accentuated here show that Ground Zero is not just about September 11. People have emotional links to the place and tourism is seen as a boon or a bane by various persons. Regardless, Ground Zero is a magnet for tourists visiting New York and is a global space. TripAdvisor has documented Ground Zero as a tourism space with conflicting views. As a result, Ground Zero acquires a tourist-centered story beyond September 11 and local development. Ground Zero is being re-culturalized. Time will tell if a consensus will emerge on how tourists should interpret and behave at the site. The contestations continue.

CONCLUSION

This chapter has shown that a tourism site like Ground Zero is being re-spatialized, re-temporalized, and re-culturalized in a Web 2.0 platform. There are a number of conclusions to draw from this study.

The first conclusion is on how social media has transformed the tourism industry. One of the transformations is the proliferation of the tourist-centric perspective of attractions, as presented in social media. Tourism mediators remain important in the industry, but tourists themselves are coming together to mediate each other's experiences.

The examination of the reviews shows how tourists understand themselves as part of a community of fellow travelers who come together to create, share, and exchange information. Tourists are not passive spectators. Tourism social media transforms tourists' communicative practices. Reviewer contributions appear in a fluid gray zone between the local and the global, between the personal and the public. They share their personal emotions but try to establish global rules of appropriate tourism behavior. They share private experiences of grief and expose them to millions of viewers. The case of Ground Zero shows how the site is being re-temporalized, -spatialized, and -culturalized. There is no tight consistency or coherence in the collection of reviews. Nevertheless, the exchanges in the virtual community reflect many of the concerns and issues tourists have and also reflect their roles as cocreators of heritage experiences.

The second conclusion, which is related to the first, is on the proliferation of the use of social media. The innovative feature of tourists' online review making is that this new form of mediation of the tourism experience cannot be fully controlled by the industry. Tourist-created content shapes experiences. Sharing digital reviews broadens the access to experiences of "touristhood" so that tourists do not only see their experiences in contrast to their own day-to-day activities, but also in many different contexts based on other travelers' experiences (Tussyadiah & Fesenmaier, 2009). As tourists are not living close to the sites, their sense of time, place, and the culture in relation to the site differ from that of locals. Tourist perspectives are now being articulated and memorialized in TripAdvisor. In other words, tourists have now found a platform to get "organized." They now have a global channel to communicate with others around the world, asserting their views and voices, laying claim to tourism sites and staking claims of legitimacy to their own interpretations. Could it be then postulated that social media quicken the emergence of new global tourism cultures? Further research is needed.

Finally, the third conclusion deals with tourism destination and attraction management organizations. A site like Ground Zero is acquiring new meanings as time flows. Practitioners and researchers alike tend to concentrate on the authenticity of the stories. That is rightly so. However, this study shows that tourists are now layering new meanings onto the historical site, and these meanings are being documented on social media platforms. This is an opportunity for market research and the creation of new narratives for historical tourist products. A more fundamental question is then: who has the authority to write and rewrite history?

This study shows that Web 2.0 is not making traditional tourism mediators redundant. Instead, social media have empowered tourists. They do not just exert their influence through their buying power now but also their ability to articulate and exchange their views at a global level. Nonetheless, their voices remain diffuse, and there is little consensus, like many other "real" societies. Thus, this chapter ends by bringing up a newer (after the memorial has been officially inaugurated) entry on Ground Zero in TripAdvisor, one that is likely to start another spatial and temporal thread in the tumbleweed. Time2Seel, from Melbourne, Australia:

> This memorial is very eloquent, humble, and respectful. You're able to spend as much time there as you like, and just read the names. It becomes a personal experience when you see the photos/notes/roses left next to some of the names. (October 25, 2011)

And the story continues and the history is in the making.

Chapter 10

Tourism Social Media and Crisis Communication: An Erupting Trend

Kristian Anders Hvass
Copenhagen Business School, Denmark

ABSTRACT

This chapter studies crisis communication within the backdrop of tourism social media. The Scandinavian airline SAS is chosen as a case study due to the recognition of the airline's social media presence during the 2010 ash cloud crisis. The study relies on netnographic and content analysis methods to examine Facebook postings throughout the life-cycle stages of the crisis as well as an interview with a social media representative at the airline. The social mediated crisis communication model is applied to situational crisis communication theory, and the findings show that social media provide a beneficial channel during a crisis. However, it is necessary for organizations to recognize stakeholders' needs during a crisis as social media presence alone does not ensure success.

Keywords: Crisis; airline; life cycle; social mediated crisis communication model; situational crisis communication theory

INTRODUCTION

During the spring of 2010, the global aviation industry experienced a widespread exogenous crisis seldom seen before. The volcanic eruption of the Icelandic volcano Eyjafjallajökull on April 14 caused enormous financial

Tourism Social Media: Transformations in Identity, Community and Culture
Tourism Social Science Series, Volume 18, 177–191
ISSN: 1571-5043/doi:10.1108/S1571-5043(2013)0000018012

and travel hardships for nearly 10 days throughout most of Europe due to flight cancellations and the requirement to maintain safe operations. The overall impact between April 14 and April 21 was progressive closure of European airspace causing the cancellation of 100,000 flights, a 30% reduction in global airline capacity, disruption to 10 million travelers, including 5 million passengers who were stranded, nearly US$2 billion in lost revenue for airlines, and an overall impact on the European economy of $5 billion (Chittenden & Swinford, 2010; *The Telegraph*, 2011).

The European Organization for the Safety of Air Navigation states that during a normal day in April there are nearly 30,000 flights in European airspace; however, during the crisis period, the lowest number of daily flights was 5,204 on April 18. As the ash cloud drifted southeast, those responsible for airspace management began to close access, with parts of the United Kingdom and Norway closing portions of their airspace on the same day as the eruption. The following day both Danish and Swedish airspace was closed by late afternoon (EUROCONTROL, 2010b). Over the course of the next two days, airspace to the south and east of Denmark was progressively closed. These decisions resulted in a shutdown of nearly all air travel to, from, and within Europe. This trend was reversed as airspace was progressively opened from the 19th of April onwards. Denmark's airspace was open to operations again on April 20. The majority of Swedish airspace was available for use by April 21 and European traffic levels were nearly 80% of normal (EUROCONTROL, 2010a). Although operations were near to normal eight days after the commencement of the event, airlines were still experiencing challenges due to the massive number of stranded passengers throughout Europe and the rest of the world; it took several weeks for airlines to remove the backlog of stranded passengers throughout their networks. All airlines with operations to, from, within, and transitioning European airspace were affected; however, airlines with home markets in affected airspace were especially hard hit. The Scandinavian airline Scandinavian Airline Systems (SAS) had to endure the brunt of airspace closures.

The Danish, Swedish, and Norwegian governments together own 50% of the airline group SAS AB. The SAS Group consists of three airline brands: Scandinavian Airline Systems, based in the three Scandinavian countries, Widerøe in Norway, and Blue1 in Finland. It is the largest airline in the Nordic region and carries nearly 25 million passengers annually with a market share in home markets between 30 and 50% (SAS Group, 2012). The airline offers more than 1,000 daily departures to nearly 130 destinations in 30 countries. The SAS Group's market was quickly impacted by the ash cloud. Between April 15 and 19, SAS had no operations, although normality came slowly from April 20 onward. The impact of the eruption on the SAS Group was a loss of nearly 25% of passengers for the month of April and approximately $100 million (Berlingske Business, 2010). This expense can be attributed to lost bookings and reimbursement for accommodation and alternative transportation. Communication plays an important role in any crisis in the aviation industry (Ray, 1999) and past events affecting SAS were dealt with in a traditional manner. The airline's website was used as a communication outlet that could provide up-to-date information while customer service representatives were available via telephone and in the airport terminal (C. Ericsson, personal communication, December 7, 2011). However, the scale of the problem tested the scalability of traditional crisis communication processes. Prior to the ash crisis, SAS had decided that social media was to play an active role in general customer service and although full implementation of it as a customer service channel had not taken place, the airline was able to utilize social media as a crisis communication tool even though this was beyond the original intentions. This chapter shows that social media have a role to play in crisis communication although there are limitations, such as recognizing stakeholder needs in relation to the crisis at hand.

SOCIAL MEDIA PRESENCE DURING A CRISIS

This chapter seeks to apply situational crisis communication theory (SCCT) and the social mediated crisis communication (SMCC) model and view them through a study of a successful, award-winning use of social media by SAS during the ash crisis (*The Financial*, 2010). The method applied is a single case study with the online social content presented during a one-month time period in April 2010 as the unit of analysis. Netnography and content analysis of the online posts, enhanced by an in-depth interview, allow the author to draw conclusions about the utilization of social media for crisis communication. This research on the theory implies that it is a relevant framework for studying communication plans, however, further developments should include an understanding of crisis typologies and subsequent user needs to improve online communication effectiveness. This allows for future research into the types of crises that would be well handled by firms with a social media presence. Within the practical field, these results show that firms need to have a pre-crisis presence on online platforms if they are to capitalize on the benefits of the media channel during externalities and that firms must recognize stakeholder needs during a crisis as social media presence alone is not a guarantee of success during such an event.

The concepts of crisis and disaster are often considered synonymous. However, researchers have identified distinguishing elements, such as the event size (Pauchant & Mitroff, 1992; Quarantelli, 1988), number affected by the event (Quarantelli, 1988), size of the organization managing an event response, such as government versus firm (Quarantelli, 1988), event catalyst (Ray, 1999), level of impact on an organization's assumptions (Pauchant & Mitroff, 1992), and perception of the event itself (Coombs, 2012). In broad terms, a disaster is often regarded as a large-scale event that affects many actors, while a crisis can be seen as a localized event. Therefore, a crisis is often regarded as local and small scale, often at the organizational level. Although the terms may be distinguishable, this chapter refers to the two as a crisis for ease of reading.

A crisis is a challenge that can raise or sink an organization, and the complex and interwoven world means that an event in a distant land may have repercussions close to home. In addition, it is often not a question of whether it *will* happen but rather *when*; as Coombs states, "a crisis is unpredictable but not unexpected" (2012, p. 3). As such, it is beneficial for organizations to have management processes in place to deal with such externalities, including a communication strategy. Whether a crisis is the result of an organization's specific, endogenous actions or an impact from exogenous factors, an organization's response communication is vital. To remain silent during a time of challenge is a pleasure organizations cannot afford without the risk of allowing external stakeholders to shape the communicative discourse.

Organizational communication can take place with various stakeholders: employees, customers, suppliers, general market, and the like. The communication content and chosen medium reflect the technological landscape. The Internet has radically transformed organizational communication during the past decades (Liu, Austin, & Jin, 2011), and the current Internet communicative cusp is social media (Jin, Liu, & Austin, 2011; Veil, Buehner, & Palenchar, 2011). The speed, unique information, and interactivity of these platforms make social media ideally suited to complement organizations' more traditional communication strategies (Liu et al., 2011; Taylor & Perry, 2005). Although it is recognized that Internet communication can trigger a crisis (Alfonso & Suzanne, 2008; Conway, Ward, Lewis, & Bernhardt, 2007; Coombs, 2012; Mei, Bansal, & Pang, 2010), several authors recognize that the benefits exceed the pitfalls (Coombs, 2012; González-Herrero & Smith, 2008; Liu & Kim, 2011; Taylor & Kent, 2007).

Life-Cycle Framework for Crisis Management

Crisis communication first entered the management literature in the 1980s (Coombs, 2007) with Mowen (1980) introducing the concept of a managed response by organizations and the link between communication and attribution theory (Kelley, 1967, 1980). Subsequently, the field has hosted two dominant theories (Kim, Avery, & Lariscy, 2009): image restoration theory and SCCT. The former is Benoit's (1997) theory that focuses on response actions to organizational crises and communication plans, which is an extension of apologia theory (Rowland & Jerome, 2004). While image restoration theory is concerned with effective response rhetoric, SCCT (Coombs, 2012) concerns itself with a holistic view of a crisis life cycle and subsequent organizational responses. A life-cycle framework is often utilized to capture the nuances found during the various stages of an externality; some argue for three stages (Coombs, 2012; Sturges, 1994), others for four (Fink, 1986; González-Herrero & Smith, 2008). The three fundamental stages are: planning and recognition, crisis, and postcrisis. Within this framework researchers are able to apply additional concepts to complement a life-cycle analysis, such as incorporation of Internet technologies (González-Herrero & Smith, 2008) and the current theoretical cusp with the social mediated crisis communication model (Liu et al., 2011).

The planning and recognition stage concerns an organization's preparation for an eventual crisis. This stage involves identification of exposure and drawing up of a plan, ranging from diagnosis to developing a management plan (Coombs, 2012). The crisis stage initially requires the identification and agreement of its existence. Coombs' three crisis dimensions—perceived importance, immediacy, and uncertainty—allow an organization to evaluate severity. Perceived importance varies directly with the perception of loss and the organizational response may vary according to stakeholders' perceptions and needs. Immediacy incorporates the perception of time and response urgency. Uncertainty addresses crisis ambiguity. It is natural for stakeholders to strive for low uncertainty, and the use of communication tools in cases of low and high uncertainty vary. The final stage is the postcrisis response once the dilemma has subsided. Crisis managers should continue their efforts once business returns to normal. This work includes monitoring sources for postcrisis data and input and an evaluation of the crisis management. Depending on its type, postcrisis management may include facilitation by the organization of respondents, such as government authorities. Although SCCT provides a framework for analyzing the life cycle of a crisis, it fails to recognize the source of communication. This is addressed by complementing SCCT with the development of the SMCC model (Liu et al., 2011).

Liu et al. (2011) have expanded on the theory of social crisis communication by incorporating social media into the mix with the model of social mediated crisis communication. Events evoke an emotional need in those affected (Macias, Hilyard, & Freimuth, 2009) and online social outlets may provide a useful channel due to their ability to provide emotional support or venting (Jin & Liu, 2010). The catalyst for development of the SMCC model has been a desire to incorporate a communication source in the event of a crisis (Liu et al., 2011). Originally referred to as the blog-mediated crisis communication model (Liu & Austin, 2010), SMCC proposes that social media have a role to play during an event in relation to three factors of persuasion: issue relevance, information seeking/sharing, and emotional venting/support (Liu et al., 2011). Three stakeholders interact with social media-created content: creators (organizations and/or individuals), followers, and inactives. An organization can either be a creator of content itself or have a direct relationship with others outside of the organization who create content during a crisis. This relationship can either be direct between an organization and creators or through social media. Subsequently, influential creators can have an offline relationship with followers and inactives (Liu et al., 2011). While creators develop content, followers consume social media content, and inactives consume information in offline channels. Despite findings by Taylor and Perry (2005) suggesting that the Internet and social media are instrumental in crisis communication, and Schultz, Utz, and Göritz's (2011) finding that social media sites play a role as information sources for social media inactives, the study of Liu et al. (2011) failed to find significant dependence on it as a source of information among a sample of university students. However, the interaction among sources (word-of-mouth, traditional media, and social media) indicates that communication source, content, and media must all be considered; there is not a one-solution-fits-all strategy, which is addressed in the SMCC model (Fig. 1).

Study Methods

A qualitative study was carried out to analyze a unique crisis situation at SAS affected by an unexpected exogenous case whose impact on customers was partly addressed using social media tools. The goal of the study was to investigate the role and meaning of this media in communicating with

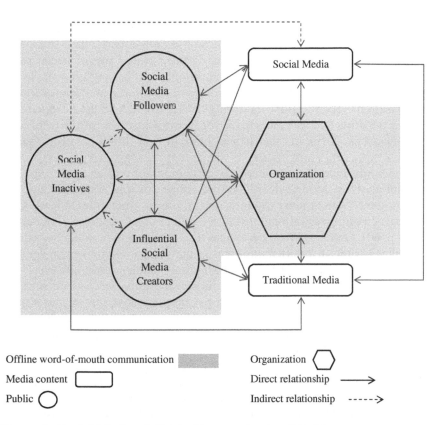

Figure 1. Social Mediated Crisis Communication Model
Source: Liu et al. (2011, p. 347)

customers during a crisis. Creswell (2003) argues that qualitative methods allow the researcher to explore and understand meanings, while quantitative methods seek to measure relationships. The latter may provide greater generalization, however, this method of analysis of the chosen phenomenon would mask peculiarities. In addition, Yin (2003) states that the case study method is preferred when examining contemporary events where inputs cannot be manipulated by the researcher. Although Coombs (2007) recognizes the role of case studies in communication research, he does acknowledge the method's limitations.

The study follows a holistic design with a single case, which lends itself to analyzing a single phenomenon in depth (Yin, 2003). It views the case as a single entity with a single unit of analysis. The unit of analysis in the study is social media content presented during a one-month time period in April 2010. This captures the status of the airline's use of social media pre, during, and postcrisis stages. The rationale for relying on a single case design is that it is unique. Although several airlines and transportation organizations used social media during the ash event, SAS used it extensively during the crisis and was recognized for its innovative use of the technology (*The Financial*, 2010); in other words, one can view this as a best-in-practice case.

The study relies on the methods of netnography (Kozinets, 2009) and content analysis (Krippendorf, 2004) of online postings and interviews with firm posters. Netnography expands on traditional ethnographic methods as "… participant-observational research based in online fieldwork" (Kozinets, 2009, p. 60). Online fieldwork provides data that are often publicly available on online forums in an often unobtrusive method. A researcher can act as an observer in the online field and be entirely anonymous; however, such behavior requires satisfying various ethical questions, such as openness on behalf of the researcher. The method has been employed in various studies, such as marketing research (Kozinets, 2002), education (Sandin, 2007), and for sensitive topics such as cosmetic surgery (Langer & Beckman, 2005), as well as wedding planning (Nelson & Otnes, 2005).

The researcher had been a fan of the official SAS Facebook group (https://www.facebook.com/SAS) since 2010, which allowed access to the site's content. This Facebook group is administered by the airline and presents posts by both SAS and fans. This study analyzes three types of posts: initial content created by SAS, initial content created by users, and responses to initial content posted by either party. Initial content is understood to be posts that can potentially start a social dialogue. Historical posts were found by scrolling through the record on the SAS Facebook group. The time period for analysis is April 1, through April 30, 2010. In order to archive this data, the content was saved as screen shots in PDF.

The netnographic method is complemented with one open, flexible interview with the manager of the Online Strategy and Communications department. The interview highlighted the history and goals of the social media team at the airline, the experiences and change in procedures that took place once the ash crisis commenced, and what lessons were learned from the experience. This interview allowed the author to analyze and compare the intended goals of the team with the results from the content analysis.

Study Findings

The ash cloud crisis that affected airline traffic to and from Europe demonstrated that social media had a relevant role to play in communication throughout the event's life cycle. The needs of stakeholders were best addressed through the immediacy and legitimization offered by social media, however addressing emotional aspects was also important. SAS was subsequently acknowledged postcrisis for its online engagement. But research shows that during the precrisis, the airline had no recognition of social media as a crisis communication tool.

Precrisis. The establishment of the official SAS Facebook site in December 2009 was intended to be a complement to traditional customer service channels, such as phone, chat, website, and email (C. Ericsson, personal communication, December 7, 2011). According to the director of Online Strategy and Communications, the overarching goal of the site was to handle and service customers in a proactive manner. This department is tasked with developing and implementing various projects in the online and communicative realms, while the Customer Contact Center (CCC), a unit of the Sales and Marketing department, is the owner of the airline's social media page on Facebook. As of this writing, CCC has approximately 20 employees responsible for customer contact via various communicative channels, including the Facebook page, and their employees rotate among the various channels.

SAS had been present and a content creator on social media prior to the ash event. Data collected by the author for previous studies (Hvass & Munar, 2011) show that SAS had nearly 10,000 fans by the end of February 2010 (as of March 2012, SAS had more than 175,000 fans) and had an unofficial platform presence since early 2009. In 2010, the airline was creating a monthly average of 13 posts, compared to an average of 9 for all airlines present on Facebook at the time (Hvass & Munar, 2011). During this time, their communicative tone on the platform had been informal and social in nature, an opportunity to build rapport and strengthen relationships with users and customers of SAS. However, the rate of posts on the official SAS site appears to be skewed toward the users rather than the airline. In the time frame leading up to the crisis, SAS initiated 12% of the posts on the platform. Among these posts, the majority were of promotion material, such as new features for frequent flyer members and awards earned by the airline. There are also posts with a focus on customer service.

For example, one SAS EuroBonus member questions the Facebook team about a missing frequent flyer card: "Hello ... I have been a SAS member for a year already and I have not gotten my card ... . when am I supposed to get it?"(if necessary, posts are translated verbatim by the author.) The issue is addressed and solved by SAS over the course of two days, and the entire conversation consisting of 12 posts is public and the Facebook fans can follow the exchanges. This type of transparent communication allows followers to get answers to similar questions without contacting the airline, while at the same time, allowing followers to see the proactive nature of customer service from the airline. The informal and social behavior of SAS on Facebook mimics the overall behavior for airlines' use of social media (Hvass & Munar, 2011), although there is inconsistency in the use of the Scandinavian and English languages. For example, a post written in English elicits an SAS response in English; however, a post written in a Scandinavian language prompts an SAS response either in that language or in English.

Crisis communication plans are in place at SAS for various channels. These plans aid employees in their handling of various situations and ensure that the airline presents an organized front to the outside world. At the onset of the project, to introduce social media to CCC, its channel was not regarded as an element in the airline's crisis communication plan. The channel was in its early stages and was intended exclusively as a customer service medium, and it had yet to become fully anchored in the organization. In fact, the official handover from the Online Strategy and Communications department to CCC was to take place on the 14th of April and the flight cancellations hindered the travel of department members to oversee the transfer of responsibility.

Crisis.   The eruption of Eyjafjallajökull on the 14th of April led to closure of some northern Scandinavian airspace the same day. However, the real impact of the problem was felt the following day as the ash cloud drifted southward. On the SAS Facebook page, there was limited communication on the day of the eruption: five posts by fans regarding various topics, and the last one by a fan, at 23:17 stating, "The ash from the volcano on Iceland has reach Norway and a few airports are already closed. So to all travelers, check out [link to Avinor, the Norwegian airport authority]." This post receives a single response from a follower 51 minutes later with an expression of gratitude. The benefits of interactivity and facilitation benefits from social media come to light as its influential creators are able to inform the followers and inactives of a potential crisis (Liu et al., 2011).

At the outset of the eruption, SAS' online behavior on Facebook suggests that the airline perceives the event as a crisis. Its first reaction to the looming event on Facebook is at 08:43 on April 15 with the following post: "Norwegian airspace is closed due to volcanic eruption in Iceland. We'll be back with more information soon. Stay tuned. Follow us on Twitter @flysas." This first post is from a mobile device, an indication that the situation requires immediacy (Coombs, 2012). Immediacy, which may be highly correlated to perceived importance, is reflected by the posting behavior of the airline, with posts nearly every quarter of an hour. In fact, the airline's second post is three minutes after its first, with updated information. At the same time, the airline often posts content in the majority of posts, also in those posts initiated by group members rather than the airline. SAS takes the time to provide individual answers, to acknowledge the question even if the airline does not know the answer, or query for more information to provide an answer. The majority of SAS-initiated posts are informational in nature, often with a link to an authoritative source with official details, which can be understood as a strategy to reduce uncertainty by providing access to information (Coombs, 2012).

While integration of links in SAS posts helped to reduce uncertainty, they can also be seen as adding credibility. Providing links to airspace or airport authorities assists in solidifying the message from SAS, often in a post regarding closure of airspace or flight cancellations causing customer disruption. Near noon on April 15, an SAS customer posts a question about the ash cloud's movement and eventual airspace disruption in continental Europe. SAS takes the time to respond: "Looks like the cloud is moving East/South-East. Brussels Airport is still open, but they are reporting some cancellations, and might have to close soon. Read more here: [link to Brussels airport provided]." The response from SAS attempts to answer a customer's question, although it may address an issue at a distant airport and outside the realm of the airline. To add credibility to the answer, SAS provides a link to the source of information. This link has the added benefit of emphasizing that SAS is not the lone airline cancelling flights; this can be important if airlines are sending conflicting messages to the public. For example, there were cases of customers insisting that SAS competitors were still flying certain routes while SAS was cancelling flights. Links to authoritative sources (such as regulators of airspace or airports) with supporting information can support SAS' statements.

The conversational tone present on social media platforms can allow for greater emotional response from a firm when compared to other communication channels. Throughout an event, it is important that a firm recognizes the emotional aspect (Jin & Liu, 2010). SAS achieves this partly by providing a response to the majority of customers who post on Facebook and partly by the content itself that is posted. Although during the ash cloud crisis there were a large number of frustrated customers, CCC took time to respond to a high volume of requests from customers. This provides a perception of personal contact even on a transparent site; it sends the message that the firm cares about its customers and takes the time for them. One example of this is from an early evening post on April 16, where a customer specifically asks for help and advice regarding cancellations and refunds. The SAS team gives specific information regarding the situation for the customer's flight, which is followed up by a subsequent question from the customer. SAS responds, "Yes, you should definitely speak to Expedia, since it is where you booked the flight. Good luck and lets keep our fingers crossed :-)." Such a response contains a tone that is personal in nature and appeals to the emotional customer who is experiencing difficulties due to a crisis. Use of a conversational tone may enable SAS to reach customers "eye-to-eye," rather than in a hierarchical relationship, which can ease communication and reduce negative backlash from the event.

During a crisis, it is important that all affected stakeholders appeal to reason, although being able to integrate emotional communication styles can strengthen the message (Jin & Liu, 2010). Many messages by SAS that provide links or answer specific questions posted by customers contain factual content; the airline continues to maintain an authoritative status among its customers, while at the same time appealing to the emotions when necessary. The frustration that many customers experienced during the crisis may be reflected in their post content. One customer posts, "The worst is that SAS abandoned all passengers in different airports. For instance, I am sitting now in the Amsterdam, my flight, like all of them, cancelled, there is no hotel available (I tried to find hotel at 14:00, but SAS representatives just gave me two telephone numbers and wished good luck in hotel finding)...." It appears as if this customer is using the site to vent frustration regarding the situation without asking specifically for any assistance. SAS is the first to respond within three quarters of an hour and appeals to the passenger's sense of reason by emphasizing that the incident is beyond the control of the airline and asks for patience. Subsequently, another customer comes to the defense of SAS with a post explaining the situation. This shows how influential social media content creators can influence the communicative dialogue in the social media realm outside of the organization and with followers and inactives (Liu et al., 2011).

Postcrisis. As airspace gradually reopened to air traffic, SAS had to cope with stranded customers scattered across the globe. A great deal of content shifted from questions regarding homeward-bound journeys to inquiries regarding reimbursement. SAS maintained a similar strategy of appealing to customers' emotions and reason with links to authoritative sources and appeals to reason. Once the crisis had waned, the activity on SAS' Facebook increased compared to before the ash event. The crisis and reliance on Facebook may have had the benefit that customers grew accustomed to looking to the social media channel for assistance, while SAS itself also appears to have become more active on the site compared to before.

In late 2010, SAS was awarded the Social Media Award for Crisis Communication at a social media event for the industry organized by SimpliFlying. The airline was recognized for the speed of the site's establishment and the use of all members of the organization. Within SAS, the use of social media garnered a great deal of attention, especially after receiving the award (C. Ericsson, personal communication, December 7, 2011). Due to the success of integration of social media in the crisis communication plan, several departments were interested in being present on the site. However, the airline concluded that the most appropriate strategy was to have one department present on Facebook as the official airline group to ensure a standardized message.

Experiences at SAS show that to successfully use social media for crisis communication, the airline should distinguish what needs arise during events. Subsequent to the ash crisis, SAS experienced two events where the use of social media as a crisis communication channel was discussed: heavier-than-normal winter snowfall in Scandinavia and the Japanese tsunami. During the winter of 2010 and the beginning of 2011, the Scandinavian region experienced heavy snowfall that disrupted operations on a large scale throughout the airline network. This meteorological event saw SAS once again relying on Facebook to communicate with customers related to the events. However, the results were dissimilar to those during the ash crisis. Here there was less need for information related to an unknown situation and more need for action by SAS staff to help rebook customers. In other words, the characteristics of Facebook as a tool to disseminate knowledge did not meet the needs of customers during the event when action was needed. Subsequently, Japan experienced the tsunami in March 2011 and there was pressure within the airline to implement the crisis plan and use social media. However, it was soon determined that this type of event, although it affected the airline's operations to a small degree, was not a crisis that demanded a great deal of attention from the airline; its overall impact on SAS customers and the firm was minimal.

CONCLUSION

Social media as a tool during a crisis situation is an important resource that firms should integrate into their communication plans. The experiences at SAS show that the platform was able to disseminate necessary information to many customers during the ash event in Europe in 2010, and was an excellent complement to more traditional communication channels. The channel allowed SAS to address stakeholder concerns at both the emotional level and through an appeal to reason. Although, there were stakeholders who were dissatisfied with the situation, the transparency of the platform allowed others to come to the defense of the airline. Through this involvement, stakeholders outside of the organization were able to become co-managers of the crisis and there were several instances of customers providing support without SAS' involvement. Such engagement during a time of crisis may extend beyond the event itself and facilitate loyalty building. Social media acts as a supplement to traditional media because it is instantaneous, transparent, two-way communication. It can be personal, while simultaneously responding to a broad audience. Those firms that choose to rely on social media during an event would benefit from having a precrisis presence on relevant platforms. For example, SAS was already present, although to a limited degree, prior to the events in April 2010. A firm's stakeholders should already be familiar with the social media presence of a firm, otherwise it may be difficult to drive traffic to the site and ramp up a team within the firm to create and respond to content.

One important observation is that it is not the crisis alone that determines the success of a social media presence, rather it is the needs of the stakeholders. Events after the ash, snow, and tsunami crises showed that the type of content required by stakeholders must match the capabilities of the social media site and organizational department responsible for the site. Stakeholders that demand information from a firm because an event creates a sense of unknown (such as the ash incident) can benefit from the use of social media. However, if a crisis creates a need other than information, for example, action on behalf of the firm, social media may not be able to deliver due to various factors, such as back-office capabilities, technological restrictions, scale of operations, and the like. For example, during the snow crisis, the volume of SAS passengers that required rebooking and used Facebook as a contact point to the airline exceeded the capabilities of the CCC department. Here the limitations of the social media platform and organizational structure showed its weakness. While the platform was ideal for dissemination time sensitive information to many people, it was less ideal in situations that required attention to individual needs on a large scale.

SCCT provides a theoretical framework to study the life cycle of a crisis, while the SMCC model allows for the integration of social media in a crisis communication plan. The life-cycle stages offer a categorization tool that allows for structured analysis. However, the framework can be complemented with a method that captures greater detail of the subject matter. This study looks at the use of three dimensions of crises and three factors of persuasion of posted content, which can be studied with more rigorous qualitative data analysis. At the same time, the SMCC model can be systematically integrated into the various life-cycle stages to provide a framework for organizations for their social media communication strategy. Finally, the field of study can be enhanced by investigating crisis typologies and stakeholder needs, which can subsequently be integrated into the SMCC model. The case of SAS is a best-in-industry example of a firm that succeeded with social media during a crisis. Although, the findings are applicable across industries, a test with multiple cases would be appropriate.

Chapter 11

Web 2.0 Innovations in Events: Human Resource Management Issues

Pamm Kellett
Deakin University, Australia

Anne-Marie Hede
Victoria University, Australia

ABSTRACT

This chapter explores how the adoption of Web 2.0 social media platforms as information communications technology (ICT) innovations is impacting organizational design, culture, and human resource management (HRM) in events. Individuals responsible for the development and implementation of social media in 12 event organizations were interviewed regarding its adoption and how it impacts work in their organizations. Three types of innovation adopters were identified: spontaneous activists, spontaneous reactors, and organized initiators. The findings demonstrate that the use of social media in event organizations is impacting event workers by creating role overload and ambiguity. This chapter discusses implications for event organizations and their employees in terms of HRM policy, performance management, workforce skill development, recruitment, and retention.

Keywords: Events; innovations; social media; human resource management (HRM)

Tourism Social Media: Transformations in Identity, Community and Culture
Tourism Social Science Series, Volume 18, 193–205
Copyright © 2013 by Emerald Group Publishing Limited
All rights of reproduction in any form reserved
ISSN: 1571-5043/doi:10.1108/S1571-5043(2013)0000018013

INTRODUCTION

The use of Web 2.0 is part of a revolution that has impacted the world (Schultz, 2011). With its suite of social media platforms, including Facebook, Twitter, and YouTube, Web 2.0 presents both opportunities and challenges for consumers and businesses alike. In the case of tourism, Web 2.0 has increased the opportunities for tourists to share their experiences, perceptions, and knowledge in consumer-to-consumer and consumer-to-business communications. With the advent of these innovations, it is expected that changes will occur in the way in which workers in the tourism industry undertake their work.

A considerable body of knowledge has emerged about human resource management (HRM) in the tourism industry, which has captured information about the casualization of the industry's human resources, employee turnover, and employee burnout (Baum, Deery, & Lockstone, 2009). Schmallegger and Carson, however, state that "… [tourism] practitioners need to understand the Web 2.0 environment" and emphasize that research is needed to inform tourism practitioners as to "how the associated applications can be employed to assist in business functions" (2008, p. 16). Though research in this area has begun to emerge in relation to marketing (Andreu, Aldas, Bigne, & Mattila, 2010; Hede & Kellett, 2012; Hvass & Munar, 2012; Munar, 2011; Wang & Fesenmaier, 2006), little attention has been directed toward exploring how the adoption of Web 2.0 and its associated social media platforms have impacted HRM. This chapter explores this issue in the events sector, where Web 2.0 and social media have been widely adopted by event organizations (Hede & Kellett, 2012). The aim here is to address a gap in the literature regarding Web 2.0 and social media and their impact on work in such organizations. In addition, as the HRM literature in events has largely focused on the motivations and management of volunteers (Elstad, 2003; Pegg, 2002; Saleh & Wood, 1998; Slaughter, 2002; Treuren & Monga, 2002), or the training of event professionals (Getz & Wicks, 1994; Tzelepi & Quick, 2002), the coverage fills a void in knowledge about HRM in this sector. The guiding research questions are: How is Web 2.0 and its social media platforms, as an ICT innovation, being used? Further, what impact is the adoption of this innovation having on HRM in this tourism sector?

INNOVATION ADOPTION IN TOURISM

Innovation is a process developed to solve a problem that involves the generation, acceptance, and implementation of new ideas, processes, products, or services (Hjalager, 2010). In tourism, ICT innovations have under-pinned many other processes. For example, the industry has been a pioneer in the adoption of a range of technological innovations (Buhalis & Law, 2008). It has seized a range of business opportunities, such as overcoming the physical barriers to reaching new markets, reducing operational costs, and improving business processes, including marketing research practices, customer service, and planning activities (Yuan, Gretzel, & Fesenmaier, 2006).

A number of theories have been put forth to better understand innovation diffusion and its impact on organizations. For example, Rogers (1995) theorized that technology innovations are diffused following a response to a problem. Innovations can be rejected or adopted; if adopted they are then implemented into an organization's processes. Rogers suggests that in the implementation stage, clarification as to how the technology is integrated into the organization and how its use is routinized occurs. Yuan et al. (2006), however, suggest that while Rogers' theory is useful, it is limited because it does not fully recognize that technology innovations may require refinement and that the process of diffusion is dynamic.

In response to this, Yuan et al. (2006) noted that Giddens' (1979) structuration theory, which recognizes the production and reproduction of a social system, provides a more appropriate lens from which to examine the diffusion of technology innovation, because it acknowledges the interplay between the organization and the technology. In this interpretation of the adoption of innovations, Giddens (1979) suggests that there are three main stages of adoption—substitution, enlargement, and reconfiguration—in which organizational structures and processes change in response to how its diffusion is occurring.

In terms of ICT innovations, Lichtenthal and Eliaz suggest that the Internet is the "most rapidly emerging and changing communication technology of the past 100 years" (2003, p. 3). Part of this emerging and changing communication technology is the second generation of the Internet, Web 2.0. It helps to address a lacuna between businesses and consumers, with its capacity to enable both to create and share information (Munar, 2011), and has been the impetus for the "creative consumer" (Berthon, Pitt, Plangger, & Shapiro, 2012).

Indeed, Web 2.0 and social media have changed the way that many tourism organizations undertake business. However, despite the potential benefits and successes related to the adoption of a range of ICT innovations, there are also a number of challenges for this industry (Lichtenthal & Eliaz, 2003; Thevenot, 2007). For example, the adoption of ICTs does not guarantee a return on investment, and Yuan et al. (2006, p. 326) go so far as to suggest that there is often a mismatch between the amount of money an organization spends on ICTs and actual improvements in business value. Although it is generally recognized that when ICT innovations are adopted and combined with other strategic and managerial measures, such as competence building and HRM, favorable impacts are attained (Hjalager, 2010). However, it has been argued that empirically derived evidence for the positive effects of ICT innovations is lacking (Tsai, Huang, & Lin, 2005).

Andreu et al. (2010) suggest that while the adoption of ICTs has empowered tourists, their findings from the travel agency sector indicate that agents' decisions to adopt this technology have largely been driven by a fear of being "left behind." It is perhaps this kind of view, and in a fast-paced and image-based industry like tourism, that the impetus for the widespread adoption of ICT innovations has been spawned by, for example, convention and visitor bureaus (Wang & Fesenmaier, 2006), destination management organizations (Munar, 2011), airlines (Hvass & Munar, 2012), and event organizations (Hede & Kellett, 2012). Munar (2012) found that Scandinavian destination management organizations were using Web 2.0 in their marketing strategies in three distinct ways: in a mimetic manner, for advertising purposes, and as a source for data analytics.

Berthon et al. suggest that the diffusion of Web 2.0 as an ICT innovation is often interpreted "to be as simple as establishing a fan page on Facebook, tweeting regularly, and perhaps placing some of a brand's ads on YouTube" (2012, p. 264). They suggest that, at least in relation to international marketing, this is not the case. While much is known about how consumers have been given greater control and more opportunities for creativity, relatively little information has been garnered about the impacts of the adoption of innovations around Web 2.0 and social media on various stakeholders (Schegg, Leibrich, Scaglione, & Ahmad, 2008). Few studies have investigated the skills required for, or the impact of, the adoption of ICTs (El-Gohary, 2012). There are, however, indications that their diffusion has the potential to impact HRM and human resources. For example, as employee and personal roles can easily become blurred in the Web 2.0 space, cases have emerged of staff being terminated for crossing "boundaries" in ways that have been perceived to be detrimental to the organization. In addition, the "24/7" nature of social media and increasing access to the Internet means that employees are often required to be online to communicate with consumers, both within and outside working hours. As these issues have not yet been fully examined in a scholarly manner within the context of tourism, the purpose of this chapter is to address this knowledge gap with a particular focus on the event sector.

Study Methods

This investigation uses a case study approach which, according to Yin (2009), can be used to *explain, describe,* or *explore* events or phenomena in the everyday contexts in which they occur. Hence case studies have the potential to develop a snapshot of reality (Healy & Perry, 2000). Twelve case studies were developed to explore insights into *how* event organizations are adopting social media, and *what* the impact is on work and workers across the sector. A cross section of organizations was included, representing cultural, community, sport, and business events. Events included those which were delivered at least once a year and on biannual bases, those privately owned or not-for-profit events, and those owned by government instrumentalities. While no claim is made that these 12 events represent the entire sector, still the sample with it diverse profiles provides a rather comprehensive picture of the real world.

First, background data, collected in 2011, were gathered via the Internet and other available promotional materials about the events. The individuals responsible for the development and implementation of social media activities in their event organizations were identified and invited to be interviewed as part of this research. Using a semi-structured interview approach, respondents were asked to reflect on their experiences of using social media in their event organizations and on the challenges they faced in using it. As the interviews were discovery based, respondents were able to provide a comprehensive "snapshot" of the ways in which their adoption of social media was impacting the organization and the way their staff were participating and responding to their adoption.

Study Findings

Web 2.0 and Social Media in the Events Sector.   Similar to Munar's (2011) findings, respondents in this study reported that they found social media to be an innovative solution to achieve a variety of strategic aims, including to increase awareness about their events, drive attendance to their events, develop databases, increase traffic to their event web sites, better understand consumers, and promote involvement and participation in virtual or actual event locations. In this way, these organizations displayed a willingness to use different Web 2.0 platforms and refine their use for their strategic purposes (Yuan et al., 2006).

Facebook and Twitter were the most commonly used platforms in the 12 event organizations that participated in this study, which reflects the incidence of adoption of social media platforms more generally (Hird, 2010; Kaplan & Haenlein, 2010). In particular, this type of adoption reflects what Munar (2011) suggests is a conservative use of social media platforms. Only three of the 12 organizations had created their own YouTube channel, but they were posting content particularly during and after their respective events, with the aim of creating and maintaining an interest in their events beyond the time frame of the event offering. Flickr was not widely used; when it was used, it tended to be for those events that were visual or content rich, such as arts and music events. In these instances, social media platforms were used in an analytic strategy (Munar, 2012) to enhance existing strategies.

Three different methods of adoption of social media were found to shape the working experience for employees in the event organizations. Of the 12 that participated in this study, five were unstructured but proactive in their approach to the practice of their social media activities. This group is described as "spontaneous activists." Another three were highly structured and proactive in their approach to the practice of their social media activities. This group is described as "organized initiators." The remaining four were unstructured and reactive in their approach to the practice of their social media activities, which are described as "spontaneous reactors."

For those organizations that were described as "spontaneous activists," the respondents reported that during the implementation stage, they constantly monitored each of the social media platforms used, posted information about events as they deemed relevant, and provided timely and appropriate responses to consumers. For example, one respondent explained "...this year we've delved into semi-regular posts on Facebook and Twitter and it's the first year that we've done that and basically the whole idea is to generate word of mouth awareness about the event... and as a channel to promote [the event]."

For the "organized initiators," their practice of social media activities, their adoption of Web 2.0 and use of social media platforms has been routinized into the organization's processes (Rogers, 1995). "Organized initiators" respondents initiated conversations on social media platforms, monitored social media sites regularly, posted specific types of information at certain times of the event's delivery (before, during, and after the event), and provided timely and appropriate responses to consumers. This approach extended beyond the traditional scope of an event's delivery, as this activity was undertaken all year round rather than only around it time. For one respondent, the collective event audience that interacted via the social media sites was considered to be a "community." As one respondent explained:

> We really are posting and nurturing the community year round. [The event organization] leverages other events that are happening that are relevant to our audience... we are posting every single day to keep the momentum.... So you don't have to see an event where it all goes for two weeks and it gets dropped until 12 months' time then it gets picked up again. We are building the audience 12 months of the year instead of just attending to them during the two weeks that the event is on.

For "spontaneous reactors" organizations, their practice meant that they monitored social media sites constantly, and provided immediate feedback to consumer responses. They seem to have the least knowledge about social media of all of the organizations in this research, and their understanding of the technology was also limited. For example, one respondent described their use of social media this way: "I just find it so time consuming. I'd have a lot more to say about it and be able to use it better if I had more time to work it out."

"Organized initiators" representatives indicated that they were aware which social media platforms were most effective across the event phases (pre-event, *in situ*, and post-event), and linked their activities to business outcomes. The organized initiators, who were highly structured in their use of social media platforms, were strategic, and as noted above, carefully planned the timing of both the collection and dissemination of information via social media platforms, and considered their social media followers as a community. Further, two of the organizations used a mimetic strategy (Munar, 2012), copying the structure and style of existing social networks and applying it to their own web sites. One organized initiator in this study, an action sport event organization, was the most experienced user of social media of all of the 12 in this study. It also developed online communities that would be consistent with Munar's (2012) findings of a fourth model of social media strategies—that of immersion. The action sport organization was comfortable with creating an online community where negative user-generated content was not censored and minimal control mechanisms were introduced.

For spontaneous activists, existing social media platform structures and channels were being utilized, but there was little strategic focus or integrated understanding of the use of social media platforms beyond promotion and advertising of their events. This is consistent with Munar's (2012) findings that mimetic and advertising strategies are the most frequently used by destination management organizations. It has already been noted that for some organizations in the travel agency sector, the use of ICTs has been driven by a fear of being "left behind" (Andreu et al., 2010). This may also be true for the event sector. For the spontaneous reactors (who were most represented in this study) as well as the spontaneous activists, the use of social media was largely driven by the need to keep pace with what they perceived other event organizations to be doing.

Emerging HRM Issues.   Event representatives reported experiencing work overload and role ambiguity. These issues have the potential to have profound impacts on recruitment and retention for an industry that is only beginning to become professionalized. Most of the informants in the study explained the nature of creating content for social media, responding to posts on social media platforms, and monitoring the platform(s) as time consuming, and saw these activities as the cause of work overload. For example, one respondent explained:

> [managing social media responsibilities] is a massive job, so just staying on top of everything and making sure you're answering your customers and being continually engaged... it's quite time consuming.

Another respondent noted:

> I struggle with it [social media] because you have to sit there and constantly have it up and constantly be checking it and having it come up on your phone... I sort of feel as though I'm looking at it all the time... I just have so much to do.

As social media allows for communication channels to the organization, and about the organization, to be open 24 hours a day, seven days per week, the attention required beyond traditional working hours was noted as being a challenge to resource. The work environment in the event sector has been described as "24/7" during events (Mair, 2009) and pulsating (Hanlon & Cuskelly, 2002; Hanlon & Jago, 2004) where the workload increases during the time immediately before, during, and after delivery of events.

Most of the research informants in this study acknowledged that working outside of normal working hours is as an expected part of working in the events sector. Although work regulations in many countries provide protection for workers in the events sector and for fair work conditions (VECCI, 2012; Weil, 2009), servicing social media in the event sector outside of traditional work hours was discussed as a regular occurrence. Most respondents indicated that the boundary between work and personal time was becoming increasingly blurred. The need to offer consumers multiple ways of engaging pre-, during, and post-event, as well extending their engagement throughout the year, has contributed to a work environment that is becoming "boundaryless." Individuals in all the 12 reported that they monitored the social media platforms multiple times a day—after hours, on weekends—often during their own personal time. They reported that they did this without any extra pay or concessions.

This approach to the adoption of ICT innovations, in parallel with the management of work and personal identities in social networks, has the potential to create role ambiguity and a blurring of personal and professional life. In other contexts, researchers have shown that the nature of Web 2.0 socio-technical structures has consequences for organizational culture and personal reputation management, as well as social dynamics at the workplace (Kaplan & Haenlein, 2010; Munar, 2012; Tapscott, 2009). It is possible that in the event sector, the use of Web 2.0 is a match for the type of work and the employment context (Mair, 2009). For example, one organization whose events are regularly held on weekends ensured that employees were aware of the commitment required of them. Weekends meant monitoring, posting, and responding on social media platforms, and the informant in this study explained, "We advertised that this was part of the requirement for this role, so that is what they do—they spend a lot of time on the weekend on their phone tweeting and updating Facebook—it's not that hard. That is part of their role." This particular organization had been using social media platforms the longest of all in this study. This was also the only one that had provided some role clarity, rather than role ambiguity, with regard to the time commitment required for social media adoption and had deliberately structured this as part of the requirements of the role. In this sense, they refined the processes around the innovation, which is reflective of Giddens' (1979) structuration theory that recognizes that innovation produces and reproduces a social system.

The workforce undertaking social media responsibilities is largely made up of members of "Generation Y," who themselves do not make clear distinctions between work and play, preferring collaborative communication that social media platforms offer (Tapscott, 2009). Tapscott (2009) suggests that for such net-generation individuals, there is little need to distinguish between work and personal spheres on social media. The extra responsibilities and requirements beyond traditional working hours are becoming more "normalized" in many sectors of society; it seems in the event sector this is also the case. Indeed, it is possible that social media assisted to reinforce a tendency that is already common in the event context (Mair, 2009). However, for the organizations in this study, it seems that social media has created a level of ambiguity with regard to employees' personal social media activities and those of the organization.

For example, employees would often "like" the event organization's platforms from their own personal Facebook accounts. For example, one respondent noted,

> on our Facebook site, there are at least 20 friends on the site
> who are actually my friends... everyone who works here has
> got a few friends and family that are linked in to it.

However, some of the 12 in the study were beginning to note that this had the potential to impact negatively on the event organization and its brand. In her study of the use of social media in destination management organizations, Munar (2012) found that there was a blurring of personal and professional use of social media platforms, which was viewed by the interviewees in her study as positive and part of "being there anyway." (2012, p. 13). However, according to Munar, this blurring was a challenge to traditional management structures and organizational cultures.

Thevenot (2007) has cautioned that the tourism today needs to recognize that while social media platforms have the potential to create positive impacts, they can also create negative ones as they offer tourists increased power and institutions/marketers decreased powers if organizations do not manage online communications appropriately. Thevenot's (2007) caution of the negative impacts of social media platforms can be extended to employees in the events sector. Organizations in the study described here were beginning to recognize the consequences of not managing the diffusion of this ICT innovation well. Respondents noted that increasingly employees needed to be encouraged to manage their personal online communications appropriately. Similar to Munar's (2012) findings, most of the respondents in this study explained that their event organizations had developed strict policies around employees' personal and professional social media presence and how these were linked to them. For example, in one organization, employees were encouraged to create and maintain a professional Facebook account that was separate from their personal Facebook account. Further, in other organizations, employees were required to sign contracts regarding the content of any personal social media posts about their workplace and colleagues so as not to bring their firms into disrepute.

The responsibility for social media activities generally lies within the marketing/advertising/promotions and communication domain of organizations (Hensel & Deis, 2010; Steinman & Hawkins, 2010). The present study also found this to be the case for event organizations. Social media is considered important in building brand communities (Cova & White, 2010), which goes some way to explaining why Web 2.0 and its associated platforms have been so readily adopted in the event sector. However, there is little known about what skills are required to drive social media activities and strategies, or what should be learned.

The study brings to light that adopting social media activities was important for the event organizations, but that expertise in this area was required for it to be successful. For example, one of the respondents noted:

> ...it can't just be anybody on Facebook and Twitter. It's not a matter of just getting an intern. You have to have a really strong understanding of public relations and media management....it's not a job for somebody that doesn't have that kind of communication background.

According to Munar (2012),to succeed in the social media space, an understanding of its culture is required beyond mere training in the actual communication tools. However, in the event sector, the question remains: Where do potential employees obtain this professional expertise? Arcodia (2009) notes that marketing and networking skills are crucial for employees in the sector, and that many event management courses do equip potential employees with such skills. Jago and Mair (2009) suggest that Generation Y will have an impact on the event workforce labor market, because it has had the opportunity to gain appropriate skills through tertiary education. Interestingly, neither Arcodia (2009) nor Jago and Mair (2009) reference the use of social media, or electronic communications as Generation Y's preferred method of interaction. The omission of social media from the monograph does not represent a weakness in the research itself—what it represents is the rapid adoption of this ICT innovation in only a few recent years, and the lack of understanding of its impact on the experience of workers in the sector.

The findings of this study suggest that while greater specificity is emerging in relation to the social media skills that event organizations are seeking in their employees, and the way in which they are recruiting desired employees, in some circumstances this is problematic in itself. In many cases, current employees were canvassed to take on the social media activities. It was reported that, for the most part, those individuals who were active on social media for their own personal use were targeted first as it was perceived that they "knew what they were doing" in the social media space (Munar, 2012). Further, if it was perceived that an individual was a good communicator, this also lent support for their selection as the social media representative. Interestingly, this led to an age and gender bias in social media personnel, as most were young female employees.

CONCLUSION

The aim of this chapter was to understand how Web 2.0 and social media are being used as an innovation in the events sector, and to examine the impact that their adoption as an ICT innovation is having on HRM in the sector. Twelve case studies were developed via a series of in-depth interviews with the marketing experts in event organizations. Three conclusions are evident. First, social media as an innovation are creating managerial, cultural, and strategic challenges for event organizations in similar ways found in other sectors of the tourism industry (Munar, 2011, 2012). Most of the event organizations that participated in this study reported that they were using social media as an innovative solution to a range of issues in events—such as creating brand awareness, increasing attendance, increasing traffic to web sites, and building community.

Second, it is clear that the use and rapid evolution of Web 2.0 has caught many event organizations "on the hop." The majority of organizations engaged in social media activities in an unstructured and spontaneous manner, with only three involved in a planned and integrative strategic approach that truly demonstrated innovative uses of social media specifically for the business of events where the ICT was itself refined. Technological innovation has been identified as a driver of competitive advantage for tourism destinations and their management (Dwyer, Edwards, Mistilis, Roman, & Scott, 2009), yet in the case of the event sector, leveraging social media for competitive advantage has thus far been limited to a small number of organizations that can appropriately resource social media activities and have developed a clear understanding of how ICTs can assist them specifically in their business functions (cf. Schmallegger & Carson, 2008).

As such, adopting social media as an innovation has potentially begun to change the peaks and troughs of event communications. This is the third major finding from this investigation. Once there was limited communication between events and target markets outside of peak event times, with social media, those communications have been made easier. The flow on effect for this is that there may be greater demand for event professionals all year round (beyond the traditional pre-event, during, and post-event phases), rather than only during the "event season." This may have positive impacts for the event workforce. The use of social media in the sector may indeed provide job responsibilities of an ongoing nature that have previously been missing. In this sector, much of the workforce is currently casualized, and event organizations have a tendency to use volunteers, as well as require their staff to multitask due to the expected and well-known pulsating nature of the industry. Innovation is a process (Hjalager, 2010), and as such, it may take some time for the event sector to realize that it needs to approach HRM differently in the future if it is to capitalize on the use of social media as an innovation in this context.

Web 2.0 is constantly evolving, and so are the ways that organizations can communicate, and be communicated with. This research has shown that the use of social media in organizations is having an impact on workers and the workforce in terms of creating overload and ambiguity, particularly for the spontaneous activists who have limited strategic planning in place with regards to social media activities. In the event sector, prior to the advent of social media, both work overload and ambiguity have been noted as common problems that lead to stress and burnout (Baum et al., 2009). Most of the organizations in this study have spent a short amount of time engaging in social media activities and it has largely been a trial and error experiment for many. The experimental nature of these activities has perhaps allowed for the human resource impacts thus far to be rendered negligible; extra social media activities may currently be perceived by workers as a tolerable short term "experiment" rather than being a burdensome extra role if it were viewed as a permanent part of their strategic responsibilities. The event sector may be setting itself up for further stress and burnout if it does not appropriately resource social media activities. This needs further monitoring and research effort.

Chapter 12

Identity and Social Media in an Art Festival

Fabrizio Montanari
University of Modena and Reggio Emilia, Italy

Annachiara Scapolan
University of Modena and Reggio Emilia, Italy

Elena Codeluppi
University of Modena and Reggio Emilia, Italy

ABSTRACT

In recent years, festivals have become prominent events in many cities throughout Europe, playing a crucial role in improving the image of the host city and enhancing its attractiveness to tourists. Festivals are temporary organizations with a short-lived and intermittent nature. Such features could raise several challenges in terms of maintaining a festival's identity and its attendees' identification during the periods of inactivity. Drawing on the literature on temporary organizations, organizational identity, and social identification, this chapter investigates how festivals can communicate their central and stable characteristics to audiences by adopting Web 2.0-based communication strategies. To explore this issue, the chapter illustrates the case of an Italian festival, *Fotografia Europea*, which has

Tourism Social Media: Transformations in Identity, Community and Culture
Tourism Social Science Series, Volume 18, 207–225
ISSN: 1571-5043/doi:10.1108/S1571-5043(2013)0000018014

changed its communication strategy from a more traditional approach to a Web 2.0-based one.

Keywords: Festivals; temporary organizations; organizational identity; Web 2.0-based communication

INTRODUCTION

Since the early 1990s, festivals have become prominent events in many cities throughout Europe (Quinn, 2005). Reasons for this proliferation may lie in a series of interconnected factors such as new approaches to urban management, the use of culture-led policies to reverse the decline of geographic areas, and the progressive culturalization or symbolicization of traditional economic sectors (Cappetta, Manzoni, & Salvemini, 2010; Scott, 2000). These factors have led to a reconceptualization of festivals as an effective strategy for cities to gain several potential economic, social, and cultural benefits (Gursoy, Kim, & Uysal, 2004; McKercher, Mei, & Tse, 2006). For example, festivals are considered to play a crucial role in improving the image of the host city, as well as enhancing both the appeal and attractiveness of a destination to tourists (Kim, Borges, & Chon, 2006). As noted by Getz (1991), festivals represent a new type of tourism, since they add vitality to a destination and contribute to attracting tourists who have a special interest in the events or themes being celebrated.

However, in order to exploit all potential benefits, festival organizations have to face several challenges. For example, the recent proliferation of festivals has increased the level of competition among different cities that want to attract potential tourists. Previous studies in the field of tourism have investigated what might induce people to attend and re-patronize a festival, highlighting the role played by different factors such as individual motivation (Dewar, Meyer, & Li, 2001), satisfaction and perceived authenticity (Chhabra, Healy, & Sills, 2003), and environmental features (Lee, Lee, Lee, & Babin, 2008). In particular, the latter study showed that the relationship between environmental cues and customer behavior may be mediated by other variables such as emotions. In this sense, Grappi and Montanari (2011) showed the important mediating role played by attendees' social identification, or the sense of connection that those attending a festival feel with other attendees (Bagozzi & Dholakia, 2006; Tajfel, 1978). In other words, people may decide to attend a festival not only for the events or themes being celebrated, but also as a means through which they construct their sense of social identity. As a result, the greater the degree of identification with a festival or other festival attendees, the more individuals will be disposed to attend or return to a festival.

Since festivals are temporary organizations with a short-lived and discontinuous nature, festival managers face several organizational issues in terms of coordinating mechanisms and human resource management. Such a discontinuity could lead to several problems from the point of view of a festival's identity, since long periods of inactivity might decrease the degree to which people identify with a festival and its attendees. Therefore, it would be interesting to investigate how festivals could preserve their stable, central, and enduring characteristics in order to maintain over time the sense of connection that a festival's attendees feel with the event itself and other visitors.

Social media are second generation Internet-based services such as social networking sites, wikis, blogs, and other communication tools that emphasize online collaboration and sharing among users (McAfee, 2006). The recent development of social media seems to open up new opportunities to festival organizations in managing the relationship with their attendees, both during the days of a festival and through the whole year. Festival organizations, in fact, could use Web 2.0 platforms to preserve their perceived identity through long periods of inactivity and sustain attendees' identification so that people may increase their willingness to attend a festival. Research investigating these issues is still lacking. This chapter contributes to filling this gap by investigating the main characteristics of the Web 2.0-based communication strategy adopted by a festival's managers and its results in terms of the festival's identity over time and attendees' social interaction with each other.

To discuss these issues, the case of *Fotografia Europea* (Festival of European Photography) is examined. The festival is held every May in Reggio Emilia, a city located in the north of Italy. Since its first year in 2006, this event has been the most popular festival in Reggio Emilia and the 2011 edition attracted over 200,000 attendees, which is significant for a city that usually has low tourist flows. Furthermore, the organizing committee adopted a Web 2.0-based strategy in 2010 and is in the process of changing it to address problems experienced over the following two years. Thus, it provides an interesting and timely setting to investigate the characteristics of Web 2.0-based communication strategies, the reasons for their adoption, and new challenges that have to be faced. The following section sequentially illustrates the theoretical background and motivation behind the study, explains the methodology used in the empirical research, and presents findings from the case study. The final section discusses the results and concludes with ideas for future research.

IDENTITY AND SOCIAL IDENTIFICATION

The term festival could refer to a multitude of events that are based on the idea of celebrating a specific theme to which the public is invited for a limited period of time (Getz, 1991; Smith, 1990). This celebration can be held annually or less frequently, and includes single events. Arts and cultural festivals, in particular, involve the celebration of themes relating to different cultural areas such as poetry, painting, film, dance, and photography. From an organizational viewpoint, festivals represent an example of a temporary organization that could be defined as "a set of diversely skilled people working together on a complex task over a limited period of time" (Goodman & Goodman, 1976, p. 494). These organizations are usually characterized as project-based (Packendorff, 1995), short-lived, discontinuous, unstable (Bechky, 2006), and ephemeral (Lanzara, 1983). In the last few decades, there has been a significant increase in the use of temporary organizations as a key approach to doing work in different industries including creative contexts (Faulkner & Anderson, 1987; Lampel, Lant, & Shamsie, 2000; Lundin & Steinthorsson, 2003; Moeran & Strandgaard Pedersen, 2011), as they provide several benefits, for instance, in terms of flexibility, capacity to deal with unexpected events, and reduced costs (Lanzara, 1983; Schwab & Miner, 2008). As Bechky summarizes, "to contend with environments that are complex and variable, temporary organizations have been found to reduce costs and control risk through the fluid movement of specialized personnel" (2006, p. 4).

However, such a temporary nature raises several organizational issues as well, which can be divided into two main groups: internal and external aspects. As far as the former is concerned, temporary organizations have to face challenges that deal with coordinating mechanisms and human resource management practices. For example, "since temporary organizations bring together a group of people who work strongly interdependently on complex tasks without being always familiar with one another's skills and abilities, [...] they have to adopt proper coordinating mechanisms in order to accomplish their goals in the face of significant uncertainty and extreme time constraints" (Bechky, 2006, p. 3). Furthermore, temporary organizations characterized by short duration and repetition may suffer from a depreciation of organizational knowledge, human capital, and social capital due to the high level of personnel turnover determined by organizational discontinuity (Rao & Argote, 2006). Such discontinuity also makes it necessary to manage internal processes of organizational regeneration to bring the entity "back to life after many months of dormancy" (Birnholtz, Cohen, & Hoch, 2007, p. 315). As far as external aspects are concerned, temporary organizations have to deal with issues in securing audiences, performance, or exhibition outlets, and relationships with key gatekeepers and other relevant stakeholders (Lampel & Meyer, 2008; Ruling, 2011). Thus, they have to adopt proper actions aimed at maintaining their organizational identity (Gioia, Schultz, & Corley, 2000), reputation (Whetten & Mackey, 2002), and legitimacy (He & Baruch, 2011).

This chapter focuses on the issue of organizational identity, which refers to those attributes that are central, distinctive, and enduring (Albert & Whetten, 1985). According to this definition of organizational identity, its key dimensions are stability and continuity over time (Booth, 1999). Moreover, since organizational identity implies "an organization's members' collective understanding of the features presumed to be central and relatively permanent" (Gioia & Pitre, 1990, p. 64), organizational memory plays a relevant role in building and maintaining an organization's identity (Booth, 1999; Rowlinson, Booth, Clark, Delahaye, & Procter, 2010). Indeed, past experience and a history of significant events contribute to casting the awareness of an organization's central and permanent traits (Gioia & Pitre, 1990). In accordance with the definition of identity as enduring or permanent, extant literature highlights that "change projects can affect core features of an organization, because changes [...] can result in misalignments with existing organizational culture [and] such misalignments produce threats to organizational identity generating uncertainty" (Jacobs, Jochen, Keegan, & Pòlos, 2008, p. 245). Furthermore, as noted by Rao and Argote (2006), unstable structures of tasks and relations might undermine organizational memory. Thus, discontinuity in temporary organizations might have a negative effect on the identity since long periods of inactivity could hamper ties between identity and organizational memory due to the decay of memories at the individual and collective level, preventing members from "recollection, or imaginative reconstruction of the past" (Rowlinson et al., 2010, p. 70).

Another stream of research has focused on how organizational identity adapts in relation to internal and external changes (Nag, Corley, & Gioia, 2007; Ravasi & Phillips, 2011). For instance, Nag and his colleagues

(2007, p. 821) have investigated "how an organization is able to transform itself in the face of a discontinuous environmental shift." These studies suggest a more dynamic and fluid notion of organizational identity, and provide some insights on how it may evolve over time. In this sense, it is important to note that it is constructed by continuous interaction between organizational members and other stakeholders such as customers, media, competitors, and public institutions (Gioia et al., 2000; Gioia, Price, Hamilton, & Thomas, 2011). The relevance of such a continuous interplay between insiders and outsiders in forging and maintaining an organizational identity implies several problems for temporary organizations, which have to take proper action aimed at sustaining such interaction in the face of their discontinuity.

These issues seem to be particularly relevant for arts and cultural festivals, since the sense of identification that attendees feel with the festival itself and other visitors could play an important role in affecting their decision to re-patronize a festival in the future (Grappi & Montanari, 2011). In cultural industries consumption preferences represent a means through which people construct their identity (Goulding & Shankar, 2004). Accordingly, people may decide to attend a festival not only for their interest in the events or themes being celebrated, but also to reinforce their individual self-image, communicate to others their desired identity, and signal allegiance to a desired social group. Such considerations are consistent with previous studies conducted in different contexts (Bagozzi & Dholakia, 2006; Bhattacharya & Sen, 2003; Scott & Lane, 2000), which suggest that the degree to which people identify with different social groups may affect their behavior. Thus, in order to enhance attendees' re-patronizing intention, it is critical to manage properly all factors that may sustain attendees' identification with the event and other attendees. In doing so, it is important to manage different communication channels adopted by a festival and promote social connections among attendees to facilitate the possibility of social exchange. In this regard, several studies have investigated the link among organizational identity, legitimacy, and communication, highlighting the role played by language (Fiol, 2002) or by external communication (He & Baruch, 2011) in the processes of maintaining (or transforming) organizational identity. For example, Corley and Gioia (2004) argue that because organizational identity consists of both labels and their underlying meanings, identity changes involve intensified sense-giving via heightened communication and symbolic action. A more recent study suggests that positive media representation fosters members' alignment around an emergent understanding of what their organization is (Kjærgaard, Morsing, & Ravasi 2011).

Accordingly, the recent development of Web 2.0 platforms could open up new opportunities for festivals (and other temporary organizations) in managing processes aimed at maintaining organizational identity via continuous interaction with external audiences. Different social media adopted by a festival (blogs, Facebook, Flickr, etc.) could play an important role since they allow both insiders and outsiders to share multiple narratives on their perceptions about relevant, stable, and significant features of an organization, even during periods of discontinuity. For instance, social media could increase the interaction with attendees who can post their comments before or after their participation in a festival's event, exchanging opinions and ideas with other attendees, thus enhancing the awareness of belonging to a social group and increasing the level of social identification.

Research on social media also highlights the fact that because they involve people banding together, social online applications like blogs, social networking, and user-generated content sites, often move in unexpected directions for organizations (Bernoff & Li, 2008). For instance, using social media, people are defining their own perspective on brands, organizations, or events, such as a festival, a view that could be at odds with the image organizations want to promote. In other words, although people are empowered by social media, organizations are losing control. Thus, in order to exploit the potential benefits of social media while avoiding the negative effects of the loss of control, organizations should figure out ways to manage this online communication channel in-house, developing a strategic framework to implement the right applications.

The case study presented in this chapter focuses on how the adoption of a Web 2.0-based communication strategy could support a festival in forging its identity, maintaining it over time, and increasing the level of attendees' social identification. The study adopts an inductive case-based approach, which is considered an appropriate way to explore new research issues (Eisenhardt, 1989; Yin, 1994). In doing so, the study pursued source triangulation, combining the following data collection methods: questionnaires, in-depth interviews, archive analysis, and direct observation. In particular, between 2008 and 2011 the festival's organizing committee was helped to survey those attending by asking a sample of attendees every year to complete a self-administered questionnaire. Attendees were approached as they left festival venues and participation was voluntary. In an attempt to obtain reasonably representative samples, the surveys were conducted for the three-day opening weekend of the festival with an equal proportion of the time of day (morning, early afternoon, and early evening).

To generate the items, an extensive literature review was conducted (Grappi & Montanari, 2011; Lee et al., 2008), focusing on attendees' demographic characteristics, perceptions of environmental cues (program content, staff behavior, locations and atmosphere, information and facilities, etc.), positive and negative emotions, social identification, satisfaction, and re-patronizing intention. Variables were measured using 7-point Likert scales (1 = strongly disagree; 7 = strongly agree). On average, about 255 usable questionnaires were collected every year.

Moreover, semistructured interviews were conducted with the City Councilor of Culture and one member of the Chamber of Commerce of Reggio Emilia in 2011. The interviews ranged from 20 to 30 minutes. Interviewees were asked information about the festival's history, evolution, main characteristics (in terms of perceived identity), and performance (in terms of attendance and impact on city image and attractiveness to tourists). Furthermore, three members of the festival's organizing committee were interviewed in 2012. The interviews ranged from 30 minutes to 1 hour. They were asked about the festival's history, main characteristics (in terms of perceived identity), and performance (in terms of attendance and impact on city image and attractiveness to tourists). They also provided information about the characteristics of the implemented web strategy with a focus on how social media have been managed over the years. The interviews were taped to provide a richer account of the data and to allow the researcher to monitor the conversation (Silverman, 1994).

Each interview was transcribed and each transcript was read carefully several times in search of emerging elements regarding aims, use, and content of the festival's web strategy. Initially, it was noted that these elements could be related to each other, outlining the evolution of the festival's communication strategy over time towards a more extensive and effective use of social media. They noted also that the main characteristics of the festival's social media strategy could be related to the evolution of managers' perceptions of its identity and its performance in terms of attendance and attractiveness to tourists. The data collected from questionnaires were reviewed and it was noted that the evolution of social media communication could be related to the evolution of attendees' main characteristics, perceptions, and behaviors, for instance, in terms of re-patronizing intention.

To collect complementary data and triangulate information that emerged through analysis of in-depth interviews and questionnaires, both before and after the interviews the study analyzed secondary sources including official documents, the official web site (www.fotografiaeuropea.it), and the social media used (the festival's Facebook fan page and the profiles on Flickr, Twitter, and YouTube). Finally, data collection involved participant observation in *Fotografia Europea* four times. This made it possible to gather additional data on the main characteristics of the festival (program content, staff behavior, locations, facilities). During these observations, informal conversations with staff, attendees, and other members of the municipality took place. These unstructured interviews provided more data on attendees' characteristics and perceptions of environmental cues, and on how local policy makers perceive the festival's identity and performance in terms of impact on the city's image and attractiveness to tourists.

Following the iterative process recommended by Strauss and Corbin (1990), the study traveled back and forth between the data and emerging theoretical arguments that could help comprehend the role of social media in a festival's communication strategy and to which this investigation might contribute. According to the literature already discussed, it was decided that studies on organizational identity, social identification, and Web 2.0-based communication could be an appropriate theoretical framework.

Fotografia Europea was established by the Municipality of Reggio Emilia in 2006. Reggio Emilia is a medium-sized city of 160,000 inhabitants and is located in northern Italy (50 km from Bologna and 130 km from Milan). The local economy is strongly based on manufacturing and agricultural activities. Reggio Emilia is home to one of the most important Italian mechanical districts, as well as famous companies operating in the food industry (some typical products such as Parmigiano Reggiano and Lambrusco are internationally renowned). Despite its tradition of industrial excellence and economic growth, the city has recently suffered the impact of the economic crisis. Numerous companies in the agricultural, livestock, and manufacturing industries have reduced their workforce or implemented work time reductions and redundancy payment schemes for their employees. Although it is not possible to conceptually place Reggio Emilia in a context of industrial decline and cultural regeneration envisaged by the literature (Bianchini & Parkinson, 1993; Garcia, 2004), local authorities are in the process of implementing public policies supporting local creative industries as initiatives that might have a positive impact on the local economy. *Fotografia Europea* represents one of the most important actions aimed at improving the image of the city and enhancing its attractiveness to tourists.

The festival's core idea consists in conceiving the art of photography "as a privileged tool for reflecting upon the complexity of contemporary living" (*Fotografia Europea*, 2012). Every year, photographers are invited to exhibit their artistic pieces related to a particular topic, which has changed yearly, for example, ranging from contemporary urban conditions to the idea of body. The 2011 event was dedicated to commemorating the 150th anniversary of Italian unification through a reflection on the identity, the history, and the future of Italy. Photographers also create new artistic pieces that the Municipality acquires for the city's public collection. *Fotografia Europea* is held in May every year. More specifically, the festival has an opening weekend at the beginning of May and then the exhibitions are open until the end of June. During the whole period of the festival, there are exhibition openings and other activities such as *lectio magistralis*, seminars, and workshops held by leading photographers and industry experts (such as journalists, critics, and academics). Moreover, local cultural associations, amateur photographers, media companies, and other actors autonomously organize smaller and more independent exhibitions, which are called "OFF exhibitions" and usually are held only on the opening weekend.

In addition to all these activities strongly related to the art of photography, other events take place during the festival: conferences (held by other artists, philosophers, writers, and the like), and music, film, and dance events. The festival events are held not only in the most renowned locations of the city (squares, theaters, museums, etc.), but also in private houses (e.g., many local photographers and artists open up their ateliers), companies' headquarters, and restored ex-industrial spaces. As a result, the whole urban fabric is involved in the festival's activities.

The festival has achieved great success over the last few years, and is now well known throughout Italy. Table 1 summarizes data on people who attended *Fotografia Europea*. It is interesting to note that the number of attendees has increased since 2006 and the 2011 event managed to attract more than 200,000 attendees for the first time. In particular, OFF exhibitions have significantly expanded since 2007 (they were not held in the first edition)

Table 1. Attendees of *Fotografia Europea*

Attendees	2006	2007	2008	2009	2010	2011
Attendees of the opening weekend	12,000	19,760	20,560	29,729	33,667	23,605
Attendees of permanent exhibitions	35,000	40,000	54,265	65,336	67,035	79,302
OFF exhibitions' attendees	–	8,300	19,541	48,384	98,140	113,653
Total	47,000	68,060	94,366	143,449	198,842	216,560

Source: Municipality of Reggio Emilia.

ranging from 8,300 attendees to 113,653. This result shows how the festival has significantly added vitality to the city and supported local community participation, as the events organized by local actors (artists, companies, cultural associations, etc.) have significantly increased over the years.

The study results show how *Fotografia Europea* has increased its ability to attract tourists, since the percentage of attendees coming from other cities has increased between 2008 and 2011 from 40% to 55%. This is an interesting result, since Reggio Emilia is not usually perceived as a tourist destination. Indeed, interviews with members of the municipality and of the local Chamber of Commerce showed how typical tourist flows mainly consist of people who come to Reggio Emilia for business reasons and stay in the city for a few days.

Therefore, *Fotografia Europea* plays an important role in the local economy, because it is the only event in Reggio Emilia that attracts tourists, even though most of them (on average 60%) come from neighboring cities (Parma, Modena, and Bologna) and thus do not stay in hotels or in other facilities. Between 2008 and 2011, graduate or higher educated respondents account for about 48% of the sample. Another interesting result regards the fact that attendees present high levels of satisfaction (on average, 5.6 on a 7-point scale: 1 = very low; 7 = very high) and re-patronizing intention (5.9), which can be defined as a pledge to repurchase (re-patronize) a product or service in the future (Oliver, 1999). Furthermore, attendees seem to appreciate all festival cues (in particular, the artistic quality of exhibitions and its pleasant atmosphere), and basically state that they want to attend the festival because of their interest in photography. However, despite this shared interest, attendees do not feel a strong sense of connection with other visitors. In 2009 and 2010, the assessment of the extent to which an attendee feels a sense of identification with other festival attendees by means of a 7-point Likert scale (Bagozzi & Dholakia, 2006) showed that attendees have low degrees of social identification (4.25 in 2009 and 4.35 in 2010).

Since the first edition, the organizing committee has allocated about 20% of the budget to communication activities. In the first years, almost all the resources were invested in traditional communication channels (commercials in newspapers and on TV and radio) with the exception of the official web site. In interviews with the organizing committee's members, it emerged that in the first years there was one person in charge of the web site and online communication, which basically consisted of banner advertising, Adwords on Google, and emailing a periodic newsletter. The web strategy was quite simple and the main goal was to use the web site as an online repository of all the information regarding the festival: official program, schedule of activities, news, information about the city (transportation, hotels, restaurants), and so on. Accordingly, the web site was updated just a couple of months before the opening weekend to provide relevant information to potential attendees, intrigue them, and create some sort of word of mouth. After the festival, organizers did not usually devote much effort to online communication; they basically advised about events (seminars, workshops, etc.) organized by the municipality that were specifically about photography by producing email newsletters and updating the web site. To illustrate, one member of the organizing committee noted:

> At the beginning, I think our approach was consistent with a Web 1.0 approach: we basically used the same "push logic" that you usually apply to more traditional communication channels. Basically, you just contact potential attendees when you get close to the event and when you want to tell them something. (Interviewee 1, February 13, 2012).

Results in terms of web site traffic were consistent with the strategy: visits tended to reach a peak in the period April–June (during the festival and in the month prior to the opening weekend), which on average counted for about 75% of annual web traffic. During the periods of festival inactivity, web site traffic was very low, since the web site was not frequently updated and thus web users were not motivated to visit it.

In 2009, the organizing committee decided to use social media to communicate with actual and potential attendees. In doing so, it decided to adopt an incremental Web 2.0-based strategy by creating a profile on one social media at a time. First, a profile was created on Flickr, because this social medium was considered the most coherent with the festival contents. Flickr is a popular photo sharing web site that allows members to upload their own photos into customizable albums that can then be labeled, organized, tagged, and publicly posted. In the case of *Fotografia Europea*, the main goal was to create an online repository of photos uploaded by the festival organizers and by attendees. Over the years, uploaded photos have created a sort of online documentation of the activities of every edition of the festival (official and OFF exhibitions, events, seminars, etc.). In June 2010, a Facebook fan page was created with the main goal of increasing festival awareness by reaching new potential attendees (especially young people), increasing the interaction between the festival and its attendees, and improving the timing of communication (in particular, information regarding some last-minute changes in the program). Another member of the organizing committee explained:

> Basically, we said: why don't we use this new communication
> channel that is free? We decided to take advantage of this new
> technological platform in order to reach new potential
> attendees with reduced communication costs. (Interviewee 2,
> February 15, 2012)

Consistent with the overall web strategy, the Facebook fan page was
managed between June 2010 and November 2011 as a repository of
information regarding the festival's program and schedule. In other terms, it
was basically used to promote the festival's events. More specifically, some
of the information already available on the official web site was just copied
onto the fan page without a precise discriminating factor. To illustrate,
according to a member of the organizing committee,

> Basically, we duplicated the official website. We just wanted to
> use Facebook as an additional communication channel aimed
> at providing some information that was already available on
> the website. Our idea was to have some synergies between the
> website and the fan page: with no additional expenditure, we
> thought to reach more potential attendees and different
> niches. (Interviewee 2, February 15, 2012)

However, results were not satisfying, since web traffic and Facebook fans
did not increase as expected. More specifically, web site traffic has continued
to be concentrated in the period between April and June, while the number
of fans has not significantly increased after the expected initial "boom."
Furthermore, fans of *Fotografia Europea's* page did not tend to interact with
the fan page administrator or with other fans. More specifically, fans tended
to leave a few comments on the fan page, not to exchange messages with
other fans, and to share little of the news posted by the fan page
administrator. One explanation is the fact that, as in the case of the official
web site, organizers used to upload posts, video, or photos on the fan page
mainly in the period between April and June. Furthermore, uploaded
material was basically aimed at promoting the festival events and not at
stimulating interactivity. Two members of the organizing committee
explained it in the interviews:

> When we created the fan page we immediately reached a
> high number of fans, but then they did not react to our posts.
> Now I can perfectly understand why. Basically, our approach

was: we tell you something related to the festival that you could find also on the website, and we tell you something when we are close to the opening weekend. We were not able to engage our fans in any interesting discourse. (Interviewee 2, February 15, 2012)

Why did people not interact with each other? We did not interact with them, so why should they with us? (Interviewee 1, February 13, 2012)

Festival organizers also created a profile on Twitter (February 2010) and one on YouTube (November 2010) that have been managed with the same logic, achieving similar results.

In November 2011, the organizing committee changed the web strategy and hired a new person as social media manager. As reported in the official document, the new web strategy's main goal is "to engage actual and potential attendees not only during the days of the festival, but also through the whole year." To achieve this goal, each web platform has a particular goal and is focused on co-producing a particular discourse with its users (Table 2).

For example, the *Fotografia Europea's* fan page is mainly focused on revealing previews of the festival's next edition and providing insights and information about the art of photography. In doing so, the social media manager tries to stimulate the debate about what is happening in contemporary photography by providing information related not just to *Fotografia Europea*, but also to events organized by other cultural institutions in Reggio Emilia and elsewhere in Europe. The rationale for this choice is that *Fotografia Europea* could increase its reputation and awareness only if it improves its legitimacy in the online discourses and narratives about photography. Therefore, the social media manager posts information at least once a week that may note anniversaries of famous photographers, photographic exhibitions organized in Reggio Emilia or in other Italian and European cities, publications of books dedicated to famous photographers, and photographic contests for amateur photographers. According to interviews, this change in the fan page's contents has contributed to solving some problems related to the difficulties previously experienced of providing new content related to *Fotografia Europea* at least once a week. In other words, it was difficult to upload new content weekly that related only to the festival's activities and events because of its very narrow focus, although it is easier to find interesting content related to the art of photography in general. It is important to note that in order to sustain

Table 2. Main Characteristics of the New Web Strategy

Web Platform	Main Purposes
Web site	To provide general information about the festival's organization and history (about us, contact info, history). To provide information about next edition (e.g., topic, official program, OFF exhibitions) To contribute to the discussion on contemporary issues of photography through interviews with experts (articles and video). Short professional training courses with video of photographers who discuss technical issues Call for volunteers who want to join the organization.
Facebook fan page	To reveal previews about the festival's next edition. To provide interesting information about what is happening in contemporary photography.
Twitter	To give updates about the festival (location of seminars, new videos uploaded on the website, deadlines, other websites that talk about *Fotografia Europea*).
Flickr	To provide an online repository of photos related to all festival editions (updated not only during the festival but during the whole year).
YouTube video	To provide an online repository of videos related to all festival editions (updated not only during the festival but during the whole year).
Newsletter	To communicate most important events.

Source: Municipality of Reggio Emilia.

interaction with users, it is critical to provide contents that are perceived as interesting by the fan page users, and when festival organizers succeed in doing so, they contribute to increasing the festival's reputation as an important gatekeeper that provides interesting information about contemporary photography.

Despite the limited period of time to test the effectiveness of the new strategy, Table 3 shows how interaction with fan page users has significantly increased in the months after the new strategy was implemented. For example, between November 2011 and February 2012 (months of festival inactivity) the number of users' comments increased from 16 to 72. It is

Table 3. Statistics about the Facebook Fan Page of *Fotografia Europea*

Month	Number of uploaded posts	Number of likes	Fans' comments	Share
November 2010	3	17	3	0
February 2011	4	26	0	0
May 2011	32	275	11	0
August 2011	6	29	1	0
November 2011	24	246	16	32
February 2012	34	519	72	190

Table 4. Web site Visitors and Number of Fans of *Fotografia Europea's* Fan Page

Month	Web site Unique Visitors	Fans on Facebook
June 2010	5,513	4,942
November 2010	867	5,511
February 2011	959	5,763
May 2011	25,818	7,022
August 2011	2,369	7,196
November 2011	3,085	7,376
February 2012	4,357	7,928

Source: Municipality of Reggio Emilia.

interesting to note also that users' comments (like other users' activities) are noticeably higher than one year before (November 2010 and February 2011).

As reported in Table 4, the new strategy also obtained positive results in terms of official web site traffic and number of fans. For example, in the four months from November 2011 to February 2012, the fan page had 552 new fans, which is about twice the increase in fan numbers achieved the previous year during the same period. Web site traffic also increased: the number of unique visitors in February 2012 is about six times higher than results achieved one year before.

Therefore, results seem to support the effectiveness of the new web strategy in sustaining interaction with actual and potential attendees. Such a result is important in terms of maintaining festival identity, also because if web users increase their interaction with official platforms and among themselves, they also contribute to fostering the "buzz" related to *Fotografia Europea* in terms of discourses that other web platforms make on the festival. In the months after the new strategy was implemented, the number of blogs specialized in photography that had uploaded at least one post about *Fotografia Europea* significantly increased (they were 6 in August 2010, 24 in February 2011, 204 in August 2011, and 272 in February 2012).

Despite positive results achieved by the new web strategy, there are still several challenges that festival organizers face. For example, the Twitter profile has only 522 followers and the YouTube channel contains 26 videos with a total of 1,242 views. Of course, since the change in web strategy is very recent and it has been focused mainly on the fan page, it is not surprising that potential benefits of other social media have not yet been fully exploited. However, these results and the comments that emerged in the interviews point to avenues for future development. For example, the organizing committee is aware that Facebook communication still presents a top-down approach and that in the future it should be aimed more at promoting collaboration among fans and encouraging spontaneous discussion. To achieve these goals, festival managers will try to promote social connections among attendees in the 2013 festival edition by providing facilities and spaces to discuss topics with other attendees, and by stimulating attendees to post their comments on the fan page before or after their participation. Furthermore, the plan is to launch a call for ideas to collect attendees' opinions about events they would like to attend and festival cues that should be improved. Moreover, festival managers will try to make a greater effort with other social media (Twitter and YouTube) to increase their perceived value.

Finally, festival managers will have to stay focused both on applications and the technologies used to implement them and on culture. They are aware that in order to exploit the potential of social media, a willingness to relinquish power to users will be required. However, in order to avoid the possible negative effects connected to the loss of control over information and contents spontaneously generated by actual and potential attendees, they will make more effort to carefully plan the right applications as well as manage them with flexibility and nimbleness. In particular, they will make more effort to listen carefully to the visitors' opinions (even when negative) since these opinions could help organizers improve the festival's attractions and the offered services. In doing so, they will use social media to communicate the changes and improvements made on the basis of visitors' suggestions and objections.

CONCLUSION

This chapter investigated how a festival could use Web 2.0 platforms during the long periods of inactivity to preserve its identity, manage relationships with attendees, and affect attendees' social identification. This is not a trivial issue since attendees' identification with the festival and other attendees plays an important role in enhancing their re-patronizing intention.

Drawing on the idea that Web 2.0 platforms could open up new opportunities for a festival in communicating its identity to external audiences and supporting the level of attendees' social identification, the chapter analyzed the case of *Fotografia Europea*. Results of the case study show how the use of different social media is not enough to sustain continuous interaction with external audiences and promote social connections among attendees themselves. In fact, during the period between June 2010 and November 2011, the web strategy did not achieve the expected results in terms of web traffic, user participation, or interaction. More specifically, actual and potential attendees did not visit the official web site and other social media during the periods of festival inactivity, and presented low degrees of interaction during the entire year. An explanation could be found in the fact that a top-down strategy contrasts with the collaborative and community-based culture that is typical of Web 2.0 users and, thus it is not effective in supporting interaction with web users and spontaneous discussion among the users themselves. When the organizing committee changed its strategy in late 2011, results started to improve. In particular, the willingness to reinforce the festival's identity and to focus online communication on issues related to the art of photography in general played an important role in increasing the interaction with web users. The new strategy appears to contribute to reinforcing the festival identity in terms of reputation within the milieu of contemporary photography. In doing so, it has achieved the goal of sustaining attendees' interest in the festival both during the period April-June and during other periods of the year.

This seems to be an interesting result for a festival that, like other temporary organizations, could be conceived of as a discontinuous organization. In fact, since organizational identity requires stability and continuity over time, the long periods of inactivity of a festival may undermine the perception of its central, distinctive, and enduring attributes by different external audiences (tourists, media, and public authorities, among others). A web strategy aimed at supporting the perception of a festival as a well-reputed actor in its artistic milieu seems to sustain a continuous interplay between insiders and outsiders, limiting the problems related to discontinuity.

In order to increase its effectiveness, it seems important to avoid a top-down approach, which may encounter some hurdles because Web 2.0 platforms are strongly grounded in some specific web cultures that are collaborative and community based. However, adopting a bottom-up approach aimed at promoting collaboration among web users and encouraging spontaneous discussion could raise challenges for organizations. Web 2.0 platforms imply several limitations to organizational control and top-down management practices (Bernoff & Li, 2008). Therefore, effective management of social media may imply also a reconfiguration of organizational routines and culture toward more collaborative and open models (McAfee, 2006).

As far as the social identification of a festival's attendees is concerned, the case study provided some provisional results that support the idea that a top-down web strategy is not able to foster social interaction among actual and potential attendees. However, the study did not measure how the new web strategy affects actual and potential attendees' social identification. This is one of the most important limitations. This research also presents a number of limitations that are typical of other exploratory case studies (Yin, 1984). However, these limitations suggest directions for future research. For example, it would be useful to investigate in the next festival editions the relationship between an attendee's social identification and her/his participation in the festival's Web 2.0 platforms. It would also be intriguing to conduct a longitudinal study to investigate how the relationship between different social media used by a festival organization, their features and contents, and attendees' social identification may change over time. Finally, it would be useful to compare the results with other festivals that are dedicated to different arts or are held in different geographical contexts.

Acknowledgment—The authors would like to thank the Reggio Emilia Councilor of Culture, Giovanni Catellani, and Elisabetta Farioli, Giovanna Righi, and Ilaria Campioli from the Municipality of Reggio Emilia for their support and valuable assistance during the data collecting process.

PART III

FUTURE PERSPECTIVES

Chapter 13

Tourism and Media Studies 3.0

Toby Miller
University of California, Riverside, USA

ABSTRACT

The term "social media" generally refers to the multi-point creation and distribution of electronic communication. It is understood in opposition to broadcasting. This chapter explains the history of media studies as a means of comprehending these newer media in the context of tourism. They need to be studied in the light of existing media, even as we seek a new form of truly interdisciplinary work that brings existing approaches together. Taking its agenda from social movements as well as intellectual ones, and its methods from social sciences and humanities, Media Studies 3.0 should focus on gender, race, class, sexuality, sustainability, and pleasure across national lines—an apt setting for those working on tourism.

Keywords: Media studies 1.0; Media studies 2.0; Media studies 3.0

INTRODUCTION

The term "social media" generally refers to the multi-point creation and distribution of electronic communication. It is understood in opposition to broadcasting (though the notion that the most popular pastime worldwide now and in the last century should be other than "social" is bizarre). This chapter explains the history of media studies, which may be of value for

Tourism Social Media: Transformations in Identity, Community and Culture
Tourism Social Science Series, Volume 18, 229–243
ISSN: 1571-5043/doi:10.1108/S1571-5043(2013)0000018015

comprehending these newer social media in the context of tourism. The chapter discusses the social media in the light of their defunct, venerable, and middle-aged counterparts.

Across history, media studies have been dominated by three topics: ownership and control, content, and audiences. Approaches to ownership and control vary between neoliberal endorsements of limited regulation by the state to facilitate market entry by new competitors, and Marxist critiques of the bourgeois media for controlling the sociopolitical agenda. Approaches to content vary between hermeneutics, which unearths the meaning of individual texts and links them to broader social formations and problems, and content analysis, which establishes patterns across significant numbers of similar texts, rather than close readings of individual ones. Approaches to audiences vary between social psychological attempts to correlate audiovisual consumption and social conduct, and critiques of imported audiovisual material threatening national and regional autonomy. These three components, fractured by politics, nation, discipline, theory, and method, are embodied in what is called here Media Studies 1.0 and Media Studies 2.0. These two formations cover a new Media Studies 3.0, and offer some examples of how the media and tourism intersect in the contemporary moment.

TOURISM AND MEDIA STUDIES

Media Studies 1.0

Media Studies 1.0 derived from the spread of new media technologies over the past two centuries into the lives of urbanizing populations and the policing questions that this posed to state and capital: What the effect on the public of these developments would be and how they would vary between those with a stake in the social order versus those seeking to transform it. By the early 20th century, academic experts had decreed media audiences to be passive consumers, thanks to the missions of literary criticism, distinguishing the aesthetically cultivated from others, and psychology, distinguishing the socially competent from others (Butsch, 2000, p. 3). The origins of social psychology can be traced to anxieties about "the crowd" in a suddenly urbanized and educated Western Europe that raised the prospect of a long-feared "ochlocracy" of "the worthless mob" (Pufendorf, 2000, p. 144) able to share popular texts. In the wake of the French Revolution, Edmund Burke was animated by the need to limit collective exuberance via restraint on popular passions (1994, p. 122). He was not alone, then or now. Consider the opening line of Baroness Orczy's famous adventure tourism novel of the Terror, *The Scarlet Pimpernel*: "A surging, seething, murmuring crowd of beings that are human only in name, for to the eye and ear they seem naught but savage creatures, animated by vile passions and by the lust of vengeance and of hate" (2009, Kindle Locations, 10488–10489). Elite theorists from both right and left emerged across the 19th century, notably Pareto (1976), Mosca (1939), Le Bon (1899), and Michels (1915). They argued that newly literate publics were vulnerable to manipulation by demagogues. Even Mill spoke of "the meanest feelings and most ignorant prejudices of the vulgarest part of the crowd" (1861, p. 144). The founder of the "American Dream," the Latino James Truslow Adams, regarded "[t]he mob mentality of the city crowd" as "one of the menaces to modern civilization." He was particularly disparaging about "the prostitution of the moving-picture industry" (1941, pp. 404, 413). These critics were frightened of socialism, democracy, and popular reason (Wallas, 1967, p. 137). With civil society growing restive, the emergence of radical politics was explained away in sociopsychological terms rather than political-economic ones. The psy-function warmed itself by campus fires, far from the crowding mass. In the United States, Harvard took charge of theorizing, Chicago observing, and Columbia enumerating the great unwashed (Staiger, 2005, pp. 21–22). Tests of beauty and truth found the popular classes wanting, and helped promulgate the idea of the newly literate and suddenly enfranchised being bamboozled by the artistically shameless and unscrupulously fluent.

The US Payne Fund studies of the 1930s investigated the impact of films on what a gaggle of sociologists labeled "'superior' adults" (this expression referred to "young college professors, graduate students and their wives") versus children from juvenile centers. Researchers wanted to know, "what effect do motion pictures have upon children of different ages?" especially on people defined as "retarded." These pioneering scholars boldly set out to discover whether "the onset of puberty is or is not affected by motion pictures" and what they called "The Big Three" narrative themes: love, crime, and sex (sound familiar?). They pondered "demonstrations of satisfying love techniques" to see whether "sexual passions are aroused and amateur prostitution ... aggravated" by the screen, gauging reactions through "autobiographical case studies," questionnaires asking whether "All Most Many Some Few No Chinese are cunning and underhand," and "skin response," as measured by psychogalvanometers attached to young people in cinemas and hypnographs and polygraphs wired to them in their beds (Charters, 1933).

The Payne Fund studies birthed seven decades of obsessive social-scientific attempts to correlate youthful consumption of popular culture with antisocial conduct, scrutinizing audiences in terms of where they came from, how many there were, and what they did as a consequence of participating (Miller, 2009). In 1951, Smythe wrote of this effects research, "[e]verybody seems to be doing it, especially those who are best qualified by virtue of the fact that 'they wouldn't have a television set in the house'" (2004, p. 318). Bob Dylan remembers the 1960s in Greenwich Village not only because he was singing in coffee shops but as a time marked by "Sociologists ... saying that TV had deadly intentions and was destroying the minds and imaginations of the young—that their attention span was being dragged down." The other dominant site of knowledge Dylan encountered was the "psychology professor, a good performer, but originality not his long suit" (2004, pp. 55, 67).

Just such purveyors of normal science continue to cast a shadow across that village, and many others. The pattern is that when cultural technologies and genres emerge, young people are identified as both pioneers and victims, simultaneously endowed by marketers and critics with power and vulner-ability. They are held to be the first to know and the last to understand the media—the grand paradox of youth, latterly on display in the digital sublime of technological determinism, as always with the super-added valence of a future citizenship in peril (American Academy of Pediatrics, Council on Communications and Media, 2009). New genres and technol-ogies are accompanied by concerns about extreme distinctions among generations. The latest manifestation of this anxiety can be found in much pop-intellectual work that divines the existence of "digital natives" (Tapscott, 2009).

Concerns about supposedly unprecedented and unholy risks deriving from new media recur with each major technological and generic innovation. Damnation was sure to follow cheap novels during the 1900s, silent then sound film of the teens and 1920s, radio in the 1930s, comic books from the 1940s and 1950s, pop music and television in the 1950s and 1960s, satanic rock and video cassette recorders of the 1970s and 1980s, and rap music, video games, the Internet, and sexting since the 1990s.

The satirical paper The Onion (2005) cleverly mocked these interdepen-dent phenomena of moral panic and commodification via a *faux* study of the impact on US youth of seeing Janet Jackson's breast in a 2004 Super Bowl broadcast. Something similar can be seen in conventional tourism research into social media, which warns corporations about how to avoid negative responses and encourage positive ones, lest the herd-like public turn against a particular company or resort (González, Gidumal, & López-Valcárcel, 2010; Pan, Xiang, Law, & Fesenmaier, 2011; Xiang & Gretzel, 2010). The audience must be controlled as if it were an unruly mob of 19th-century socialists. This anxiety and desire for surveillance has particular force when the social media are identified as causal agents, or at least facilitators, of child sex tourism (George & Panko, 2011).

Effects studies suffer all the disadvantages of ideal-typical psychological reasoning. They rely on methodological individualism and fail to account for cultural norms, let alone the arcs of history that establish patterns of text and response inside politics, war, ideology, and discourse. Each laboratory test, based on, as the refrain goes, "a large university in the Midwest [of the United States]," is countered by a similar experiment, with conflicting results. As politicians, grant-givers, and pundits call for more and more research to prove that the media make you stupid, violent, and apathetic— or the opposite—academics line up at the trough to indulge their contempt for popular culture and their rent-seeking urge for public money. Media Studies 1.0 rarely interrogates its own conditions of existence—namely, governments, religious groups, business leeches, and the media themselves account for social problems by diverting blame onto popular culture. It takes each new medium and genre as an opportunity to affirm its omniscient agenda (Miller, 2009).

Whereas effects research focuses on the cognition and emotion of individual human subjects via observation and experimentation, another way of considering audiences looks to the customs and patriotic feeling exhibited by collective human subjects, the grout of national culture. In place of psychology, it is concerned with politics. The media do not make you a well- or ill-educated person, a wild or self-controlled one. Rather, they make you a knowledgeable and loyal national subject or a *naïf*, ignorant of local tradition and history. Cultural belonging, not psychic wholeness, is the touchstone of this model. Instead of measuring responses electronically or behaviorally, it interrogates the geopolitical origin of popular texts and the themes and styles they embody, with particular attention to the putatively nation-building genres of drama, news, sport, and current affairs. Adherents hold that local citizens should control television, for instance, because they can be counted on to be patriotic in the event of war. Many nations prohibit foreigners owning TV licenses. The United States is a prominent example.

In addition to audience research and cultural policy, Media Studies 1.0 also includes political economy, which focuses on infrastructure rather than audiences, and critical theory, which is concerned that the audiovisual sector turns people away from artistic and social traces of authentic intersubjectivity and toward control of individual consciousness. Both work from the *nostrum* that the media are all powerful. Political economy is more policy oriented and political in its focus on institutional power. Critical theory is more philosophical and aesthetic in its desire to develop modernism and the avant-garde. They began as one with lamentations for the triumph of industrialized cultural production and the loss of a self-critical philosophical address. The two approaches are also linked via a distaste for what they deride as mass culture. Because demand is dispersed and supply centralized, the media supposedly operate via an administrative logic. Far from reflecting already-established and -revealed preferences of consumers in reaction to tastes and desires, they manipulate audiences from the apex of production. Coercion is mistaken for free will, and culture is one more industrial process subordinated to the dominant economic forces within society. It seeks a maximum of standardization and a minimum of risk. The only element that might stand against this leveling sameness is said to be individual consciousness. But that consciousness has itself been customized to enable efficient media production (Adorno & Horkheimer, 1977).

Media Studies 2.0

For Media Studies 2.0, popular culture represents the apex of modernity. Far from being supremely alienating, it embodies the expansion of civil society, the first moment in history when political and commercial organs and agendas became receptive to, and part of, the popular classes; when the general population counted as part of the social, rather than being excluded from political-economic calculations. At the same time, there was a lessening of authority, the promulgation of individual rights and respect, and the development of intense but large-scale human interaction (Hartley, 2003; Shils, 1966). This perspective has offered a way in to media audiences that differs from Media Studies 1.0 and its faith in the all-powerful agency of the media. For in Media Studies 2.0, the all-powerful agent is the audience. It claims that the public is so clever and able that it makes its own meanings, outwitting institutions of the state, academia, and capitalism that seek to measure and control it. In the case of children and the media, for example, anxieties from 1.0 about turning Edenic innocents into rabid monsters, capitalist dupes, or mental Americans have been challenged by a new culturalist perspective. This formation has animated research into the generic features and intertexts of children's news, drama, action-adventure, education, cartooning, and play and how children distinguish between fact and fiction and talk about the media as part of social interaction (Buckingham, 2000).

Faith in the active audience can reach cosmic proportions. It has been a *donnée* of 2.0 that the media are not responsible for anything. This position is a virtual *nostrum* in some research into fans, who are thought to construct connections with celebrities and actants in ways that mimic friendship, make sense of human interaction, and ignite cultural politics. Media Studies 2.0 commonly attacks opponents of commercial culture for misrecognizing its capacity to subvert patriarchy, capitalism, and other forms of oppression. The popular is held to have progressive effects, because it is decoded by people in keeping with their social situations. The active audience is said to be weak at the level of cultural production, but strong as an interpretative community. All this is supposedly evident to scholars from their perusal of audience conventions, web pages, discussion groups, quizzes, and rankings, or by staring at screens with their children. Consumption is the key to Media Studies 2.0—with production discounted, labor forgotten, consumers sovereign, and governments there to protect them.

Cybertarian technophiles, struck by the digital sublime, attribute magical properties to contemporary communications, and cultural technologies that obliterate geography, sovereignty, and hierarchy in an alchemy of truth and beauty. Cybertarians see omniscient, omnipotent audiences outwitting the efforts of capital, the state, and parents to understand and corral them. The new-media *savants* who construct the latter model routinely invoke precapitalist philosophers, dodging questions of state and capital by heading for aesthetics (Cogburn & Silcox, 2008). A deregulated, individuated media world supposedly makes consumers into producers, frees the disabled from confinement, encourages new subjectivities, rewards intellect and competitiveness, links people across cultures, and allows billions of flowers to bloom in a post-political cornucopia. It is a kind of Marxist/Godardian wet dream, where people fish, fornicate, film, and finance from morning to midnight. At such moments, one can say that what Eagleton (1982) sardonically named The Reader's Liberation Movement is in the house. In his survey of this work, Mosco rightly argues that such "myths are important both for what they reveal (including a genuine desire for community and democracy) and for what they conceal (including the growing concentration of communication power in a handful of transnational media businesses)" (2004).

In tourism, the aggregated effect of collective knowledge via social media that is associated with personal recommendations of destinations is a good example of these claims (Popescu & Grefenstette, 2011). Such findings excite 2.0 advocates, as per the unseemly way that tourism experts egged on by social media salivate over wealthy foreigners; a typical instance is the discourse of Chinese consumers liberated from the state (Arlt & Thraenhart, 2011). Such sanctioned greed is some distance from research that illustrates how the social media function as surveillance-and-control devices in places as diverse as China and Australia (Qiu, 2007) or the World Privacy Forum proposing that people are in a "one-way mirror society," where power accretes to corporations through the supposedly even-handed tool of interactivity (Dixon, 2010).

The fundamental dilemma for adherents of Media Studies 2.0 is this: Can fans or tourists be said to make rational evaluations of core questions of social justice such as labor exploitation, patriarchy, racism, climate change, and neo-imperialism—or in some specifiable way make a difference beyond their own selves—when they interpret TV unusually, each other about romantic frustrations, play pirated versions of Scrabble on Facebook, or take a cruise based on amateur recommendations?

Has the society gone too far in supplanting the panicky Woody Allen nebbishness of 1.0 ("I'm kind of bothered that ... ") with the Panglossian Pollyanna nerdiness of 2.0 ("Cool stuff")? Keen, a lapsarian prophet of the Internet, argues that the new landscape is abuzz with noise and ignorance rather than subtlety and knowledge (2007, p. 12). He sees a dreary world of constant clatter and frenzied imagery denaturing aesthetics in favor of uninterrupted stimulus. This is no 2.0 utopia! Postrel, then editor of the libertarian *Reason* magazine and later a *New York Times* economics journalist, wrote a *Wall Street Journal* op-ed welcoming 2.0 as "deeply threatening to traditional leftist views of commerce ... lending support to the corporate enemy and even training graduate students who wind up doing market research" (1999).

Media Studies 3.0

One needs more *frottage* between Media Studies 1.0 and 2.0, breaking down the binary between them. Media Studies 1.0 should register struggle, and 2.0 should register structure. Currently, 1.0 draws one's attention to audience inoculation and corporate control, but leaves out productive labor and environmental implications. Media Studies 2.0 uptakes and adds responses, but again marginalizes these key topics. Media Studies 1.0 misses moments of crisis and hope, presenting a subject-free picture of structure but no agency, other than psychological response, shareholder maximization, and managerial rationality. Its nationalistic cultural policies often deny the banality of protected cinema, the futility of quota-driven television, and the partiality of who is chosen to create national images and appear in them. Media 2.0 misses forms of domination and exploitation, presenting an institution-free picture with agency but no structure, other than fan creativity and reader imagination. Further, both 1.0 and 2.0 are doggedly tied to nativist epistemologies that must be transcended. The nativism is especially powerful in the United States, the United Kingdom, and their academic satellites such as Israel and Australia, where effortless extrapolations from very limited experience support totalizing theories and norms, due to the hegemony of English-language publishing and scholarly links to the warfare, welfare, and cultural bureaucracies. The following remark (paid for by Vodafone) encapsulates 2.0:

> Mobile phones have become affective technologies. That is, objects which mediate the expression, display, experience and communication of feelings and emotions. ... They are an extension of the human body ... building and maintaining ... groups and communities. (Lasén, 2004)

This will not do. Thankfully it is challenged by a remark that could come from 3.0—funded by a nongovernment organization of Mexican electronics workers:

> The increasingly faster and more versatile computers, appealing mobile phones, high-definition TVs, Internet, tiny music players, ingenious photo cameras, entertaining games consoles and even electronic pets give us the idea of a developed, pioneering and modern world. It is indeed a new era for many; but the dark side of this prosperous world reveals a very different reality, that far from taking us to the future, takes us back to a darker past. (Centro de Reflexión y Acción Laboral, 2006)

Media Studies 3.0 is as much about experiences as technologies or institutions. The media color the world. They give it meaning; and the process is reciprocal. The sounds, stories, and pictures that *are* the media— whether social or antisocial—actually come from people. Old stories from oral traditions become commercial narratives. Letters to the editor tell newspapers what interests their readers. Audience measurements and focus groups instruct producers on which TV shows are likely to succeed and why.

Fans become creators as they write zines that in turn become story ideas. Marketers trawl street fairs, clubs, and fan sites to uncover emergent trends. Coca-Cola hires African Americans to drive through the inner city selling soda and playing hip-hop. AT&T pays San Francisco buskers to mention the company in their songs. Street performance poets rhyme about Nissan cars for cash, simultaneously hawking, entertaining, and researching. Subway's sandwich commercials are marketed as made by teenagers. Cultural studies graduates become designers, and graduate students in New York and Los Angeles read scripts for producers and pronounce on whether they tap into audience interests.

Semiotics textbooks that critically deconstruct commercial culture adorn advertising executives' bookcases. Precariously employed part-timers prowl the streets with DVD players under their arms to ask target audiences what they think of trailers for upcoming movies, or while away their time in theaters spying on how their fellow spectators respond to coming attractions. Opportunities to vote in the Eurovision Song Contest or a reality program determine both the success of contestants and the profile of active viewers who can be monitored and wooed. In all these instances, audience creativity is important. It informs and frightens producers, simultaneously offering them leads on stories and trends and daunting them with its changeability and friskiness. End-user licensing agreements ensure that players of corporate games online and contributors to official discussion groups about film or television sign over their cultural moves and access. Such topics frequently elude 1.0 and 2.0. They do not fit those models.

Studying tourism through the media and vice versa must blend ethnographic, political-economic, and aesthetic analyses in a global and local way, establishing links among the key areas of cultural production around the world (Africa, the Americas, Asia, Europe, and the Middle East) and diasporic and dispossessed communities engaged in their own cultural production. Media 3.0 needs to be a media-centered version of area studies, with diasporas as important as regions. It must be animated by collective identity and power: how human subjects are formed and experience cultural and social space. Taking its agenda from social movements as well as intellectual ones, and its methods from economics, politics, communications, sociology, literature, law, science, medicine, environmental studies, anthropology, history, and art, Media Studies 3.0 should focus on gender, race, class, sexuality, sustainability, and pleasure, across national lines—an apt setting for those working on tourism.

One can gain some tips on doing this from the history of theorizing culture. It has usually been studied in two registers: via the social sciences and the humanities—truth versus beauty. Culture has been a marker of differences and similarities in taste and status, as explored interpretatively or methodically. In the humanities, cultural texts have long been judged by criteria of quality, as practiced critically and historically. For their part, the social sciences have focused on religions, customs, times, and spaces, as explored ethnographically or statistically. Thus, whereas the humanities articulate differences through symbolic norms (e.g., which classes have the cultural capital to appreciate high culture and which do not), the social sciences articulate differences through social norms (such as, which peoples cultivate agriculture in keeping with spirituality and which do not) (Benhabib, 2002; Wallerstein, 1989). This distinction feeds into the Cartesian dualism separating thought from work. It assumes that humans have two distinct natures: the intelligent and the corporeal. One is focused on action, the other on reason. That binary has dominated media studies, posing oppositions of society versus economy and audience versus meaning. It haunts 1.0 and 2.0.

For all its sticky origins in Cartesianism, this bifurcation and silencing of labor and culture cannot and should not hold. Historically, the best critical political economy and the best cultural studies have worked through the imbrication of power and signification. Blending them can heal the fissure between fact and interpretation, the social sciences and the humanities, and truth and beauty, under the sign of a principled approach to cultural democracy. Grossberg recommends "politicizing theory and theorizing politics" by combining abstraction and grounded analysis (1997). That requires a focus on the contradictions of organizational structures, their articulations with everyday living and textuality and their intrication with the polity and economy, addressing production, consumption, and social stratification. Half a century ago, Smythe studied TV texts as "a group of symbols" that "serve as a medium of exchange between the mass media and the audience." He recognized that analyses of infrastructure and content must be supplemented by accounting for the conditions under which culture is made, circulated, received, interpreted, and criticized: "The produced program is ... more than the sum of the program ingredients" because it is encrusted with "contextual and explicit layers of meaning" that emerge during its creation and consumption (1954, p. 143).

Relevant work toward 3.0 is already underway. Rajagopal notes that because the television, the telephone, the Internet, the neoliberal, and the outgoing tourist are relatively new to India, "markets and media generate new kinds of rights and new kinds of imagination ... novel ways of exercising citizenship rights and conceiving politics" (2001). For Winocur

(2002), women's talkback radio in Latin America since the fall of US-backed dictatorships has offered a simultaneously individual and social forum for new expressions of citizenship in the context of decentered politics, emergent identities, minority rights, and gender issues—a public space that transcends the subordination of difference and the privileging of elite experience. Mosco (2004) starts from the power of mythology then "builds a bridge to political economy" in his investigation of neoliberal *doxa* about empowerment, insisting on "the mutually constitutive relationship between political economy and cultural studies" as each mounts "a critique of the other." One can note similar intent animating such innovations as Sarai, the Free Software Foundation, and the Alternative Law Forum—exemplary instances of Media Studies 3.0 in formation. They blend internationalism, political economy, ethnography, and textual analysis, and resist the binarism of 1.0 and 2.0.

The art world can incarnate this approach in its critical views of tourism. For instance, Amsterdam's urbanscreens.org uses electronic billboards as public space to encourage active citizenship, as do Ars Electronica of Linz and Melbourne's Federation Square. Artists draw attention to personal multimedia messaging services and corporate occupancy of public space by placing passersby on billboards, as per Zhang Ga's Times Square *People's Portrait*, for all the world a throwback to Judy Holliday's moment of celebrity in the classic Hollywood film *It Should Happen to You* (George Cukor, 1954), when she buys advertising space in Columbus Circle to promote herself.

Anderson and Wolff (2010), lapsed sacerdotal zealots of the new media from *Wired* magazine, say the web is dead because social networks and software applications are supplanting the old fantasy of an open frontier with a new hegemony of a few institutions. Schiller (2007) challenges social media enthusiasts to query the way that economic inequalities fuel new consumer needs, as people rush to purchase inferior services at high cost. In the United States, for instance, the decline in governmental oversight of the media since World War II has diminished the quality and regulation of competition, allowing telecommunication companies to exploit the need for connectedness in times of fragmentation.

CONCLUSION

To understand media infrastructure, it is necessary to address technological innovation, regulation, labor, ownership, control, and environmental impact, utilizing ethnographic, political-economic, scientific, and public-policy research. To understand content, one must address production and undertake content and textual analysis, combining statistical and hermeneutic methods. To understand audiences, ratings, uses-and-gratifications, effects, active-audience, ethnographic, and psychoanalytic traditions, combining quantitative and qualitative measures should be standard.

Two examples from 3.0 can be used to show the relationship between the media and tourism. They concern major tourist spots thematized in films. Each involves environmental destruction and popular responses to corporate malevolence. They blend older and newer media in artful ways appropriate to 3.0.

Much of Fox Studios' *Titanic* (Cameron, 1997) was shot in the Mexican village of Popotla. During the making of the picture, the national film studio Churubusco was renovated and a National Film Commission established, with satellites across the country providing *gabacho* moguls trips in governors' helicopters, among other services. Restoring Mexico to the Hollywood map gained the film's director Cameron the Order of the Aztec Eagle from a grateful government. *Titanic* was, in this context, a screen testimony to the 1994 North American Free Trade Agreement/Tratado de Libre Comercio, which has seen offshore film and television production in Mexico increase thanks to easy shipment of technology, especially for low-budget shoots. Studio owner Rupert Murdoch approvingly cited the number of workers invisibly employed in making the film:

> this cross-border cultural co-operation is not the result of regulation, but market forces. It's the freedom to move capital, technology and talent around the world that adds value, invigorates ailing markets, creates new ones.

Meanwhile, local Mexican film production spiraled downwards, from 747 titles in the decade prior to the agreement/tratado to 212 the following decade (Maxwell & Miller, 2006; Miller, Govil, McMurria, Maxwell, & Wang, 2005, pp. 164–65).

There is a cruel irony to this liquid globalization of cultural labor: the cost of the film could have provided safe drinking water to 600,000 people for a year. People submerged in the credits to *Titanic* (or not listed at all) supposedly benefited from the textualization of a boat laden with wealthy tourists and *lumpen* steerage that had been sunk by invisible ice and business bombast 80 years earlier. During filming, Popotla was cut off from the sea and local fisheries by a 6-feet-high and 500-feet long movie wall, built to keep citizens away. Fox's chlorination of surrounding seawater deci-mated sea urchins, which locals had long harvested, and reduced overall fish levels by a third (Kushner, 1998; Miller et al., 2005, p. 165). Today, Popotla is promoted as a destination for smiling foreigners eager to see where their favorite drowning sequences were shot at the charmingly named "Foxploration" (http://www.bajatours.org/about_rosarito_beach; http://www.rosaritoinn.com/foxtour.htm).

Such arrogant despoliation has not gone unanswered. In collaboration with artists like Jim Bliesner, the Popotlanos decorated the wall with rubbish to ridicule the filmmakers, and adopted the rallying cry *mariscos libre* (free-dom for shellfish). (Photographs are available at rtmark.com/popotlaimages. html.) This nifty environmental critique has largely eluded journalistic and scholarly analysis. Ars Electronica awarded the Popotlanos a prize for "symbolic low-tech resistance to real high-tech destruction" that was in keeping with the movie's textual—if not industrial—class politics. But the award was a fraction of the money Ars Electronica gave the film's producers for their innovative special effects. Resistance has come from groups using social media to pose as officials from the World Trade Organization to underscore the damage done to livelihoods and the environment. The Popotlanos' view of Cameron's putatively green, pro-indigenous, anti-imperialist *Avatar* (2009) is not on record, but their town is currently vilified by the likes of *The Washington Times* as a site for "illegals" seeking to enter the United States (Coombe & Herman, 2000; gatt.org/popotla.html; Kushner, 1998; *Popotla vs. Titanic*, n.d.; Sekula, 2001; Spagat, 2010).

Cameron acknowledges the need to change filmmaking in light of the ecological crisis. He is quick to point out that "*Avatar* was an enormous battle film that took place in a rainforest but was 100% C[omputer-] G[enerated]" (Cheney, 2010; quoted in Miller, 2010). When he castigated the Pacific Northwest for extracting oil from tar sands, the *Edmonton Sun* editorialized in best un-Canadian fashion "James Cameron is a Hypocrite" for working in California, where energy comes from power companies that use coal from elsewhere (*Edmonton Sun*, 2010).

Three years after *Titanic*, Fox made *The Beach* (Boyle, 2000), where a modern-day Asian Eden suddenly turns nasty for jaded tourists. Like the earlier film, it starred the environmental moralist Leonardo DiCaprio (Biggs, 2000). *The Beach* was shot in Maya Beach, part of Thailand's Phi Phi Islands National Park. Natural scenery was bulldozed because it did not fit the company's fantasy of a tropical idyll: sand dunes were relocated, flora rearranged, and a new strip of coconut palms planted. The producers paid off the government with a donation to the Royal Forestry Department, and campaigned with the Tourism Authority to twin the picture as a promotion for the country. The damaged sand dunes of the region collapsed in the next monsoon, their natural defenses against erosion destroyed by Hollywood bulldozers. Thai environmental and pro-democracy activists publicized this arrogant despoliation, while the director claimed the film was "raising environmental consciousness" among a local population whose appreciation of these things lagged "behind" US "awareness" (Law, Bunnell, & Ong, 2007; Miller et al., 2005; Shoaib, 2001; Tzanelli, 2006). Director Boyle heroically announced his intention to "give something back to Thailand" by hiring Thai apprentices but then complained that "[w]e were hauling 300 fucking people around wherever we went. And you know how hard it is to learn Thai names. Every lunchtime was like a prime minister's reception" (quoted in Gilbey, 2002). Before the film was released—but no doubt after having had their consciousness raised—the Ao Nang Tambon Administration Organization, the Krabi Provincial Administration Organization, and various environmental groups filed a suit against Fox and local officialdom for contravening the National Parks Act and the Environmental Protection Act. It took seven years, but the Thai Supreme Court found in their favor in 2006 (*The Nation*, 2006). The reaction of the "300 fucking people" who were being "hauled around" during production is not on record.

The political-economic background to such ecologically destructive filmmaking implicates tourism. Structural adjustment as peddled by neoliberal high priests at the World Bank, the International Monetary Fund, the World Trade Organization, and the sovereign states that dominate them has encouraged the Global South to turn away from subsistence agriculture and toward tradable services, beyond manufacturing capacity and in the direction of human exchange. In much of Southeast Asia, these policies pushed people into littoral regions in search of work. Fish-farming corporations created a new aquaculture, displacing the natural environment of mangroves and coral reefs that protect people and land. The requirement to reconstitute themselves as entertaining heritage sites and decadent tourism playgrounds induced Thailand, Indonesia, and Malaysia to undertake massive construction projects. They built resorts at the point where high tides lap, attracting more and more workers and decimating more and more natural protection. Areas that had not been directed to remove natural barriers suffered dramatically fewer casualties in the 2004 tsunami (Bidwai, 2005; Sharma, 2005; Shiva, 2005). That ugly side to tourism and the media is something 3.0 can specify, engage, and struggle against. Doing so might make for a truly social media.

Chapter 14

Critical Digital Tourism Studies

Ana María Munar
Copenhagen Business School, Denmark

Szilvia Gyimóthy
Aalborg University, Denmark

ABSTRACT

This chapter analyzes the subject of critical digital tourism studies and envisions an agenda for technology research and education. Inspired by the insights of this book and the work of scholars in digital humanities and communication (Baym, 2010; Hayles, 2012), the study presents "embedded cognition" as a framework to comprehend the interdependencies between people's actions and discourses, and technological affordances. It introduces the concept of "turistus digitalis," discusses theories for conceptualizing society and technology relations, and examines the challenges of transdisciplinarity. This investigation contributes to increasing research reflexivity in understanding how tourism is enacted through digital worlds and how digital technologies evolve through tourism practices.

Keywords: Embedded cognition; methodology; education; digital studies

INTRODUCTION

The tourist is different with a smartphone in her hand; the smartphone is different with her holding it. She is another

Tourism Social Media: Transformations in Identity, Community and Culture
Tourism Social Science Series, Volume 18, 245–262
Copyright © 2013 by Emerald Group Publishing Limited
All rights of reproduction in any form reserved
ISSN: 1571-5043/doi:10.1108/S1571-5043(2013)0000018016

> subject because she holds the smartphone; the smartphone is another subject because it has entered into a relationship with her; the social world is different because they have entered this relationship with one another. (paraphrasing Latour, 1999)

Tourists and the world of tourism have entered into a special relationship with digital technologies. This relationship provides the ground on which new questions pertaining to what digital tourism is or how it evolves can be formulated. Technological tools are not passive objects; they carry affordances enabling as well as shaping tourist behavior. A tourist with a smartphone in her hand is a hybrid with a number of new action possibilities: capable of calling others, paying entry tickets, sharing touristic moments across time and space, and listening to audioguides. However, by enabling Facebook status updates or checking in on 4Square or QR-code scans, the smartphone discloses the physical location of its bearer, which may allow the virtual harvesting and distribution of personal information. In other words, digital technology fundamentally changes one's social world and has the potential to enact new tourism realities. The contributions presented in this volume attempt to address the following questions: How can this emerging new world and the digitally hybrid human activity—the *turistus digitalis* (the digital tourist)—be known? How do dialogic and rhizomatic (multiple and non-hierarchical) relations among technological objects, systems, and humans change tourism? What are the biological, environmental, societal, cultural, and ethical consequences of these emergent hybridities? How can research and educational agendas capable of embracing these new phenomena be formulated?

This concluding discourse takes these four questions as the point of departure. By discussing the insights presented in the preceding chapters, it analyzes the ways in which social digital technologies transform tourism and also set the stage for the development of the new field of digital tourism studies. Through the novel framing of problems, innovative methodological considerations, and the critical analysis and discussions introduced, a new landscape for this subject is presented. At its heart is the use of research paradigms based on critical and interpretivist traditions of thought. These traditions are essentially multidisciplinary or transdisciplinary, relying on a rich mixture of humanities and social sciences characterized by an extensive use of qualitative methodologies.

DIGITAL TOURISM

A novel view on the individual tourist appears through the reading of the different contributions in this volume. Many of the authors argue for abandoning the established conceptualization of the tourist as a vulgar, hedonistic consumer or as an experience "junkie." Instead, the tourist is seen as a complex technology-enabled agent. New roles appropriated and performed by tourists are presented in this book. Ooi and Munar explain how tourists become reflexive cocreators of heritage experiences and thereby empowered agents of interpretation. How technological evolution has opened new landscapes for human action and decisionmaking is presented in Hvass' discussion of tourists as comanagers of communication strategies and Budeanu's explanation of tourists as agents of change in social and political power relations. Adopting new forms of responsibility, tourists perform managerial activities once secluded within organizations. They become creators of new markets, as they expose and construct destinations based on popular culture, as explored by Lexhagen and her colleagues studying Twilight Tourism. Digitally enabled human beings negotiate flexible and fluid identities and processes of identification with touristic events and objects, as seen in the cases of *Fotografia Europea* and the Roskilde Festival.

The *turistus digitalis* interacts with and creates new social spaces and virtual communities. Inherently different from traditional bounded communities, these are ephemeral, fragmented, imagined, fluid, and liminal. As Ek's contribution suggests, these communities of strangers may be a consequence of the missing community in the contemporary tourism. As presented in Munar, digital social interaction is not neutral or "democratic"; it also enables exploitation and reification, new systems of inclusion and exclusion, new demarcations of "otherness," and the emergence of the digitally illiterate. Digital presence is not to be confounded with reflexivity, wisdom, or responsible action, as indicated by Miller's critical views. A digitally enabled human has accessed the possibility to gain "digital capital" and has become digital capital herself. This possibility entails gains in social reputation, cultural knowledge, emotional influence, and economic advantages. As such, the *turistus digitalis* becomes a capital asset for tourist organizations and for other tourists. Therefore, critical digital tourism studies should aim at expanding the ontological fundament of this field with simultaneous enquiries on the nature of the hybridity between humans and technical tools and systems. While this volume contributes to mapping the features of *turistus digitalis* and her conceptualization as an agent of change, more research effort and empirical contributions are required to understand the complexity of the technical tools/material in this complex relationship. Further development of the concept of *turistus digitalis* will expand the tourism knowledge field in the areas of *embedded cognition* and *technogenesis.*

Cognition, the study of how humans think, is at the core of the philosophy of science and theories of traditional disciplines in social sciences and humanities, from the concepts of *Homo Faber* to *Homo Economicus.* In trying to grasp human cognition, scholars such as Habermas (1987) and Giddens (1987) have identified language and action as the means by which humans make sense of their world and are able to adapt and perform in modern societies. The powerful attraction of the discursive (language and communication) lies in its ability to represent the self-aware and reflexive conscious human. For theorists focusing on language, this is the medium by which societies reach understanding, coordinate action, and socialize individuals (Habermas, 1987).

In the past 20 years, science and technology scholars such as Latour (1999) and Law (2002) have suggested that knowledge should not only be conceptualized as discoursive, but as embodied. The spatial turn asserts a crucial role for the environment, acknowledging its qualities as an enabler for human cognition. Space is no longer an inanimate, absolute, three-dimensional container, but a relational agent (Thrift, 2007). Challenging a conceptual division between mind and body as separate entities, embedded cognition claims that human language and actions are bodily enacted, and that the affordances and attributes of objects in the environment support and extend memory, idea production, and complex thinking (Hutchings cited in Hayles, 2012, pp. 92–93). Additionally, embedded cognition acknowledges that a large part of the process of thinking does not take place at the level of the conscious mind (or self-awareness) but at the level of the non-conscious and unconscious (Hayles, 2012), as conceptualized in Thrift's non-representational theory. The focus is now given to the study of individual actions and to the environment, including the technological tools that allow these actions to take place. Embedded cognition is a critical response to what Ek describes as "the mechanisms of dualism: human/nonhuman, knowing subjects/objects of knowledge, social/natural, active/passive entities" (Law, 2004, p. 132). The concept of *turistus digitalis* recognizes the complexity and hybrid nature of embedded cognition and that tourists' perception, evaluation, and relation to their social and material worlds are transformed, thanks to the possibilities embedded in new technological tools.

Bauman (2000), in his book *Liquid Modernity*, provides a vivid description of a global elite represented by two business tourists. They are archetypes of a hyper-mobile *turistus digitalis*. Bauman's report is an example of the consequences of embedded cognition through the interrelations of discourse, action, and technology, as well as an indication of how information and communication technologies profoundly transform spaces and social relations:

> A few months ago I sat with my wife in an airport bar waiting for the connecting flight. Two men in their late twenties or early thirties circled around the next table, each armed with a cellular telephone. Through about an hour and a half of waiting, they did not exchange a word with each other, though they both spoke without interruption—to the invisible conversationalist on the other end of the phone connection. Which does not mean that they were oblivious to each other's presence. As a matter of fact, it was the awareness of that presence which seemed to motivate their actions. The two men were engaged in competition—as intense, frenzied, and furious as competition could be. Whomever finished the cellular conversation while the other was still talking, searched feverishly for another number to press; clearly the number of connections, the degree of "connectedness," the density of the respective networks which made them into nodes, the quantity of other nodes they could link to at will, were matters of utter, perhaps even superior, importance to both: indices of social standing, position, power and prestige. Both men spent that hour and a half in what was, in its relation to the airport bar, an outer space. When the flight they were both to take was announced, they simultaneously locked their briefcases with identical synchronized gestures and left, holding their telephones close to their ears. I am sure they hardly noticed me and my wife sitting two yards away and watching their every move. As far as their *Lebenswelt* was concerned, they were (after the pattern of orthodox anthropologists censured by Lèvi-Strauss) physically close to us yet spiritually and infinitely remote. (2000, pp. 153–154; italics in the original)

But has the technology really exceeded humanity, confirming Einstein's concerns from decades ago? This volume addresses and nuances the digitally enabled multi-presence described by Bauman, through critical and rich analyses of the dynamics between discursive practices, actions, and tools. For example, the chapters by Ek and Miller warn about the limits of reflexivity and explain how social and environmental consequences of IT tools or media production are often ignored; Lexhagen et al. discuss how highly engaged consumer tribes develop new social spaces; Kellett and Hede denounce "boundaryless" work environments; while Gyimóthy and Munar explore how tourists' capacity of action and socialization are extended, shaped, and inhibited, due to the steering properties embedded in social media platforms.

The idea of embedded cognition claims the relevance of the environment in which discourse and action take place. Hence, this volume calls for bringing back (rather than abandoning) space and spatiality to digital tourism studies. The idea of technogenesis puts emphasis on the "dynamic interplay between the kinds of environmental stimuli created in information-intensive environments and the adaptative potential of cognitive faculties in concert with them" (Hayles, 2012, p. 97). Contemporary technogenesis posits a strong link in the adaptation of technics and humans, for example, creating new media or transforming these media into revolutionary tools of social mobilization (as in the case of the Arab Spring or the Occupy Wall Street movement). Thanks to this dynamic interplay, Hayles (2012) argues that late-modern societies are experiencing changes in cognitive modes. At the heart of this interplay lies the transformation of selective attention from traditional deep attention to an increased relevance of hyper attention. Deep attention is needed when coping with complex cultural or scientific works. Hyper attention is characteristic of someone scanning webpages and associated with hyper reading; on the other hand, deep attention is a human capacity cultivated through centuries and correlated to deep reading. Hyper attention is fast, flexible, and useful in switching between textual and visual data materials, to quickly provide an overview of digital spaces, as in the case of tourists surfing review sites and looking for hotels. "Surfing," a metaphor popularly used when referring to web usage, reflects the speed and the lightness of this attentive mode, but also its shallowness and lack of attention to detail. The increased importance of hyper attention has consequences for how tourists search, create, and obtain meaning from the retrieved information. It also has radical consequences for tourism education and scholarship. Due to digital technologies, a continuum of different levels of attention unfolds and a complex interplay of the multiple tourism literacies of the *turistus digitalis* takes shape.

Mediated Tourism

The world of tourism is a mediated world. Since its dawn, long before digital technologies, landscapes have been artistically portrayed by poets, play-wrights, and painters. These mediated images triggered historical travelers to flock to attractions and produce uncountable cover versions of these representations that in turn inspired the travelers seeking them. Digitally mediated tourism behavior follows a similar pattern, aptly demonstrated by Lexhagen, Larson, and Lundberg, who highlight the links between popular culture, destination choice, and social media communications.

The *turistus digitalis* as a hybrid actant takes on a central role in augmenting and circulating enacted versions of destinations. The touristic "circuit of culture" is both reproduced and extended further in social media. Arguably, Facebook, Twitter, and other digital platforms are more than additional channels for communication. Bearing upon the capacity of reconstructing meanings, they qualitatively alter the way in which tourist activities and destinations are remediated. Ooi and Munar as well as Montanari and his colleagues point out that dialogues on social media do not solely wrap historical attractions or events in virtual layers, but also re-spatialize, re-culturalize and re-temporalize them. Ghazali and Cai indicate how the essence of image formation and spatial identity is changed with the emergence of new, global tourism cultures and socially networked, digital touristhoods. Fluid time–space relationships transform established reference systems and introduce new temporalities in mediating tourism interactions between providers and tourists, tourists and places/cultures/societies, and tourists and tourists. Communications once characterized by pulsating, seasonal fluctuations are now evolving into continuous or atemporal dialogues.

Digital touristhoods are communicatively constituted virtual commu-nities with sense-making taking place parallel to physical and virtual worlds. These communities can be conceptualized as "networked publics" or "networked imagined communities" (Boyd, 2011, pp. 40–41). Networked publics, structured by digital technologies, are simultaneously a space and a collection of people (Boyd, 2011). These technologies change the way in which information flows and tourists can interact with each other. They provide spaces for the shaping of "world views" in tourism that, as mentioned in Lexhagen et al., "enable social actors in terms of practices, procedures, and perspectives." The fluid time–space relationships allow for bonding across geographical, cultural, and institutional boundaries, as well as managerial and consumption agendas.

The roles of tourists are changing, from consumers to part-time marketers or politically active citizen-consumers. Virtual communities are embedded and juxtaposed between local and global sociocultural practices or tastes and hence are capable of launching new market trends initially independent of commercial activities. Such trends are inevitably marked by collective consumption phenomena (such as Couchsurfing or Home-Exchange) enabled by digital platforms. The collective power of virtual communities is further explored by Budeanu, who argues how social media may empower collective action with significant consequences on tourism organizations and governance. Nevertheless, one is only beginning to grasp the collective constitutive dynamics, identity creation, and stratification processes in these communities. Learning from the diversities illustrated by the case chapters in this volume, further conceptualization in this field is called for—while building on multidisciplinary insights.

This volume also provides a critical assessment pertaining to the ambivalent potential of social media. Rather than accepting the naive claim of social media being egalitarian and non-hierarchical, authors claim that it transforms power structures in tourism and creates new hierarchies, latent ties, and inequalities. Digital platforms are potentially emancipatory but also conflictive and negotiated spaces, full of disputes, exclusions, hypocrisy, and maligning. The control and role of the invisible "Other" on digitally mediated platforms is an unresolved political and ethical issue, which paradoxically, as Ek claims, leads to a weak or loose sociality, loneliness, and illusionary social relations. Munar draws attention to the dark side of social media with autocommunicative tendencies, imagined audiences, and disembodied and/or multiple pseudoidentities, and indirectly calls for further research investigating these aspects.

As knowledge is historically rooted and interest bound (Habermas, 1987), ideologies play an active role in the shaping of academic knowledge. A task that lies ahead is the examination of the ideological argumentations that characterize technology and digital media research in tourism. Researchers adopt specific ideological frames when selecting their research problems and topics, when arguing the relevance of their research contribution, and when deciding on their recommendations to the industry and to the academic world. Dominant ideologies act as powerful forces in research production. Specific ideological frameworks contribute both to knowledge production and to defining which interests are to be heard in tourism, what tourism is, and what it should be. They can advocate specific epistemologies, act as gatekeepers, and represent "taken-for-granted" assumptions. To date still the ideological and political dimensions of digital technologies are seldom explored.

Frameworks for Conceptualizing Society and Technology Relations

The preceding chapters expand the field of tourism research interested in analyzing the relationship between human agency, society, and technology. Baym (2010) suggests that in the field of social studies of science and technology, there are three prevalent theoretical frameworks examining the causal links between society and technology: technological determinism, the social construction of technology, and the social shaping of technology. The most traditional among these frameworks is the first one.

Determinists see technologies as the main agents of change that act as transformative forces in society with individuals having little control or power over them. This tendency often dominates social debates in the beginning of a technical revolution. Often based on *Luddite* or *technopian* ideological positions (Kozinets, 2008), technological determinism understands technology either as destructive of more authentic ways of life or as a path for an enhanced and better society. Determinism prevails in popular narratives used to make sense of technological change—utopian tales of a world reborn and dystopian visions of an unhuman world (Nye cited in Baym, 2010, pp. 28–29).

In utopian narratives, the tourism experience can be brought to a perfected state with proper utilization of science and its tools. In Miller's words, these are the utopian visions of cybertarian technophiles. The utopian descriptions of virtual communities are abundant. For example, TripAdvisor announces that their site allows individuals to "plan the *perfect* trip" (emphasis added) and CouchSurfing explains that, because of their efforts, "the appreciation of diversity spreads tolerance and creates a global community." Technological change is portrayed in dystopian narratives as wild, dangerous, or alienating. Review sites are accused of including lies and being "out-of-control," social networks are fluid on-and-off communities without real commitment, media sharing sites distribute banal content for entertaining purposes, and pervasive interactive technologies nurture addiction disorders. The branding campaign of Wales, which promotes the destination as "an area of outstanding bad mobile reception," plays with dystopian narratives—a tourism experience without technology is believed to be more authentic. Determinism also reflects a naive belief that people are able to avoid technological influence by avoiding the technology itself.

A critique of the deterministic framework can be seen in the Gyimóthy's advocacy to adopt a cocreation paradigm and abandon mechanistic views where tourists are passive recipients in the hands of technology or marketers. She indicates the problems of treating social media communications as mechanistic systems, where "given the right design and choice architecture (or conditional stimulus), individuals will respond in a predictable way."

In a deterministic framework, customers are reduced to being seen as an empowered "asset" to create value for the provider and digital platforms are nothing more than technological tools of creative tourist exploitation and control. As Hvass so aptly illustrates in the volcano crisis case, customers are surrogate agents of service recovery and comanagers of crisis communications. Organizational boundaries are more porous than ever and the customer is indeed a cocreator of value, carrying the seeds of organizational learning and development. However, one must critically assess and problematize the "technology has the power" approaches by asking searching questions. Who is the customer in a digitally networked (and boundaryless) tourism organization? What is her role and responsibility and how is she compensated for creative and informative contributions? Who controls (manages) the cocreation process and what new roles and functions can be formulated? Does the dyadic model of provider/customer interaction still make sense? What are the prerequisites of egalitarian and mutually beneficial relationships and what may be the consequences of new power constellations behind the service-minded facades of customer-oriented corporate structures?

The social construction of technology argues that the power lies in the hand of individuals and that people are the primary source of change in technology. In tourism research, positions close to the social construction of technology are often adopted by technology optimists who see individuals using technology to achieve better tourism experiences or to foster new collaborations and communities across borders. Bødker and Browning's chapter indicates that prevalent views in the field of technology design conceptualize the tourist as the active, empowered agent mastering space through technology. They criticize how this conceptualization privileges an organizing (and orderly) tourist gaze.

The social construction framework looks at how technology arises from social processes and it is consistent with the theory of self-directed connectivity (Castells, 2001). As Munar's chapter suggests, self-directed connectivity is a source of individual empowerment and freedom. Digital technologies are seen as transformative tools providing collective action and meaning. They allow individuals to express their identities and to create and maintain social relations online. People can use technology to tailor tourism experiences to individual needs. Technological systems are portrayed as instrumental tools in the human pursuit after better markets, happier lives, more fulfilling experiences, and more effective organizations. Tourism has been regarded as an agent of change, playing a liberating role in modern societies (Jafari, 1987). Technologically enhanced tourism expands feelings of freedom and release from the constraints often related to tradition, place boundaries, routines, and norms.

Budeanu's analysis of sustainability and social media points to the weaknesses of the "people have the power" narrative. Promises of empowerment and agency of local communities often excluded in decisionmaking processes are still to be delivered by digital technologies. According to her, "although individuals have a dominant presence on social media, their presence may not represent a sufficient input base for a sustainable tourism." Individual agency and the liberating potential of digital worlds are also challenged by organizational cultures. Montanari et al. discuss the difficulties for event organizations in finding the right strategies to deal with novel technological channels. The situation of the managers of the festival *Fotografia Europea* is not one of powerful control over technological processes; on the contrary, it looks like a trial-and-error negotiation with ongoing evaluations about how technology mediates the relationship between the organizers of the festival and the tourists. One of the respondents in Hede and Kellett's study is another example of the limitations of the libertarian utopian vision of the individual as "master of technology":

> I struggle with it [social media] because you have to sit there
> and constantly have it up and constantly be checking it and
> having it come up on your phone ... I sort of feel as though
> I'm looking at it all the time ... I just have so much to do.

Certainly, this account is a personal, deterministic perspective: the individual victimized by technological change. Digital technologies may become powerful tools of consumer exploitation and employee control suitable for the latent machinations of global information capitalism.

The third framework presented by Baym (2010) is the "social shaping of technology." This theoretical approach sees the relationship between technology and individuals as interdependent with influence flowing in both directions. The insights nurtured in this volume show the complex and paradoxical nature of this relationship. As indicated in the above discussions of *turistus digitalis* and mediated tourism, technologies' affordances and materialities influence but do not dictate the possibilities of social change. This book advocate a research agenda which examines the societal circumstances that give rise to tourist technologies, the specific constraints and possibilities of these technologies, and the actual use of these technologies once they are enacted by tourists and tourism organizations.

Digital Methodologies and Transmethodology

Previous studies of the relationships between tourists and virtual/mobile technologies tend to singularize and compartmentalize the digital aspect of tourism consumption characterized by a *ceteris paribus* mindset in tourism social media studies. This decontextualized approach prevents a deeper understanding of how social media interactions are related to broader social and cultural processes. As already noted, popular culture, tourism consumption, and social media communications mutually impact each other, calling for more innovative and radical methods to fully investigate this phenomenon. The authors in this book point out the advantages and affordances of alternative approaches, such as ethnomethodology, exploratory, and experimental methods (Ek), longitudinal studies (Montanari), as well as historical methods (Miller). Others introduce and explore the potential of methods developed elsewhere. For instance, Gyimóthy introduces symbolic convergence theory and its capacity to trace discursive processes in digital polilogues. Ooi and Munar adapt netnographic methods to the study of review making. Furthermore, Bødker and Browning call for approaches capable of exploring the sensuality and emotionality of contemporary technologically augmented tourist practices.

The methods presented in this volume also show that there is a world of possibilities to develop novel methodological approaches in digital tourism studies. Processes of transdisciplinarity and interdisciplinarity often observed in the contemporary research result in processes of "transmethodology," which entails the transgression of methodological traditions. It reflects the fast expansion and increasing diversity of the methods toolkits of digital scholars. Deep knowledge of a subject is still as relevant as ever, both to ask the right questions and to analyze patterns and relationships, but these scholars often challenge quantitative/qualitative divides and method hegemony. Quantitative methods can be applied to traditional fields usually dominated by qualitative approaches such as cultural studies (and vice versa) and methods born into humanities can be adapted and transformed to the study of digital data, machines, tools, and technological practices. In digital studies, there is an increased cross-fertilization among methodological traditions. Kozinets' (2002) development of ethnography into netnography is an example of anthropological methods applied to digital studies, while Hayles' (2012) advocacy of the use of programming for text analysis (with such programs as Wordle, RapidMiner, or the advanced version of Hermetic Word Frequency) in literary studies shows the advancement of quantitative techniques applied in fields traditionally dominated by qualitative approaches. Transmethodology is obvious in the presentation title by Jockers, a researcher in literary studies that uses big data methods: "Computing and Visualizing the 19th-Century Literary Genoma" (Lohr, 2013).

Transmethodology pushes scholars out of their disciplinary comfort zones and often encounters opposition from academic traditions. Some of the methodological tools are developed in the field of software engineering. Scholars such as Ek advocate the use of multiple methodological lenses to study technological materialities (like mapping the geographies of the metals present in a computer). An example of how innovative methods open new research avenues is the study conducted by Pentland (2008) on "honest signals." Pentland developed a digital sensor (a sociometer) that enabled his team of researchers to monitor the subtle unconscious patterns of signaling that people use when interacting with other people and that revealed their attitudes, intentions, goals, and values. These measurements are able to accurately predict the outcomes of diverse social situations ranging from job interviews to first dates. While the theories of social signaling and embedded cognition have a negative resonance, as they challenge the often strong belief in the power of human agency and consciousness, they also open a new landscape of enquiry into the relevance of the "non-discursive" (feelings, emotions, the unconscious) to understand how tourists think and how tourism is experienced and performed. Additionally, novel methods pose diverse ethical dilemmas in research practices, such as the need for informed consent when analyzing tourist-created content. The use of and access to digital data possess new ethical challenges and demands of the academic community a higher reflexivity on what is appropriate and just behavior for researchers.

Digital Tourism Education

The dominance of managerial approaches in the field of new digital technologies is mirrored in educational programs and courses. Usually the linkage between technology and tourism, both at undergraduate and graduate levels, takes place in marketing and managerial courses introducing the development of e-tourism and the impacts of IT on tourism production and consumption. Eventually, specific courses on e-business with a major focus on IT management are offered. As a reminder of traditional and pervasive disciplinary divisions established in the industrial era between engineering/technical studies and social sciences or humanities, knowledge on the making and designing of digital systems, including coding and programming, are seldom part of the tourism curriculum. Additionally, it is infrequent to see teams of social science or humanities scholars working collaboratively with IT researchers to develop educational activities aiming to address the production and implementation of high-end technologies in tourism processes. The result is that the study of technological change is conceptualized and taught as a silo in tourism education or reduced to a few chapters in a textbook.

Therefore, adopting a new ontological approach to tourism social media implies challenging tourism curricula, managerial frameworks, and pedagogical styles. As Kellett and Hede point out, new digital platforms generate significant organizational challenges and long-term social media presence requires organizational capabilities that many firms lack. Tourism and event organizers are still experimenting and stumble in the darkness as contemporary management and marketing frameworks fall short of providing assistance to integrate social media in human resources management, relationship marketing, and crisis communications. This tension is reflected in hybrid concepts (such as market orientation, perceived service quality, mass customization, and part-time marketers), which arguably assign a more active role to the customer, but leave the ontological assumptions of value cocreation unchallenged. There is an urgent need to let the new map redraw the landscape; that is, real and digital organizational structures must be reconceptualized in order to accommodate a more seamless customer involvement. This entails adopting and going beyond the tenets of the so-called service-dominant logic, proposed by Vargo and Lusch (2004). The goal is still short of a comprehensive theoretical "language," which leads to the creative recycling of concepts from an outdated production-dominant ontology with rigid organizational boundaries separating consumers from producers. This rigidity is mirrored in a tourism curriculum that often follows course structures that in many cases mimic traditional management education, with divisions, such as marketing, strategy, and the like, that are unable to grasp the transdisciplinarity of the technical–societal–individual tourism phenomenon. There are several consequences of this narrow perspective on the relationship between technology and tourism.

First, the technological field is isolated from major knowledge areas in tourism. Digital technology appears relevant for those parts of the curriculum dealing with the business of tourism but mostly absent in those areas where tourism is understood as a broader social phenomenon. There is a factual separation between those who are trained to achieve competences in the development of technological solutions and those who are taught to analyze and reflect on the problems of tourism. Despite this isolation, the use and development of technology is a crucial, embedded element of the phenomenon of late-modern tourism in all its multiple and complex dimensions, from the transformation of the ways in which the movement of people in space takes place, to the ways in which individuals can dream and fantasize about travel. Technical tools have the capacity to catalyze exponential change in social, political, cultural, or economic processes. As Lash indicates:

> In the first modernity we were faced with relatively mutually exclusive and exhaustive systems: of (Parsonian) social systems, on the one hand, and engineering-like technical systems, on the other. The second modernity's totally normal chaos is regulated by non-linear systems. It is also regulated by an extraordinarily powerful interlacing of social and technical systems: by precisely, socio-technical systems. It is at the interface of the social and the technical that we find the second-modernity's individual. It is at this interface that we take on the precarious freedom of a "life of our own"; that we "invent the political," that we take on ecological responsibility. The individual in the second modernity is profoundly a socio-technical subject. (2002, p. xiii)

The challenge for the academic community is to design a tourism education system that acknowledges this complexity and provides students with cognitive and practical tools to understand and further develop this interface.

Second, the way in which digital technology is designed into the curriculum reflects the supremacy of a specific managerial narrative. Boterrill, in his presentation entitled "Making the case for tourism higher education" (2012), suggests that advocacy for tourism education is approached through three narratives that prioritize different skills: building leadership and management capacity in the visitor economy (such as project planning, time management); understanding global complexity through tourism (including critical thinking, political and historical sensitivity); and making a difference through action in tourism (like emotional intelligence, interventions). While often important as part of the first narrative, social media and IT studies are less visible in the other two.

Third, digital technologies transform the world of tourism and also have a transformative power in the world of learning. The problem faced by tourism education is that scholars often approach technology for teaching and technology in the phenomenal world of tourism as two separate entities. There is a factual division between digital technologies for pedagogic use, on the one hand, and knowledge sharing and technology as object of analysis in its own right, on the other. For example, a program may use interactive technologies in the classroom and open source materials as part of the readings; however, the study of the sociocultural consequences of the same technical systems in the tourism phenomenon are not evaluated or explored. It is possible to envision a more advanced stage of technological usage and understanding by digital tourism scholars that may result in a higher convergence of the pedagogical and the tourism-specific dimensions of technology and where these dimensions are holistically integrated in the curriculum and in the classroom. Scholars develop their careers in media-rich and information-heavy environments and both teachers and students in developed countries use relevant amounts of their leisure time in digital media. These new social practices produce new social spaces and interrelations. However, there is little transfer from leisure or research activities in digital media to classroom instruction or vice versa.

Adopting embedded cognition and transmethodological approaches in digital tourism education will entail a rethinking of curriculum design. It demands a curriculum framework that emphasizes plurality in methods and the crossing of disciplinary borders and addresses the need to provide students with skills and competences in multiple literacies (in a continuum that goes from deep to hyper reading skills). Digitization processes of text and information allow for new ways of teaching and studying, as they allow for new ways of making and sharing tourism experiences. These are not minor processes, but radical in nature. A large part of the academic community is no longer able to imagine higher education or research without access to the web or to computers. Digital texts, despite presenting aesthetic similarities with analogue documents, differ radically in their potentialities and reach (issues such as navigation, hypertext links, hierarchies of screen displays, and much more). Some examples of this holistic integration that tourism scholars can use as inspiration come from the emergent field of digital humanities (Hayles, 2012).

Social media transforms the nature of public life in academia. These media can challenge the staging and performing of traditional academic roles, blur the distinction between private and public spheres, alter research communication, and introduce complex and multilayered audiences. Through personal strategic choices, scholars negotiate their private and public spheres, reflect upon imagined audiences, evaluate risks, promote their research, and redefine their professional roles. Virtual practices are shaped by the architecture and affordances of social media, but also by the traditions, context, and practices of higher education institutions. The making and transforming of digital identities provides insights into existential and ethical questions of the self and reveals how scholars redefine the boundaries of privacy and publicness. Social media expansion impacts the daily-life practices, curriculum delivery and development, and expected performance of academics. Interactive media provide opportunities for emancipation, value creation, and socialization in higher education, but also for increased institutional control and commercialization of social relations.

It is possible to draw a parallel between the critique made by Miller in his Media Studies 3.0, and how tourism scholars approach curriculum building in this field. Also in the case of IT in tourism studies, there are spectacular gaps of knowledge, for example, in critical analysis of the political and ethical consequences of digital tourism practices. The contributors of this volume provide an attempt to highlight some of these gaps.

CONCLUSION

Narratives of economic benefit, efficiency, and market development that have dominated the research enquiries in the field of information technologies and tourism are expanded and challenged throughout this volume. This discourse advocates that it is time to encourage plural research perspectives and a critical approach to studying digital sociotechnical systems and virtual mediation in tourism. Critical digital tourism studies open a new cross-disciplinary field where the sociality of virtual tourism interactions is examined (entailing the study of structures, social rules, ideologies, power relations, sustainability dimensions, ethics, and cultural values shaping digital tourism). This volume contributes to increasing research reflexivity in understanding how tourism is enacted through digital worlds and how digital technologies evolve through tourism practices. Critical thinking and sociopolitical engagement is applied to examine the development of the web and contested concepts of human interaction in touristic cyberspaces such as equality, anonymity, transparency, democratization, and publicity culture.

The renewal of methods to approach technological studies is increasingly complex, multidirectional, and transgresses the borders of traditional disciplines. Tourism researchers who need to extract knowledge from the phenomenal world of tourism often use a qualitative/quantitative examination of discursive arguments and practices (e.g., people's answers in a survey or the longer explanations of interviews or focus groups). Additionally, scholars also use observation (through field work, for instance) and other methodological tools to examine the actions and conduct of tourists. Both discourse and action are often predominant in methodological practices. However, a major focus on embedded cognition in tourism demands innovative methodological practices that go beyond the "mechanisms of dualism" and try to comprehend the interdependences and influences between people's actions and discourses and technological affordances and materialities. This crucial task in the development of digital tourism studies is still in the making.

In many ways, contemporary education and curriculum are a reflection of the disciplinary limitations, tribal tendencies, and insularity of the tourism academic world. Today's digital tourism studies cannot and should not be confined to a managerial dimension of tourism. The contributions in this book are meant as a step in a new direction. They show, among other things, that an advanced knowledge of the relationship between individuals and technology demands the expansion and distribution of this field throughout different curricular courses and fields, and that the reality of today's tourism cannot be conceived without envisioning the technological dimensions of traditional courses such as tourism impacts, sustainable tourism, and tourism policy.

Many research challenges and opportunities are ahead. Scholars should aim at revealing the complex relationship of technological change with power relations, justice, and the establishment and transformation of norms, values, and beliefs; the impacts of technological change in human cognition; digital mediation of humor, love, and emotion; the complex interrelationship of technology with nature and environment; and how all these different phenomena are embedded in and transformed through tourism. This new landscape remains unexplored, with some inroad in the making, as signaled in this volume.

References

Abowd, G., Atkeson, C., Hong, J., Long, S., Kooper, R., & Pinkerton, M.
(1997). Cyberguide: A mobile context-aware tour guide. *Wireless Networks*, *3*(5), 421–433.

Adams, J.
(1941). *The epic of America*. New York, NY: Triangle Books.

Adanhounme, A.
(2011). Corporate social responsibility in postcolonial Africa: Another civilizing mission? *Journal of Change Management*, *11*(1), 91–110.

Adkins, B., & Grant, E.
(2007). Backpackers as a community of strangers: The interaction order of an online backpacker notice board. *Qualitative Sociology Review*, *3*(2), 188–201.

Adorno, T., & Horkheimer, M.
(1977). The culture industry: Enlightenment as mass deception. In J. Curran, M. Gurevitch & J. Woollacott (Eds.), *Mass communication and society* (pp. 349–383). London: Edward Arnold.

Ahmed, Z.
(1991). The influence of the components of a state's tourist image on product positioning strategy. *Tourism Management*, *12*, 331–340.

Albert, S., & Whetten, D.
(1985). Organizational identity. In L. Cummings & B. Staw (Eds.), (Vol. 7, pp. 263–295). Greenwich: JAI Press.

Alfonso, G., & Suzanne, S.
(2008). Crisis communications management on the web: How internet-based technologies are changing the way public relations professionals handle business crises. *Journal of Contingencies and Crisis Management*, *16*(3), 143–153.

Alford, P., & Clarke, S.
(2009). Information technology and tourism a theoretical critique. *Technovation*, *29*(9), 580–587.

American Academy of Pediatrics, Council on Communications and Media.
(2009). Policy statement – Media violence. *Pediatrics*, *124*(5), 1495–1503.

Anderson, C., & Wolff, M.
(2010). *The web is dead: Long live the internet*. Retrieved from wired.com/magazine/2010/08/ff_webrip/all/1. Accessed on August 17, 2010.

Andrejevic, M.
(2011). Social network exploitation. In Z. Papacharissi (Ed.), *A networked self: Identity, community, and culture on social network sites* (pp. 82–102). New York, NY: Routledge.

Andreu, L., Aldas, J., Bigne, J., & Mattila, A.

(2010). An analysis of e-business adoption and its impact on relational quality in travel agency–supplier relationships. *Tourism Management, 31,* 777–787.

Andrews, J., Durvasula, S., & Akhter, S.

(1990). A framework for conceptualizing and measuring the involvement construct in advertising research. *Journal of Advertising, 19*(4), 27–40.

Arcodia, C.

(2009). Event management employment in Australia: A nationwide investigation of labour trends in Australian event management. In T. Baum, M. Deery & L. Lockstone (Eds.), *People and Work in Events and Conventions: A Research Perspective* (pp. 17–28). Wallingford, Oxon, UK: CABI Publishing.

Arlt, W., & Thraenhart, J.

(2011). Social media tourism marketing in China. In R. Conrady & M. Buck (Eds.), *Trends and issues in global tourism 2011* (pp. 149–154). Berlin: Springer.

Arnaboldi, M., & Spiller, N.

(2011). Actor-network theory and stakeholder collaboration: The case of cultural districts. *Tourism Management, 32*(3), 641–654.

Arsal, I., Baldwin, E., & Backman, S.

(2009). Member reputation and its influence on travel decisions: A case study of an online travel community. *Information Technology and Tourism, 11*(3), 235–246.

Arsal, I., Woosnam, K., Baldwin, E., & Backman, S.

(2010). Residents as travel destination information providers: An online community perspective. *Journal of Travel Research, 49*(4), 400–413.

Aspan, M.

(2008). *How sticky is membership on Facebook? Just try breaking free.* Retrieved from http://www.nytimes.com/2008/02/11/technology/11facebook. html. Accessed on June 21, 2009.

Axup, J., Viller, S., MacColl, I., & Cooper, R.

(2006). Lo-fi matchmaking: A study of social pairing for backpackers. In P. Dourish & A. Friday (Eds.), *Ubicomp 2006: Proceedings of the eighth international conference* (Vol. 4206, pp. 351–368). Lecture Notes in Computer Science. Orange County, CA: Springer-Verlag.

Ayeh, J., Leung, D., Au, N., & Law, R.

(2012). Perceptions and strategies of hospitality and tourism practitioners on social media: An exploratory study. In M. Fuchs, F. Ricci, & L. Cantoni (Eds.). *Information and communication technologies in tourism 2012* (pp. 1–12.). *Proceedings of the international conference*, Helsinborg, Sweden, January 25–27, 2012. Wien: Springer-Verlag.

Bærenholdt, J., Haldrup, M., Larsen, J. & Urry, J.
(2004). *Performing tourist places*. New Directions in Tourism Analysis. Aldershot, Hants: Ashgate Publishing Limited.

Bagozzi, R., & Dholakia, U.
(2002). Intentional social action in virtual communities. *Journal of Interactive Marketing, 16*(2), 2–21.

Bagozzi, R., & Dholakia, U.
(2006). Antecedents and purchase consequences of customer participation in small group brand communities. *International Journal of Research in Marketing, 23*, 45–61.

Bagozzi, R., & Lee, K.
(2002). Multiple routes for social influence: The role of compliance, internalization, and social identity. *Social Psychology Quarterly, 65*(3), 226–247.

Bakhtin, M.
(1981). *The dialogic imagination: Four essays*. In M. Holquist (Trans.), C. Emerson, & M. Holquist (Eds.). Austin, TX: University of Texas Press.

Bales, R.
(1970). *Personality and interpersonal behavior*. New York, NY: Holt, Rinehart & Winston.

Baloglu, S., & Brinberg, D.
(1997). Affective images of tourism destinations. *Journal of Travel Research, 36*, 11–15.

Baloglu, S., & McCleary, K.
(1999). A model of destination image. *Annals of Tourism Research, 26*(4), 868–897.

Banerjee, S., Chico, V., & Mir, R. (Eds.).
(2009). *Organizations, markets and imperial formations: Towards an anthropology of globalization*. Cheltenham, UK: Edward Elgar.

Barkhuus, L., & Polichar, V.
(2010). Empowerment through seamfulness: Smart phones in everyday life. *Personal and Ubiquitous Computing, 16*(6), 629–639.

Basu, R., Mok, D., & Wellman, B.
(2007). Did distance matter before the internet? *Social Networks, 29*(3), 430–461.

Baum, T., Deery, M., & Lockstone, L.
(2009). *People and work in events and conventions: A Research perspective*. Wallingford, Oxon, UK: CABI Publishing.

Bauman, Z.
(1998). *Globalization: The human consequences*. Cambridge: Polity Press.

Bauman, Z.
(2000). *Liquid modernity*. Cambridge: Polity Press.

Bauman, Z.
(2002). *Society under siege*. Cambridge: Polity Press.

Baym, N.
(2010). *Personal connections in the digital age.* Cambridge: Polity Press.
Bechky, B.
(2006). Gaffers, gofers and grips: Role-based coordination in temporary organizations. *Organization Science, 17*(1), 3–21.
Beck, U.
(1993). *Risk society: Towards a new modernity [Risikogesellschaft.].* London: Sage.
Beck, U., & Beck-Gernsheim, E.
(2002). *Individualization.* London: Sage.
Beerli, A., & Martin, J.
(2004). Tourists' characteristics and the perceived image of tourist destinations: A quantitative analysis – A case study of Lanzarote, Spain. *Tourism Management, 25*(5), 623–636.
Beeton, S.
(2005). *Film-induced tourism.* Clevedon, UK: Channel View.
Beeton, S.
(2008). Partnerships and social responsibility: Leveraging tourism and international film tourism. In T. Coles & M. Hall (Eds.), *International business and tourism – Global issues, contemporary interactions* (pp. 256–272). London: Routledge.
Beeton, S.
(2010). The advance of film tourism. *Tourism and Hospitality Planning & Development, 7*(1), 1–6.
Benckendorff, P., Moscardo, G., & Murphy, L.
(2005). High tech versus high touch: Visitor responses to the use of technology in tourist attractions. *Tourism Recreation Research, 30*(3), 37–47.
Benckendorff, P., Moscardo, G., & Murphy, L.
(2006). Visitor perceptions of technology use in tourist attraction experiences. *Proceedings of the travel and tourism research association 37th annual conference, cutting edge research in tourism: New Directions, challenges and applications*, June 6–9, Guildford, Surrey, UK (pp. 1–17).
Benhabib, S.
(2002). *The claims of culture: Equality and diversity in the global era.* Princeton, NJ: Princeton University Press.
Benoit, W.
(1997). Image repair discourse and crisis communication. *Public Relations Review, 23*(2), 177–186.
Berger, C., & Calabrese, R.
(1975). Some explorations in initial interaction and beyond: Toward a developmental theory of interpersonal communication. *Human Communication Research, 1*, 99–112.

Berlingske Business.
   (2010). *Askesky koster SAS knap en halv milliard.* (*Ash cloud costs SAS approximately a half billion*). Retrieved from http://www.business.dk/transport/ askesky-koster-sas-knap-en-halv-milliard. Accessed on August 24, 2011.
Berlo, D.
   (1960). *The process of communication: An introduction to theory and practice.* San Francisco, CA: Rhinehart.
Bernoff, J., & Li, C.
   (2008). Harnessing the power of the oh-so-social web. *MIT Sloan Management Review, 49*(3), 35–42.
Berthon, P., Pitt, L., Plangger, K., & Shapiro, D.
   (2012). Marketing meets Web 2.0, social media, and creative consumers: Implications for international marketing strategy. *Business Horizons, 55*(3), 261–271.
Bhattacharya, C., & Sen, S.
   (2003). Consumer-company identification: A framework for understanding consumers' relationships with companies. *Journal of Marketing, 67*(2), 76–88.
Bianchini, F., & Parkinson, M.
   (1993). *Cultural policy and urban regeneration: The West European experience.* Manchester: Manchester University Press.
Bidwai, P.
   (2005). *Prevent, prepare and protect.* Retrieved from in.rediff.com/news/2005/ jan/04bidwai.htm. Accessed on January 4, 2005.
Biggs, B.
   (2000). *The two faces of Leo.* Retrieved from motherjones.com/environment/ 2000/02/two-faces-leo. Accessed on February 4, 2000.
Birnholtz, J., Cohen, M., & Hoch, S.
   (2007). Organizational character: On the regeneration of camp poplar grove. *Organization Science, 18*(2), 315–332.
Bødker, M., & Browning, D.
   (2012). Beyond destinations: Exploring tourist technology design spaces through local-tourist interactions. *Digital creativity. 23*(3–4), 204–224
Booth, W.
   (1999). Communities of memory: On identity, memory, and debt. *The American Political Science Review, 93*(2), 249–263.
Bormann, E.
   (1972). Fantasy and rhetorical vision: The rhetorical criticism of social reality. *Quarterly Journal of Speech, 58*, 396–407.
Bormann, E.
   (1983). Symbolic convergence: Organizational communication and culture. In L. Putnam & M. Pacanowsky (Eds.), *Communication and organizations: An interpretive approach* (pp. 99–122). Beverly Hills, CA: Sage.

Bormann, E.
   (1985). Symbolic convergence theory: A communication formulation. *Journal of Communication, 35*(4), 128–138.
Bormann, E., & Bormann, N.
   (1990). *Small group communication: Theory and practice.* New York, NY: Harper & Row.
Bormann, E., Cragan, J., & Shields, D.
   (1994). In defense of symbolic convergence theory: A look at the theory and its criticism after two decades. *Communication Theory, 4*(4), 259–294.
Bormann, E., Cragan, J., & Shields, D.
   (1996). An expansion of the rhetorical vision concept of symbolic convergence theory: The cold war paradigm case. *Communication Monographs, 63,* 1–28.
Bormann, E., Cragan, J., & Shields, D.
   (2001). Three decades of developing, grounding, and using symbolic convergence theory (SCT). *Communication Yearbook, 25,* 271–313.
Bormann, E., & Itaba, Y.
   (1992). Why do people share fantasies? An empirical investigation of the symbolic convergence theory in a sample of Japanese subjects. *Human Communication Studies, 20,* 1–25.
Bormann, E., Knutson, R., & Musolf, K.
   (1997). Why do people share fantasies? An empirical investigation of a basic tenet of the symbolic convergence communication theory. *Communication Studies, 48,* 254–276.
Botterill, D.
   (2012). Making the case for tourism higher education. Paper presented at ATHE Annual Conference 2012, Re-invigorating the tourism curriculum, 6–7 December 2012, Selwyn College, Cambridge.
Bourdieu, P.
   (1984). *Distinction: A social critique of the judgment of taste* (R. Nice, Trans.). Cambridge, MA: Harvard University Press.
Boyd, D.
   (2011). Social network sites as networked publics: Affordances, dynamics and implications. In Z. Papacharissi (Ed.), *A networked self: Identity, community, and culture on social network sites* (pp. 39–58). New York, NY: Routledge.
Boyd, D., & Ellison, N.
   (2008). Social network sites: Definition, history and scholarship. *Journal of Computer-Mediated Communication, 13,* 210–230.
Brereton, P.
   (2006). Nature tourism and Irish films. *Irish Studies Review, 14*(4), 407–420.

Brogan, C., & Smith, J.
(2009). *Trust agents: Using the web to build influence, improve reputation, and earn trust.* Hoboken, NJ: Wiley.

Bronner, F., & de Hoog, R.
(2011). Vacationers and eWOM: Who posts, and why, where, and what? *Journal of Travel Research, 50*(1), 15 26.

Broom, C., & Avanzino, S.
(2010). The communication of community collaboration: When rhetorical visions collide. *Communication Quarterly, 58*(4), 480–501.

Brown, B., & Chalmers, M.
(2003). Tourism & mobile technology. In K. Kuutti, E. Karsten, G. Fitzpatrick, P. Dourish, & K. Schmidt (Eds.), *Proceedings of the 8th European conference on computer supported cooperative work*, Norwell, MA: Kluwer (pp. 335–354).

Brown, S., Kozinets, R., & Sherry, J., Jr.
(2003). Teaching old brands new tricks: Retro branding and the revival of brand meaning. *Journal of Marketing, 67*, 19–33.

Browning, D., Benckendorff, P., & Bidwell, N.
(2009). Capturing visitor experiences using egocentric PoV Video. In V. Platenkamp, R. Isaac & A. Portegies (Eds.), *Voices in tourism development.* Breda, Netherlands: NHTV.

Browning, D., Bidwell, N., Hardy, D., & Standley, P.
(2008). Rural encounters: cultural translations through video. *Proceedings of OzCHI 2008: 20th Australasian conference on computer-human interaction: Designing for habitus and habitat.* Cairns, Australia: ACM (pp. 148–155).

Browning, D., Bødker, M., Bidwell, N., van Erp, M., & Turner, T. A. J.
(2009). *Designing for a naturally engaging experience. in human-computer interaction – INTERACT 2009. 12th IFIP TC 13 international conference*, Uppsala, Sweden, August 24–28, 2009, Proceedings, Part II, Springer (pp. 961–962).

Buchanan, R.
(1992). Wicked problems in design thinking. *Design Issues, 8*(2), 5–21.

Buchmann, A.
(2010). Planning and development of film tourism: insights into the experience of Lord of the Rings Film Guide. *Tourism and Hospitality Planning and Development, 7*(1), 77–84.

Buchmann, A., Moore, K., & Fisher, D.
(2010). Experiencing film tourism: Authenticity and fellowship. *Annals of Tourism Research, 37*(7), 229–248.

Buckingham, D.
(2000). *After the death of childhood: Growing up in the age of electronic media.* Cambridge: Polity Press.

Budeanu, A.
(2007). Sustainable tourist behavior – A discussion of opportunities for change. *Journal of Consumer Studies*, *31*(5), 499–508.
Buhalis, D., & Law, R.
(2008). Progress in information technology and tourism management: 20 years on and 10 years after the Internet – The state of eTourism research. *Tourism Management*, *29*(4), 609–623.
Burke, E.
(1994). The restraints on men are among their rights. In P. Clarke (Ed.), *Citizenship* (pp. 121–123). London: Pluto Press.
Burnes., B.
(2005). Complexity theory and organizational change. *International Journal of Management Reviews*, *7*(2), 73–90.
Burrell, J.
(2009). The field site as a network: A strategy for locating ethnographic research. *Field Methods*, *21*(2), 181.
Buss, A., & Strauss, N.
(2009). *Online communities handbook: Building your business and brand on the web*. Berkeley, CA: New Riders.
Butler, R.
(1999). Sustainable tourism: A state-of-the-art review. *Tourism Geographies*, *1*(1), 7–25.
Butsch, R.
(2000). *The making of American audiences: From stage to television, 1750–1990*. Cambridge: Cambridge University Press.
Button, G.
(2000). The ethnographic tradition and design. *Design Studies*, *21*(4), 319–332.
Buur, J., & Soendergaard, A.
(2000). Video card game: An augmented environment for user centred design discussions. In *Proceedings of DARE 2000 – Designing augmented reality environments*, New York, NY: ACM (pp. 63–69).
Byrne, D.
(1998). *Complexity theory and the social sciences: An introduction*. London: Routledge.
Cai, L., Feng, R., & Breiter, D.
(2004). Tourist purchase decision involvement and information preferences. *Journal of Vacation Marketing*, *10*(2), 138–148.
Callon, M., & Latour, B.
(1995). Agency and the hybrid "collectif.". *South Atlantic Quarterly*, *94*(2), 481–507.
Campbell, B.
(2009). Guinea and Bauxite-Aluminium: The challenges of development and poverty reduction. In B. Campbell (Ed.), *Mining in Africa: Regulation and development* (pp. 66–118). London: Pluto Press.

Campbell, N.
(2005). Producing America: Redefining post-tourism in the global media age. In D. Crouch, R. Jackson & F. Thompson (Eds.), *The media and the tourist imagination: Converging cultures* (pp. 198–214). New York, NY: Routledge.

Cappetta, R., Manzoni, B., & Salvemini, S.
(2010). Value drivers for cultural events: Empirical evidence from Italy. *International Journal of Arts Management, 12*(2), 4–16.

Casaló, L., Flavián, C., & Guinalíu, M.
(2010). Determinants of the intention to participate in firm-hosted online travel communities and effects on consumer behavioral intentions. *Tourism Management, 31*(6), 898–911.

Castells, M.
(1997 [1996]). *The rise of the network society* (Reprinted ed.). Malden, MA: Blackwell Publishers.

Castells, M.
(2001). *La galaxia internet: Reflexiones sobre internet, empresa y sociedad. [The internet galaxy: Reflections on the internet, business and society.].* Barcelona: Plaza & Janés.

Centro de Reflexión y Acción Laboral.
(2006). *New technology workers: Report on working conditions in the Mexican electronics industry.* Retrieved from sjsocial.org/fomento/proyectos/plantilla.php?texto = cereal_m

Chan, K., & Li, S.
(2010). Understanding consumer-to-consumer interactions in virtual communities: The salience of reciprocity. *Journal of Business Research, 63*, 1033–1040.

Chan, N., & Guillet, B.
(2011). Investigation of social media marketing: How does the hotel industry in Hong Kong perform in marketing on social media websites? *Journal of Travel and Tourism Marketing, 28*(4), 345–368.

Chang, H., & Chuang, S.
(2011). Social capital and individual motivations on knowledge sharing: Participant involvement as a moderator. *Information and Management, 48*, 9–18.

Charters, W.
(1933). *Motion pictures and youth: A summary.* New York, NY: Macmillan.

Chen, P.
(2007). Sport tourists' loyalty: A conceptual model. *Journal of Sport and Tourism, 11*(3/4), 1–37.

Cheney, J.
(2010). Celebritology 2.0. *Washington Post*, August 27. Retrieved from voices.washingtonpost.com/celebritology/2010/08/talking_with_james_cameron_abo.html

Cheung, C., & Lee, M.
>   (2010). A theoretical model of intentional social action in online social networks. *Decision Support Systems, 49*, 24–30.

Chhabra, D., Healy, R., & Sills, E.
>   (2003). Staged authenticity and heritage tourism. *Annals of Tourism Research, 30*, 702–719.

Chittenden, M., & Swinford, S.
>   (2010). *Volcanic ash grounds Britain for days to come.* Retrieved from http://www.timesonline.co.uk/tol/travel/news/article7101162.ece. Accessed on August 16, 2011.

Chon, K.
>   (1991). Tourism destination image modification process: Marketing implications. *Tourism Management, 12*, 68–72.

Chung, J., & Buhalis, D.
>   (2008a). Information needs in online social networks. *Information and communication technologies in tourism-applications, methodologies, techniques, 10*(4), 267–281.

Chung, J., & Buhalis, D.
>   (2008b). Web 2.0: A study of online travel community. In P. O'Connor, W. Höpken, & U. Gretzel (Eds.), *Information and communication technologies in tourism.* Proceedings of the International Conference in Innsbruck, Austria, Springer-Verlag, Wien.

Cogburn, J., & Silcox, M.
>   (2008). *Philosophy through video games.* London: Routledge.

Cohen, J.
>   (1988). *Statistical power analysis for the behavioral sciences* (2nd ed.). Hillsdale, NJ: Lawrence Earlbaum Associates.

Cohen, S.
>   (2010). Personal identity (de)formation among lifestyle travellers: A double-edged sword. *Leisure Studies, 29*(3), 289–301.

Connell, J.
>   (2005). Toddlers, tourism and tobermory: Destination marketing issues and television-induced tourism. *Tourism Management, 26*(5), 763–776.

Conrad Advertising.
>   (2011). *Mapping the travel mind: The influence of social media.* Conrad Advertising. Retrieved from http://www.conrad.co.uk/viewpoint-mapping-travel-mind. Accessed on July 10, 2012.

Conway, T., Ward, M., Lewis, G., & Bernhardt, A.
>   (2007). Internet crisis potential: The importance of a strategic approach to marketing communications. *Journal of Marketing Communications, 13*(3), 213–228.

Cook, S.
>   (2008). The contribution revolution: Letting volunteers build your business. *Harvard Business Review, 86*(10), 60–69.

Coombe, R., & Herman, A.
(2000). Trademarks, property, and propriety: The moral economy of consumer politics and corporate accountability in the World Wide Web. *DePaul Law Review, 50*, 597–632.

Coombs, W.
(2007). Attribution Theory as a guide for post crisis communication research. *Public Relations Review, 33*(2), 135–139.

Coombs, W.
(2012). *Ongoing crisis communication*. Thousand Oaks, CA: Sage.

Corley, K., & Gioia, D.
(2004). Identity ambiguity and change in the wake of a corporate spin-off. *Administrative Science Quarterly, 49*(2), 173–208.

CouchSurfing.
(2011). *Homepage*. Retrieved from http://www.CouchSurfing.org/. Accessed on October 14, 2011.

Cova, B., & Cova, V.
(2002). Tribal marketing – The tribalisation of society and its impact on the conduct of marketing. *European Journal of Marketing, 36*(5/6), 595–620.

Cova, B., Kozinets, R. V., & Shankar, A.
(2007). Tribes, Inc.: The new world of tribalism. In B. Cova, R. V. Kozinets & A. Shankar (Eds.), *Consumer tribes* (pp. 3–26). Oxford, UK: Butterworth-Heinemann.

Cova, B., & White, T.
(2010). Counter-brand and alter-brand communities: The impact of Web 2.0 on tribal marketing approaches. *Journal of Marketing Management, 26*(3/4), 256–270.

Cragan, J., & Shields, D.
(1981). *Applied communication research: A dramatistic approach*. Prospect Heights, IL: Waveland Press.

Cragan, J., & Shields, D.
(1992). The use of symbolic convergence theory in corporate strategic planning: A case study. *Journal of Applied Communication Research, 20*(2), 199–218.

Cragan, J., & Shields, D.
(1995). *Symbolic theories in applied communication research: Bormann, Burke, and Fisher*. Cresskill, NJ: Hampton.

Craik, J.
(1997). The culture of tourism. In C. Rojek & J. Urry (Eds.), *Touring cultures: Transformations of travel and theory* (pp. 113–136). London: Routledge.

Creswell, J.
(2003). *Research design qualitative, quantitative, and mixed methods approaches* (2nd ed.). London: Sage.

Crouch, D., Jackson, R., & Thompson, F.
(2005). *The media and the tourist imagination: Converging cultures.* London: Routledge.

Croy, W.
(2010). Planning for Film Tourism: Active Destination Image Management. *Tourism and Hospitality Planning and Development, 7*(1), 21–30.

Currie, R., Wesley, F., & Sutherland, P.
(2008). Going where the Joneses go: Understanding how others influence travel decision-making. *International Journal of Culture, Tourism and Hospitality Research, 2*(1), 12–24.

Dahlberg, L.
(2001). The internet and democratic discourse: Exploring the prospects of online deliberative forums extending the public sphere. *Information, Communication and Society, 4*(4), 615–633.

Davies, N., Mitchell, K., & Cheverst, K.
(1998). *GUIDE: Context-sensitive mobile multimedia support for city visitors.* Mobile Computing Research Team. Retrieved from http://www.guide.lancs. ac.uk/GuideOverview.html. Accessed on Feburary 28, 2012.

DeLanda, M.
(2002). *Intensive science and virtual philosophy.* London: The Athlone Press.

Delanty, G.
(2005). *Social science: Philosophical and methodological foundations* (2nd ed.). Maidenhead, UK: Open University Press.

Dellarocas, C.
(2003). The digitization of word of mouth: Promise and challenges of online feedback mechanisms. *Management Science, 49*(10), 1407–1424.

Dewar, K., Meyer, D., & Li, W.
(2001). Harbin, lanterns of ice, sculptures of snow. *Tourism Management, 22*(5), 523–532.

Dholakia, U., Bagozzi, R., & Klein Pearo, L.
(2004). A social influence model of consumer participation in network- and small-group-based virtual communities. *International Journal of Research in Marketing, 21*(3), 241–263.

Dickinger, A.
(2011). The trustworthiness of online channels for experience- and goal-directed search tasks. *Journal of Travel Research, 50*(4), 378–391.

Diken, B.
(2007). Houellebecq, or, the carnival of spite. *Journal for Cultural Research, 11*(1), 57–74.

Diken, B.
(2010). Fire as a metaphor of (im)mobility. *Mobilities, 6*(1), 95–102.

Diken, B.
(2012). *Revolt, revolution, critique: The paradox of society*. Abingdon, UK: Routledge.
Diken, B., & Laustsen, C.
(2005). *The culture of exception: Sociology facing the camp*. Abingdon, UK: Routledge.
Dixon, P.
(2010). *The one-way mirror society: Privacy implications of the new digital signage networks*. World Privacy Forum. Retrieved from worldprivacyforum. org/pdf/onewaymirrorsocietyfs.pdf
Doh, S., & Hwang, J.
(2009). How consumers evaluate eWOM (Electronic Word-of-Mouth) messages. *Cyber Psychology and Behavior, 12*(2), 193–197.
Dourish, P.
(2006). Implications for design. *Proceedings of the ACM conference on human factors in computing systems, CHI 2006*, Montreal, Canada (pp. 541–550).
Dourish, P., Anderson, K., & Nafus, D.
(2007). Cultural mobilities: Diversity and agency in urban computing. In *Human-computer interaction–INTERACT 2007, 11th IFIP TC 13 international conference*, Rio de Janeiro, Brazil, September 10–14, 2007, Proceedings, Part II, pp. 100–113.
Dwyer, L., Edwards, D., Mistilis, N., Roman, C., & Scott, N.
(2009). Destination and enterprise management for a tourism future. *Tourism Management, 30*(1), 63–74.
Dylan, B.
(2004). *Chronicles* (Vol. 1). New York, NY: Simon and Schuster.
Dyllick, T., & Hockerts, K.
(2002). Beyond the business case for corporate sustainability. *Business Strategy and the Environment, 11*(2), 130–141.
Eagleton, T.
(1982). The revolt of the reader. *New Literary History, 133*(3), 449–452.
Echtner, C., & Ritchie, B.
(1991). The meaning and measurement of destination image. *The Journal of Tourism Studies, 14*(1), 37–48.
Edmonton Sun.
(2010). *James Cameron is a hypocrite*. Retrieved from edmontonsun. com/comment/editorial/2010/09/28/15510431.html. Accessed on September 29, 2010.
Eisenhardt, K.
(1989). Building theories from case study research. *Academy of Management Review, 14*(1), 532–550.

El-Gohary, H.
  (2012). Factors affecting e-marketing adoption and implementation in tourism firms: An empirical investigation of Egyptian small tourism organizations. *Tourism Management, 33*, 1256–1269.
Elstad, B.
  (2003). Continuance commitment and reasons to quit: A study of volunteers at a jazz festival. *Event Management: An International Journal, 8*(2), 99–108.
Elstad, O., Widing, A., Bonde, H., Bring, G., Edvinsson, J., Rosenquist, J., & Englund, A.
  (1998). *Miljöbelastningsbedömning av vissa energi- och materialflöden vid Mitthögskolan.* Rapport 1998, Working Paper No. 13, University of Mitthögskolan, Östersund.
Enoch, Y., & Grossman, R.
  (2010). Blogs of Israeli and Danish backpackers to India. *Annals of Tourism Research, 37*(2), 520–536.
ePractice Media.
  (2010). *Social media.* Retrieved from http://epracticemedia.com/dental-facebook-marketing/. Accessed on February 24, 2011.
EUROCONTROL.
  (2010a). *Update on European air traffic situation – 10.30 CET.* Retrieved from http://www.eurocontrol.int/news/update-european-air-traffic-situation-1030-cet-0. Accessed on August 16, 2011.
EUROCONTROL.
  (2010b). *Volcanic ash cloud timeline – 2010 events.* Retrieved from http://www.eurocontrol.int/articles/volcanic-ash-cloud-timeline-2010-events. Accessed on August 16, 2011.
European Commission.
  (2003a). *Basic orientations for the sustainability of European tourism.* Brussels: Communication of the European Commission.
European Commission.
  (2003b). *Structure, performance and competitiveness of European tourism and its enterprises.* Brussels: European Commission, Directorate-General Enterprise, The Tourism Unit.
European Consumer Choice.
  (2012). *Top 10 Destinations in Europe.* Retrieved from http://www.european consumerschoice.org/travel/european-best-destination-2012. Accessed on June 10, 2012.
Evjemo, B., Akselsen, S., & Schürmann, A.
  (2007). User acceptance of digital tourist guides lessons learnt from two field studies. Human-Computer Interaction. *Interaction Design and Usability, 4550*, 746–755.

Facebook Press Room.
  (2011). *Newsroom*. Retrieved from http://www.facebook.com/press/info.php?
  statistics. Accessed on January 28, 2011.
Faulkner, R., & Anderson, A.
  (1987). Short-term projects and emergent careers: Evidence from Hollywood.
  American Journal of Sociology, 92(4), 879–909.
Fesenmaier, D., & Cook, S.
  (2009). *Travellers' use of the internet*. Washington, DC: U.S. Travel Association.
Fink, S.
  (1986). *Crisis management: Planning for the inevitable*. New York, NY:
  American Management Association.
Fiol, C.
  (2002). Capitalizing on paradox: The role of language in transforming
  organizational identities. *Organization Science, 13*(6), 653–666.
Fischer, W.
  (1984). Narration as a human communication paradigm: The case of public
  moral argument. *Communication Monographs, 51*(1), 1–22.
Forsyth, T.
  (1996). Sustainable tourism: Moving from theory to practice. World Wildlife
  Fund.
Foster-Fishman, P., Berkowitz, S., Lounsbury, D., Jacobson, S., & Allen, N.
  (2001). Building collaborative capacity in community coalitions: A review
  and integrative framework. *American Journal of Community Psychology, 29*,
  241–261.
Fotis, J., Buhalis, D., & Rossides, N.
  (2012). Social media use and impact during the holiday travel planning
  process. In M. Fuchs, F. Ricci, & L. Cantoni (Eds.), *Information and
  communication technologies in tourism 2012. Proceedings of the international
  conference in Helsinborg*, Sweden, January 25–27, 2012. Wien: Springer-Verlag
  (pp. 13–24).
Fotografia Europea.
  (2012). Retrieved from www.fotografiaeuropea.it/about/
Fournier, S., & Avery, J.
  (2011). The uninvited brand. *Business Horizons, 54*(3), 193–207.
Franklin, A.
  (2003a). *Tourism: An introduction*. London: Sage.
Franklin, A.
  (2003b). The tourist syndrome: An interview with Zygmunt Bauman. *Tourist
  Studies, 3*(2), 205–217.
Franklin, A.
  (2004). Tourism as an ordering: Towards a new ontology of tourism. *Tourist
  Studies, 4*(3), 277–301.

Franklin, A.
(2009). On loneliness. *Geografiska Annaler B: Human Geography, 91*(4), 343–354.

Frost, W.
(2006). From backlot to runaway production: Exploring location and authenticity in film-induced tourism. Paper presented at Second International Tourism and Media Conference, Monash University, Department of Management, Melbourne, Australia. Working Paper Series ISSN 1327-5216.

Frost, W.
(2009). From backlot to runaway production: Exploring location and authenticity in film-induced tourism. *Tourism Review International, 13*(2), 85–92.

Füller, J.
(2010). Refining virtual co-creation from a consumer perspective. *California Management Review, 52*(2), 98–122.

Gaines-Ross, L.
(2010). Reputation warfare. *Harvard Business Review, 88*(12), 70–76.

Gallarza, M., Saura, I., & Garcia, H.
(2002). Destination image, towards a conceptual framework. *Annals of Tourism Research, 29*(1), 56–78.

Garcia, B.
(2004). Cultural policy and urban regeneration in Western European cities: Lessons from experience, prospects for the future. *Local Economy, 19*(4), 312–326.

Gartner, W.
(1993). Image formation process. *Journal of Travel and Tourism Marketing, 2*(2/3), 191–215.

George, B., & Panko, T.
(2011). Child sex tourism: Facilitating conditions, legal remedies, and other interventions. *Vulnerable Children and Youth Studies, 6*(2), 134–143.

Getz, D.
(1991). *Festivals, special events, and tourism.* New York, NY: Van Nostrand Reinhold.

Getz, D., & Wicks, B.
(1994). Professionalism and certification for festival and event practitioners. *Festival Management and Event Tourism, 2*(2), 103–109.

Giddens, A.
(1979). *The constitution of society: Outline of the theory of structuration.* Los Angeles, CA: University of California Press.

Giddens, A.
(1987). *Social theory and modern sociology.* Oxford: Polity Press.

Giddens, A.
(1990). *The Consequences of Modernity.* Cambridge: Polity.

Giddens, A.
(2009). *The politics of climate change.* Cambridge: Polity.
Gilbey, R.
(2002). *Danny Boyle: 'Yes, we did betray Ewan'.* Independent. Retrieved from independent.co.uk/arts-entertainment/films/features/danny-boyle-yes-we-did-betray-ewan-608347.html. Accessed on October 25, 2002.
Gioia, D., & Pitre, E.
(1990). Multiparadigm perspectives on theory building. *Academy of Management Review, 15*(4), 584–602.
Gioia, D., Price, K., Hamilton, A., & Thomas, J.
(2011). Forging an identity: An insider-outsider study of processes involved in the formation of organizational identity. *Administrative Science Quarterly, 55,* 1–46.
Gioia, D., Schultz, M., & Corley, K.
(2000). Organizational identity, image and adaptive instability. *Academy of Management Review, 25*(1), 63–81.
Gitelson, R., & Crompton, J.
(1983). The planning horizons and sources of information used by pleasure vacationers. *Journal of Travel Research, 21*(2), 2–7.
Goffman, E.
(1967). *On face work: Interaction ritual. Essays in face-to-face behavior.* Chicago, IL: Aldine.
Goldman-Segall, R.
(1989). Thick descriptions: A tool for designing ethnographic interactive videodiscs. *SIGCHI Bulletin, 21*(2), 118–122.
González, S., Gidumal, J., & López-Valcárcel, B.
(2010). La participación de los clientes en sitios web de valoración de servicios turísticos. El caso de Tripadvisor. *Revista de Análisis Turístico, 10,* 17–22.
González-Herrero, A., & Smith, S.
(2008). Crisis communications management on the Web: How internet-based technologies are changing the way public relations professionals handle business crises. *Journal of Contingencies and Crisis Management, 16*(3), 143–153.
Goodman, R., & Goodman, L.
(1976). Some management issues in temporary systems: A study of professional development and manpower – The theater case. *Administrative Science Quarterly, 21,* 493–501.
Goulding, C., & Shankar, A.
(2004). Age is just a number: Rave culture and the cognitively young "thirty something". *European Journal of Marketing, 38*(5/6), 641–658.
Grappi, S., & Montanari, F.
(2011). The role of social identification and hedonism in affecting tourist re-patronizing behaviours: The case of an Italian festival. *Tourism Management, 32*(5), 1128–1140.

Gretzel, U.
(2011). Intelligent systems in tourism: A social science perspective. *Annals of Tourism Research, 38*(3), 757–779.
Gretzel, U., Kang, M., & Lee, W.
(2008). Differences in consumer-generated media adoption and use: A cross-national perspective. *Journal of Hospitality and Leisure Marketing, 17*(1-2), 99–120.
Grossberg, L.
(1997). *Bringing it all back home: Essays on cultural studies.* Durham, NC: Duke University Press.
Guex, V.
(2010). A sociological view of the cybertourists. In U. Gretzel, R. Law, & M. Fuchs, (Eds.), *Information and communication technologies in tourism 2010, Proceedings of the ENTER conference.* Vienna: Springer-Verlag (pp. 417–428).
Gunn, C.
(1988). *Vacationscape: Designing tourist regions* (2nd ed.). New York, NY: Van Nostrand Reinhold.
Gursoy, D., Kim, K., & Uysal, M.
(2004). Perceived impacts of festivals and special events by organizers: An extension and validation. *Tourism Management, 25*(2), 171–181.
Gursoy, D., & McCleary, K.
(2004). An integrative model of tourists' information search behavior. *Annals of Tourism Research, 31*(2), 353–373.
Gursoy, D., & Umbreit, W.
(2004). Tourist information source behaviour: Cross-cultural comparison of European Union member states. *International Journal of Hospitality Management, 23*(1), 55–70.
Habermas, J.
(1984). *Theory of communicative action* (Vol. 1). Boston, MA: Beacon Press.
Habermas, J.
(1987). *Theory of communicative action* (Vol. 2). Boston, MA: Beacon Press.
Hagen, P., & Robertson, T.
(2010). *Social technologies: Challenges and opportunities for participation.* Paper presented at the Proceedings of the 11th Biennial Participatory Design Conference, New York, NY, pp. 31–40. doi:10.1145/1900441.1900447
Hair, J. F., Anderson, R. E., Tatham, R. L., & Black, W. C.
(1998). *Multivariate data analysis* (5th ed.). NY: Hall International.
Haldrup, M., & Larsen, J.
(2010). *Tourism, performance and the everyday: Consuming the Orient.* London: Routledge.
Hall, M.
(2005). *Tourism: Rethinking the social science of mobility.* Harlow, UK: Pearsons Education Ltd.

Hall, M.

(2011). A typology of governance and its implications for tourism policy analysis. *Journal of Sustainable Tourism, 19*(4/5), 437–457.

Hand, M.

(2008). *Making digital cultures: Access, interactivity, and authenticity* (1st ed.). Hampshire: Ashgate Publishing Limited.

Hanlon, C., & Cuskelly, G.

(2002). Pulsating major sport event organizations: A framework for inducting managerial personnel. *Event Management: An International Journal, 7*(4), 231–244.

Hanlon, C., & Jago, L.

(2004). The challenge of retaining personnel in major sport event organizations. *Event Management: An International Journal, 9*(1–2), 39–49.

Hanna, R., Rohm, A., & Crittenden, V.

(2011). We're all connected: The power of the social media ecosystem. *Business Horizons, 54*(3), 265–273.

Harrison, D.

(2001). Tourism and less developed countries: Key issues. In D. Harrison (Ed.), *Tourism and the less developed world: Issues and case studies* (pp. 23–46). London: CABI.

Harrison, S., & Dourish, P.

(1996). Re-place-ing space: The roles of place and space in collaborative systems. *Proceedings of the 1996 ACM conference on computer supported cooperative work*. New York, NY: ACM (pp. 67–76).

Hart, J., Ridley, C., Taher, F., Sas, C., & Dix, A.

(2008). Exploring the Facebook experience: A new approach to usability. *Proceedings of the 5th Nordic conference on human-computer interaction: Building bridges*, New York, NY: ACM (pp. 471–474). Retrieved from http://dl.acm.org/citation.cfm?doid=1463160.1463222

Hartley, J.

(2003). *A short history of cultural studies.* London: Sage.

Hayles, N. K.

(2012). *How we think: Digital media and contemporary technogenesis.* Chicago, IL: The University of Chicago Press.

He, H., & Baruch, Y.

(2011). Organizational identity and legitimacy under major environmental changes: Tales of two UK building societies. *British Journal of Management, 21*, 44–62.

Healy, M., Beverland, M., Oppewal, H., & Sands, S.

(2007). Understanding retail experiences: The case for ethnography. *International Journal of Market Research, 49*(6), 751–778.

Healy, M., & Perry, C.

(2000). Comprehensive criteria to judge validity and reliability of qualitative research within the realism paradigm. *Qualitative Market Research: An International Journal, 3*(3), 118–126.

Hede, A.-M., & Kellett, P.
  (2012). Building online brand communities: Exploring the benefits, challenges and risks in the Australian event sector. *Journal of Vacation Marketing*, *18*(3), 239–250.
Held, D., McGrew, A., Goldblatt, D., & Perraton, J.
  (1999). *Global transformations*. Cambridge: Polity Press.
Hensel, K., & Deis, M. H.
  (2010). Using social media to increase advertising and improve marketing. *Entrepreneurial Executive*, *15*, 87–97.
Hetherington, K., & Law, J.
  (2000). After networks. *Environment and Planning D: Society and Space*, *18*(2), 127–132.
Hird, J.
  (2010). *20+ mind-blowing social media statistics*. Retrieved from http://econsultancy.com/blog/5324-20+-mind-blowing-social-mediastatistics-revisited. Accessed on August 1, 2012.
Hjalager, A.-M.
  (2010). A review of innovation research in tourism. *Tourism Management*, *31*, 1–12.
Hollinshead, K.
  (1999). Surveillance of the worlds of tourism: Foucault and the eye-of-power. *Tourism Management*, *20*(1), 7–23.
Holloway, J., & Robinson, C.
  (1995). *Marketing for tourism* (3rd ed.). Harlow: Longman.
Holquist, M.
  (1981). Glossary. In M. Bakhtin, tr. C. Emerson & M. Holquist (Eds.), *The dialogic imagination: four essays* (pp. 423–434). Austin, TX: University of Texas Press.
Hsu, M., Ju, T., Yen, C., & Chang, C.
  (2007). Knowledge sharing behavior in virtual communities: The relationship between trust, self-efficacy, and outcome expectations. *International Journal of Human-Computer Studies*, *65*(2), 153–169.
Huang, C.-J., Chou, C.-J., & Lin, P. C.
  (2010). Involvement theory in constructing bloggers' intention to purchase travel products. *Tourism Management*, *31*(4), 513–526.
Huebner, A.
  (2011). Who came first – Dracula or the tourist? New perspectives on Dracula tourism at Bran Castle. *European Journal of Tourism Research*, *4*(1), 55–65.
Hughes, G.
  (1995). The cultural construction of sustainable tourism. *Tourism Management*, *16*(1), 49–59.

Hunt, J.
  (1975). Image as a factor in tourism development. *Journal of Travel Research*, *13*, 1–7.
Hvass, K., & Munar, A.
  (2010). *Airlines Web 2.0: The challenge of social media, center for international businesses and emerging markets.* Working Paper Series, November 2011, Copenhagen Business School, Copenhagen.
Hvass, K., & Munar, A.
  (2011). *Let's be social at 30,000 feet.* Retrieved from http://www.aerlines.nl/wp-content/uploads/2011/01/49_Hvass_social_media1.pdf. Accessed on September 13, 2012.
Hvass, K., & Munar, A.
  (2012). The takeoff of social media in tourism. *Journal of Vacation Marketing*, *18*(2), 93–103.
Ingold, T.
  (2010). *Being alive: Essays on movement, knowledge and description.* London: Routledge.
International Telecommunication Union.
  (2009). *Measuring the information society: The ICT development index.* Retrieved from http://www.itu.int/ITU-D/ict/publications/idi/2009/material/IDI2009_w5.pdf. Accessed on April 1, 2010.
Ishii, K.
  (2006). Implications of mobility: The uses of personal communication media in everyday life. *Journal of Communication*, *56*, 346–365.
Israel, S.
  (2009). *Twitterville: How businesses can thrive in the new global neighborhoods.* New York, NY: Portfolio.
Iwashita, C.
  (2006). Media representations of the UK as a destination for Japanese tourists: Popular culture and tourism. *Tourist Studies*, *6*(1), 59–77.
Jackson, R.
  (2005). Converging cultures: Converging gazes. In D. Crouch, R. Jackson & F. Thompson (Eds.), *The media and the tourist imagination: Converging cultures* (pp. 183–197). New York, NY: Routledge.
Jacobs, G., Jochen, C., Keegan, A., & Pòlos, L.
  (2008). Reactions to organizational identity threats in times of change: Illustrations from the German police. *Corporate Reputation Review*, *11*(3), 245–261.
Jacobsen, J., & Munar, A.
  (2012). Tourist information search and destination choice in a digital age. *Tourism Management Perspectives*, *1*(1), 39–47.
Jafari, J.
  (1987). Tourism models: The sociocultural aspects. *Tourism Management*, *8*(2), 151–159.

Jafari, J.

(1990). Research and scholarship: The basis of tourism education. *Journal of Tourism Studies, 1*(1), 33–41.

Jago, L., & Mair, J.

(2009). Career theory and major event employment. In T. Baum, M. Deery, C. Hanlon, L. Lockstone & K. Smith (Eds.), *People and work in events and conventions: A research perspective* (pp. 65–74). Wallingford, UK: CABI Publishing.

Jamal, T., Hartl, C., & Lohmer, R.

(2010). Socio-cultural meanings of tourism in a local-global context: Implications for planning and development. *Pranjana: The Journal of Management Awareness, 13*(1), 1–15.

Jamal, T., & Hollinshead, K.

(2001). Tourism and the forbidden zone: The underserved power of qualitative inquiry. *Tourism Management, 22*(1), 63–82.

Jansen, B., Zhang, M., Sobel, K., & Chowdury, A.

(2009). Twitter power: Tweets as electronic word of mouth. *Journal of the American Society for Information Science and Technology, 60*, 2169–2188.

Jansson, A.

(2002). Spatial phantasmagoria: The mediatization of tourism experience. *European Journal of Communication, 17*(4), 429–443.

Jeong, E., & Jang, S.

(2010). Restaurant experiences triggering positive electronic word-of-mouth (eWOM) motivations. *International Journal of Hospitality Management, 30*(2), 356–366.

Jepsen, A.

(2006). Information search in virtual communities: Is it replacing use of off-line communication? *Journal of Marketing Communications, 12*(4), 247–261.

Jiang, H., Mills, J., & Stepchenkova, S.

(2008). Digital identity management and satisfaction with virtual travel communities. *Information Technology and Tourism, 10*(1), 43–58.

Jin, Y., & Liu, B.

(2010). The blog-mediated crisis communication model: Recommendations for responding to influential external blogs. *Journal of Public Relations Research, 22*(4), 429–455.

Jin, Y., Liu, B., & Austin, L.

(2011). Examining the role of social media in effective crisis management: The effects of crisis origin, information form, and source on publics' crisis responses. *Communication Research*, 1–21.

Jóhannesson, G.

(2005). Tourism translations: Actor-network theory and tourism research. *Tourist Studies, 5*(2), 133–150.

Johnston, R., & Tyrrell, T.
    (2005). A dynamic model of sustainable tourism. *Journal of Travel Research*, *44*(2), 124–134.
Jones, D., & Smith, K.
    (2005). Middle-Earth Meets New Zealand: Authenticity and Location in the Making of The Lord of the Rings. *Journal of Management Studies*, *42*(5), 923–945.
Kanellopoulos, D.
    (2006). The advent of semantic web in tourism information systems. *Tourismos: An International Multidisciplinary Journal of Tourism*, *1*(2), 77–93.
Kaplan, A., & Haenlein, M.
    (2010). Users of the world, unite! The challenges and opportunities of social media. *Business Horizons*, *53*(1), 59–68.
Keen, A.
    (2007). *The cult of the amateur: How today's internet is killing our culture and assaulting our economy.* London: Nicholas Brealey Publishing.
Kelley, H.
    (1967). *Attribution theory in social psychology.* Nebraska Symposium on Motivation. Lincoln, Nebraska, 15 (proceedings), pp. 192–238.
Kelley, H.
    (1980). Attribution Theory and Research. *Annual Review of Psychology*, *31*, 457–501.
Kietzmann, J., Hermkens, K., McCarthy, I., & Silvestre, B.
    (2011). Social media? Get serious! Understanding the functional building blocks of social media. *Business Horizons*, *54*(3), 241–251.
Kim, H., Borges, M., & Chon, J.
    (2006). Impacts of environmental values on tourism motivation: The case of FICA. *Brazil. Tourism Management*, *27*(5), 957–967.
Kim, H., & Richardson, S.
    (2003). Motion picture impacts on destination images. *Annals of Tourism Research*, *30*(1), 216–237.
Kim, N.-S., & Chalip, L.
    (2004). Why travel to the FIFA World Cup? Effects of motives, background, interest, and constraints. *Tourism Management*, *25*(6), 695–707.
Kim, S., Avery, E., & Lariscy, R.
    (2009). Are crisis communicators practicing what we preach?: An evaluation of crisis response strategy analyzed in public relations research from 1991–2009. *Public Relations Review*, *35*(4), 446–448.
Kirkpatrick, G.
    (2008). *Technology and social power.* New York, NY: Palgrave Macmillan.
Kirshenblatt-Gimblett, B.
    (1998). *Destination culture: Tourism, museums, and heritage.* Berkeley, CA: University of California Press.

Kjærgaard, A., Morsing, M., & Ravasi, D.
(2011). Mediating identity: A study of media influence on organizational identity construction in a celebrity firm. *Journal of Management Studies, 48*(3), 514–543.

Kleinman, D.
(2005). *Science and technology in society: From biotechnology to the internet.* Oxford: Blackwell.

Kozinets, R.
(1999). E-tribalized marketing? The strategic implications of virtual communities of consumption. *European Management Journal, 17*(3), 252–264.

Kozinets, R.
(2002). The field behind the screen: Using netnography for marketing research in online communities. *Journal of Marketing Research, 39*(1), 61–72.

Kozinets, R.
(2008). Technology/Ideology: How ideological fields influence consumers' technology narratives. *Journal of Consumer Research, 34*(6), 865–881.

Kozinets, R.
(2009). *Netnography: Doing ethnographic research online.* Thousand Oaks, CA: Sage.

Kozinets, R., de Valck, K., Wojnicki, A., & Wilner, S.
(2010). Networked narratives: Understanding word-of-mouth marketing in online communities. *Journal of Marketing, 74*(2), 71–89.

Krippendorf, K.
(2004). *Content analysis: An introduction to its methodology* (2nd ed.). Thousand Oaks, CA: Sage.

Krosche, J., Baldzer, J., & Boll, S.
(2004). Mobidenk-mobile multimedia in monument conservation. *IEEE Multimedia, 11*(2), 72–77.

Kushner, D.
(1998). *Titanic vs. Popotla.* Retrieved from wired.com/culture/lifestyle/news/1998/08/14294. Accessed on August 7, 1998.

Kwan, M.
(2007). Mobile communications, social networks, and urban travel: Hypertext as a new metaphor for conceptualizing spatial interaction. *The Professional Geographer, 59*(4), 434–446.

Lam, T., & Hsu, C.
(2006). Predicting behavioral intention of choosing a travel destination. *Tourism Management, 27*(4), 589–599.

Lampel, J., Lant, T., & Shamsie, J.
(2000). Balancing act: Learning from organizing practices in cultural industries. *Organization Science, 11*(3), 263–269.

Lampel, J., & Meyer, A.
(2008). Field-configuring events as structuring mechanisms: How conferences, ceremonies, and trade shows constitute new technologies, industries, and markets. *Journal of Management Studies, 45*(6), 1025–1035.

Lane, G.
(2003). Urban tapestries: Wireless networking, public authoring and social knowledge. *Personal and Ubiquitous Computing, 7*(3/4), 169–175.

Langer, R., & Beckman, S.
(2005). Sensitive research topics: Netnography revisited. *Qualitative Market Research: An International Journal, 8*(2), 189–203.

Lanier, C., & Hampton, R.
(2008). Consumer participation and experiential marketing: Understanding the relationship between co-creation and the fantasy life cycle. *Advances in Consumer Research, 35*, 44–48.

Lanzara, G.
(1983). Ephemeral organizations in extreme environments: Emergence, strategy, extinction. *Journal of Management Studies, 20*(1), 71–95.

Larsen, J.
(2008). De-exoticizing leisure travel. *Leisure Studies, 27*(1), 21–34.

Larson, M., & Gyimóthy, S.
(2012). *Social media and festivals: Co-creating the experience.* Workshop paper presented at the ENTER conference, Helsingborg, Sweden, January 24–27, 2012.

Lasén, A.
(2004). *Affective technologies – Emotions and mobile phones.* Receiver 11. Retrieved from receiver.vodafone.com/11/articles/index03.html

Lash, S.
(2002). Foreword: Individualization in a non-linear mode. In U. Beck & E. Beck-Gernsheim (Eds.), *Individualization* (pp. vi–xix). London: Sage.

Latin American Herald Tribune.
(2012, March 14). *Greenpeace launches campaign against Mexican resort project.* Retrieved from http://www.laht.com/article.asp?ArticleId = 478655&-CategoryId = 14091. Accessed on August 15, 2012.

Latour, B.
(1986). The power of association. In J. Law (Ed.), *Power, action and belief: A new sociology of knowledge?* (pp. 264–280). London: Routledge.

Latour, B.
(1991). Technology is society made durable. In J. Law (Ed.), *A sociology of monsters: Essays on power, technology and domination* (pp. 103–131). London: Routledge.

Latour, B.
(1999). *Pandora's hope: Essays on the reality of science studies.* Cambridge, MA: Harvard University Press.

Latour, B.
(2005). *Reassembling the social: An introduction to actor-network-theory.* Oxford: Oxford University Press.

Law, J.
(2002). Objects and spaces. *Theory, Culture and Society, 19*(5/6), 91–105.

Law, J.
(2004). *After method: Mess in social science research.* Abingdon: Routledge.

Law, J., & Mol, A.
(2001). Situating technoscience: An Inquiry into spatialities. *Environment and Planning: Society and Space, 19*(5), 609–621.

Law, J., & Singleton, V.
(2005). Object lessons. *Organization, 12*(3), 331–355.

Law, L., Bunnell, T., & Ong, C.-E.
(2007). The Beach, the gaze and film tourism. *Tourist Studies, 7*(2), 141–164.

Law, R.
(2006). Internet and tourism – Part XXI: TripAdvisor. *Journal of Travel and Tourism Marketing, 20*(1), 75–77.

Law, R., Leung, R., & Buhalis, D.
(2009). Information technology applications in hospitality and tourism: A review of publications from 2005 to 2007. *Journal of Travel and Tourism Marketing, 26*(5), 599–623.

Le Bon, G.
(1899). *Psychologie des foules.* Paris: Alcan.

Lee, G., & Tussyadiah, I.
(2010). Textual and visual information in eWOM: A gap between preferences in information search and diffusion. *Information Technology and Tourism, 12*(4), 351–361.

Lee, J., & Ingold, T.
(2006). Fieldwork on foot: Perceiving, routing, socializing. In P. Collins & S. Coleman (Eds.), *Locating the field: Space, place and context in anthropology* (pp. 67–86). Oxford, UK: Berg.

Lee, Y., Lee, C., Lee, S., & Babin, B.
(2008). Festivalscapes and patrons' emotions, satisfaction, and loyalty. *Journal of Business Research, 61*(6), 56–64.

Leech, N., Barrett, K., & Morgan, G.
(2005). *SPSS for intermediate statistics* (2nd ed.). London: Lawrence Erlbaum Associates.

Lichtenthal, J., & Eliaz, S.
(2003). Internet integration in business marketing tactics. *Industrial Marketing Management, 32*(1), 3–13.

Light, D.
(2007). Dracula tourism in Romania: Cultural identity and the state. *Annals of Tourism Research, 34*(3), 746–765.

Light, D.
(2009). Performing Transylvania: Tourism, fantasy and play in a liminal place. *Tourist Studies*, *9*(3), 240–258.

Lindgren, S.
(2005). Populärkultur: Teorier, metoder och analyser. [Pop culture: Theories, methods, and analysis.]. Malmö: Liber.

Litvin, S., Crotts, J., & Hefner, F.
(2004). Cross-cultural tourist behavior: A replication and extension involving Hofstede's uncertainty avoidance dimension. *International Journal of Tourism Research*, *6*, 29–37.

Litvin, S., Goldsmith, R., & Pan, B.
(2008). Electronic word-of-mouth in hospitality and tourism management. *Tourism Management*, *29*(3), 458–468.

Liu, B., & Austin, L.
(2010). *How publics use social media to communicate during crises: Proposing the social-mediated crisis communication model.* Public Relations Society of America: Educators Academy, 2010 Proceedings, Washington, DC.

Liu, B., Austin, L., & Jin, Y.
(2011). How publics respond to crisis communication strategies: The interplay of information form and source. *Public Relations Review*, *37*(4), 345–353.

Liu, B., & Kim, S.
(2011). How organizations framed the 2009 H1N1 pandemic via social and traditional media: Implications for U.S. health communicators. *Public Relations Review*, *37*(3), 233–244.

Liu, Z.
(2003). Sustainable tourism development: A critique. *Journal of Sustainable Tourism*, *11*(6), 459–475.

Lo, I., McKercher, B., Lo, A., Cheung, C., & Law, R.
(2011). Tourism and online photography. *Tourism Management*, *32*(4), 725–731.

Lohr, S.
(2013). In search for cultural insight, technology that lets no phrase go unparsed. *International Herald Tribune*, p. 18.

Lu, Y., Zhao, L., & Wang, B.
(2010). From virtual community members to C2C e-commerce buyers: Trust in virtual communities and its effect on consumers' purchase intention. *Electronic Commerce Research and Applications*, *9*(4), 346–360.

Lueg, C.
(2003). Knowledge sharing in online communities and its relevance to knowledge management in the e-business era. *International Journal of Electronic Business*, *1*(2), 140–151.

Lundin, R., & Steinthorsson, R.
(2003). Studying organizations as temporary. *International Journal of Management*, *19*, 233–250.

Macbeth, J.
(2005). Towards an ethics platform for tourism. *Annals of Tourism Research*, *32*(4), 962–984.

MacCannell, D.
(1999). *The Tourist – A new theory of the leisure class*. Los Angeles, CA: University of California Press.

Macias, W., Hilyard, K., & Freimuth, V.
(2009). Blog functions as risk and crisis communication during Hurricane Katrina. *Journal of Computer-Mediated Communication*, *15*(1), 1–31.

Mack, R., Blose, J., & Pan, B.
(2008). Believe it or not: Credibility of blogs in tourism. *Journal of Vacation Marketing*, *14*(2), 133–144.

Maffesoli, M.
(1996). *The time of the tribes: The decline of individualism in mass society*. Thousand Oaks, CA: Sage.

Mair, J.
(2009). The events industry: The employment context. In T. Baum, M. Deery, C. Hanlon, L. Lockstone & K. Smith (Eds.), *People and work in events and conventions: A research perspective* (pp. 3–16). Wallingford, UK: CABI Publishing.

Mangold, G., & Faulds, D.
(2009). Social media: The new hybrid element of the promotion mix. *Business Horizons*, *52*, 357–365.

Markham, A.
(2004). Internet communication as a tool for qualitative research. In D. Silverman (Ed.), *Qualitative research: Theory, method and practice* (pp. 95–124). London: Sage.

Maxwell, R., & Miller, T.
(2006). Film and globalization. In O. Boyd-Barrett (Ed.), *Communications media, globalization and empire* (pp. 33–52). Eastleigh: John Libbey.

McAfee, A.
(2006). Enterprise 2.0. *MIT Sloan Management Review*, *47*, 20–28.

McCarthy, J., Wright, P., Wallace, J., & Dearden, A.
(2006). The experience of enchantment in human-computer interaction. *Personal and Ubiquitous Computing*, *10*(6), 369–378.

McIntosh, A., & Prentice, C.
(1999). Affirming authenticity: Consuming cultural heritage. *Annals of Tourism Research*, *26*, 589–612.

McKercher, B., Mei, W., & Tse, T.
(2006). Are short duration cultural festivals tourist attractions? *Journal of Sustainable Tourism*, *14*, 55–66.

Meaney, S., & Robb, J.
(2006). Shooting Ireland: The American tourism market and promotional film. *Irish Geography*, *39*(1), 129–142.

Mei, J., Bansal, N., & Pang, A.
(2010). New media: A new medium in escalating crises? *Corporate Communications: An International Journal*, *15*(2), 143–155.

Merman Scott, D.
(2011). *The New Rules of Marketing & PR* (3rd ed.). Chichester, UK: Wiley.

Michels, R.
(1915). *Political parties. A sociological study of the oligarchical tendencies of modern democracy* (E. and C. Paul, Trans.). London: Jarrold & Sons.

Mill, J.
(1861). *Considerations on representative government*. Retrieved from constitution.org/jsm/rep_gov.htm

Miller, L., & Christakis, N.
(2011). Tapping the power of social networks. *Harvard Business Review*, *89*(9), 28.

Miller, T.
(2009). Media effects and cultural studies: A contentious relationship. In R. Nabi & M. Oliver (Eds.), *The Sage handbook of media processes and effects* (pp. 131–143). Thousand Oaks, CA: Sage.

Miller, T.
(2010). *Television studies: The basics*. London: Routledge.

Miller, T., Govil, N., McMurria, J., Maxwell, R., & Wang, T.
(2005). *Global Hollywood 2*. London: British Film Institute.

Minca, C.
(2012). No country for old men. In C. Minca & T. Oakes (Eds.), *Real tourism: Practice, care and politics in contemporary travel culture* (pp. 12–37). Abingdon, UK: Routledge.

Minelli, F.
(2008). *Facebook, Contradictions, Bamako, Mali*. Photograph. Retrieved from http://www.filippominelli.com/contradictions/

Mintel Group.
(2003, October). *Film tourism – International*. London: Mintel International Group.

Moeran, B., & Strandgaard Pedersen, J.
(2011). Introduction. In B. Moeran & J. Strandgaard Pedersen (Eds.), *Negotiating values in the creative industries. Fairs, festivals and competitive events* (pp. 1–32). Cambridge: Cambridge University Press.

Mohrmann, G.
(1982). An essay on fantasy theme criticism. *Quarterly Journal of Speech*, *68*, 109–132.

Mol, A., & Law, J.
(1994). Regions, networks and fluids: Anaemia and social topology. *Social Studies of Science*, *24*(4), 641–671.

Mordue, T.
(2001). Performing and directing resident/Tourist cultures in heartbeat country. *Tourism Studies, 1*(3), 233–252.

Mordue, T.
(2009). Angling in modernity: A tour through society, nature and embodied passion. *Current Issues in Tourism, 12*(5-6), 529–552.

Mosca, G.
(1939). *The ruling class* (H. D. Kahn, Trans, A. Livingston, Ed.). New York, NY: McGraw-Hill.

Moscardo, G.
(2008). *Building community capacity for tourism development*. Wallingford, UK: CABI.

Mosco, V.
(2004). *The digital sublime: Myth, power, and cyberspace*. Cambridge, MA: MIT Press.

Mowen, J.
(1980). Further information on consumer perceptions of product recalls. *Advances in Consumer Research, 7*, 519–523.

Müller, D.
(2006). Unplanned development of literary tourism in two municipalities in rural Sweden. *Scandinavian Journal of Hospitality and Tourism, 6*(3), 214–228.

Munar, A.
(2009). Challenging the brand. In L. Cai, W. Gartner, & A. Munar (Eds.), *Tourism branding: Communities in action* (Vol. 1, pp. 17-35). Bridging Tourism Theory and Practice. Bingley, UK: Emerald Group.

Munar, A.
(2010a). Digital exhibitionism: The age of exposure. *Culture Unbound, 2*, 401–422.

Munar, A.
(2010b). *Technological mediation and user created content in tourism*. Center for International Business and Emerging Markets Working Papers Series, April 2010, Copenhagen Business School, Copenhagen.

Munar, A.
(2011). Tourist-created content: Rethinking destination branding. *International Journal of Culture, Tourism and Hospitality Research, 5*(3), 291–305.

Munar, A.
(2012). Social media strategies and destination management. *Scandinavian Journal of Hospitality and Tourism, 12*(2), 101–120.

Munar, A., & Ooi, C.-S.
(2012). The truth of the crowds: Social media and the heritage experience. In L. Smith, E. Waterton & S. Watson (Eds.), *The cultural moment in tourism* (pp. 255–273). London: Routledge.

Muñiz, A., & Schau, H.
(2007). Vigilante marketing and consumer-created communications. *Journal of Advertising, 36*(3), 35–50.

Murdoch, J.
(2006). *Post-structuralist geography: A guide to relational space.* London: Sage.

Murnan, C.
(2006). Expanding communication mechanism: They're not just emailing anymore. *Proceedings of the 34th annual ACM SIGUCCS fall conference.* New York, NY: ACM Press (pp. 267–272).

Musser, J., O'Reilly, T., & O'Reilly Radar Team, X.
(2007). *Web 2.0: Principles and best practices.* Sebastopol, CA: O'Reilly Radar.

Nag, R., Corley, K., & Gioia, D.
(2007). The intersection of organizational identity, knowledge, and practice: Attempting strategic change via knowledge grafting. *Academy of Management Journal, 50*(4), 821–847.

Nelson, M., & Otnes, C.
(2005). Exploring cross-cultural ambivalence: A netnography of intercultural wedding message boards. *Journal of Business Research, 58*(1), 89–95.

Novelli, M., Schmitz, B., & Spencer, T.
(2006). Networks, clusters and innovation in tourism: A UK experience. *Tourism Management, 27*(6), 1141–1152.

Nunnally, J.
(1978). *Psychometric theory* (2nd ed.). New York, NY: McGraw-Hill.

O'Connor, P.
(2010). Managing a hotel's image on TripAdvisor. *Journal of Hospitality Marketing and Management, 19*(7), 754–772.

Oliver, R.
(1999). Whence consumer loyalty? *Journal of Marketing, 63*(1), 33–44.

Olufwote, J.
(2006). Rousing and redirecting a sleeping giant. Symbolic convergence theory and complexities in the communicative constitution of collective action. *Management Communication Quarterly, 19*(3), 451–492.

Ooi, C.-S.
(2001). Tourist historical products: packaged past of Denmark and Singapore. *Scandinavian Journal of Hospitality and Tourism, 1*(2), 113–132.

Ooi, C.-S.
(2002a). *Cultural tourism and tourism cultures: The business of mediating experiences in Copenhagen and Singapore.* Copenhagen: Copenhagen Business School Press.

Ooi, C.-S.
(2005). A theory of tourism experiences. In T. O'Dell & J. Bindloss (Eds.), *Experiencescapes: Tourism, culture and economy.* Copenhagen: Copenhagen Business School Press.

Ooi, C.-S., & Ek, R.
   (2010). Culture, work and emotion. *Culture Unbound, 2*, 303–310.
Orczy, B.
   (2009). *The scarlet pimpernel: The ultimate spy collection* (Seven Books). Douglas and Kindle Editions.
O'Reilly, N., Rahinel, R., Foster, M., & Patterson, M.
   (2007). Connecting in megaclasses: The netnographic advantage. *Journal of Marketing Education, 29*(1), 29–69.
O'Reilly, T.
   (2005). *What is Web 2.0: Design patterns and business models for the next generation of software.* Retrieved from http://www.oreillynet.com/pub/a/oreilly/tim/news/2005/09/30/what-is-web-20.html. Accessed on 15, 2011.
Organization for Economic Cooperation and Development (OECD).
   (2007). *Participative web: User-generated content.* Lugano: OECD.
Otnes, C., & Maclaran, P.
   (2007). The consumption of cultural heritage among a British Royal Family brand tribe. In B. Cova, R. Kozinets & A. Shankar (Eds.), *Consumer tribes* (pp. 51–66). Oxford, UK: Butterworth-Heinemann.
Packendorff, J.
   (1995). Inquiring into the temporary organization: New directions for project management research. *Scandinavian Journal of Management, 11*(4), 319–333.
Paget, E., Dimanche, F., & Mounet, J.-P.
   (2010). A tourism innovation case: An actor-network approach. *Annals of Tourism Research, 37*(3), 828–847.
Paivio, A.
   (1969). Mental imagery in associative learning and memory. *Psychological Review, 76*(3), 241–263.
Pan, B., Xiang, Z., Law, R., & Fesenmaier, D.
   (2011). The dynamics of search engine marketing for tourist destinations. *Journal of Travel Research, 50*(4), 365–377.
Papathanassis, A., & Knolle, F.
   (2010). Exploring the adoption and processing of online holiday reviews: A grounded theory approach. *Tourism Management, 32*(2), 215–224.
Pareto, V.
   (1976). *Sociological writings* (D. Mirfin, Trans., S. E. Finer, Ed.). Oxford: Basil Blackwell.
Pariser, E.
   (2011). When the internet thinks it knows you. *International Herald Tribune*, May 23, p. 8.
Park, D.-H., Nam, T., & Shi, C.
   (2006). Designing an immersive tour experience system for cultural tour sites. In *CHI'06 extended abstracts on human factors in computing systems* (pp. 1193–1198). New York, NY: ACM

Park, D.-H., Lee, J., & Han, I.
(2007). The effect of on-line consumer reviews on consumer purchasing intention: The moderating role of involvement. *International Journal of Electronic Commerce, 11*(4), 125–148.

Parks, M.
(2011). Social network sites as virtual communities. In Z. Papacharissi (Ed.), *The networked self: Identity, community, and culture on social network sites* (pp. 105–123). New York, NY: Routledge.

Parra-López, E., Bulchand-Gidumal, J., Gutiérrez-Tano, D., & Diaz-Armas, R.
(2011). Intentions to use social media in organizing and taking vacation trips. *Computers in Human Behaviour, 27*(2), 640–654.

Pauchant, T., & Mitroff, I.
(1992). *Transforming the crisis-prone organization: Preventing individual, organizational, and environmental tragedies.* San Francisco, CA: Jossey-Bass.

Pearce, P.
(1982). Perceived changes in holiday destinations. *Annals of Tourism Research, 9*, 145–164.

Pearce, P.
(2005). Tourist behaviour: Themes and conceptual schemes. In *Aspects of tourism* (Vol. 27). Clevedon, UK: Channel View Books.

Pegg, S.
(2002). Satisfaction of volunteers involved in community events: Implications for the event manager. Paper presented at the Events and Placemaking: International Event Research Conference, Sydney, July 2002.

Pekkola, S., Robinson, M., Korhonen, J., Hujala, S., Toivonen, T., & Saarinen, M.
(2000). An architecture for virtual reality, audio, video, text, and document handling in applications supporting multi-person interactions. *Proceedings of the 26th euromicro conference,* 2000, 2, pp. 150–157.

Pentland, A.
(2008). *Honest signals: How they shape our world.* Cambridge, MA: MIT Press.

Peters, G., & Pierre, J.
(2001). Developments in intergovernmental relations: Towards multi-level governance. *Policy and Politics, 29*(2), 131–135.

Petersen, S.
(2008). Loser generated content: from participation to exploitation. *First Monday 13*(3). Retrieved from http://www.uic.edu/htbin/cgiwrap/bin/ojs/index.php/fm/article/view/2141/1948. Accessed on March 12, 2012.

PhoCusWright.
(2010). How big is social media in travel? *FYI Newsletter,* April 5, 2010.

Pierce, D.
(2008). *Contradictions.* Retrieved from http://www.filippominelli.com/contradictions/. Accessed on May 10, 2012.

Pike, S.
(2002). Destination image analysis. *Tourism Management, 23*, 541–549.
Pingdom AB.
(2012). Retrieved from http://royal.pingdom.com/2012/01/17/internet-2011-in-numbers/
Pink, S.
(2007). *Doing visual ethnography: Images, media and representation in research.* London: Sage.
Pink, S.
(2009). *Doing sensory ethnography.* London: Sage.
Popescu, A., & Grefenstette, G.
(2011). Mining social media to create personalized recommendations for tourist visits (May 23–25). COM. Geo 2011. Washington, DC.
Popotla vs. Titanic.
(n.d.). Retrieved from rtmark.com/popotla.html
Poster, M.
(2006). *Information please.* London: Duke University Press.
Postrel, V.
(1999). The pleasures of persuasion. *Wall Street Journal*, August 2, p. A18.
Prensky, M.
(2001). Digital natives, digital immigrants. *On the Horizon, 9*(5), 1–6. Retrieved from http://www.marcprensky.com/writing/Prensky%20-%20Digital%20 Natives,%20Digital%20Immigrants%20-%20Part1.pdf. Accessed on January 12, 2011.
Prentice, R.
(2004). Tourist familiarity and imagery. *Annals of Tourism Research, 31*(4), 923–945.
Prentice, R., & Andersen, V.
(2007). Interpreting heritage essentialisms: Familiarity and felt history. *Tourism Management, 28*(3), 661–676.
Pritchard, A., Morgan, N., & Ateljevic, I.
(2011). Hopeful tourism: A new transformative perspective. *Annals of Tourism Research, 38*(3), 941–963.
Pudliner, B.
(2007). Alternative literature and tourist experience: Travel and tourist weblogs. *Journal of Tourism and Cultural Change, 5*(1), 46–59.
Pufendorf, S.
(2000). *On the duty of man and citizen according to natural law* (M. Silverthorne, Trans., J. Tully, Ed.) Cambridge: Cambridge University Press.
Qiu, J.
(2007). Mobile messaging service as a means of control. *International Journal of Communication, 1*, 74–91.

Qu, H., & Lee, H.
> (2011). Travelers' social identification and membership behaviors in online travel community. *Tourism Management, 32*(6), 1262–1270.

Qualman, E.
> (2009). *Socialnomics: How social media transforms the way we live and do business.* Hoboken, NJ: Wiley.

Quarantelli, E.
> (1988). Disaster crisis management: A summary of research findings. *Journal of Management Studies, 25*(4), 373–385.

Quinn, B.
> (2005). Arts festivals and the city. *Urban Studies, 42*(5/6), 927 943.

Rajagopal, A.
> (2001). *Politics after television: Religious nationalism and the reshaping of the Indian public.* Cambridge: Cambridge University Press.

Rao, R., & Argote, L.
> (2006). Organizational learning and forgetting: The effects of turnover and structure. *European Management Review, 3*(2), 77–85.

Rasche, A.
> (2010). Collaborative governance 2.0. *Corporate Governance, 10*(4), 500–511.

Ravasi, D., & Phillips, N.
> (2011). Strategies of alignment: Organizational identity management and strategic change at Bang & Olufsen. *Strategic Organization, 9*(2), 103–135.

Ray, S.
> (1999). *Strategic communication in crisis management: Lessons from the airline industry.* Westport, CT: Quorum Books.

Reisch, L.
> (2001). The internet and sustainable consumption: Perspectives on a Janus face. *Journal of Consumer Policy, 24*(3/4), 251–286.

Ren, C.
> (2011). Non-human agency, radical ontology and tourism realities. *Annals of Tourism Research, 38*(3), 858–881.

Ren, C., Pritchard, A., & Morgan, N.
> (2010). Constructing tourism research: A critical inquiry. *Annals of Tourism Research, 37*(4), 885–904.

Rheingold, H.
> (1993). *The virtual community: Homesteading on the electronic frontier.* New York: Harper Perennial.

Riley, R., Baker, D., & Van Doren, C.
> (1998). Movie induced tourism. *Annals of Tourism Research, 25*(4), 919–935.

Riley, R., & Van Doren, C.
> (1992). Movies as tourism promotion: A push factor in a pull location. *Tourism Management, 13*(3), 267–274.

Ritzer, G., & Jurgenson, N.
    (2010). Production, consumption, prosumption. *Journal of Consumer Culture*, *10*(1), 13–36.
Robertson, R.
    (1995). Glocalization: Time-space and homogeneity-heterogeneity. In M. Featherstone, S. Lash & R. Robertson (Eds.), *Global modernities* (pp. 25–44). London: Sage.
Rodger, K., Moore, S., & Newsome, D.
    (2009). Wildlife tourism, science and actor network theory. *Annals of Tourism Research*, *36*(4), 645–666.
Rogers, E.
    (1995). *Diffusion of innovations* (4th ed.). New York, NY: The Free Press.
Rotmans, J., & Martens, P.
    (2002). Transitions in a globalizing world: What does it all mean? In J. Rotmans & P. Martens (Eds.), *Transitions in a globalizing world* (pp. 117–131). Lisse: Swets & Zeitlinger Publishers.
Rowland, R., & Jerome, A.
    (2004). On organizational apologia: A reconceptualization. *Communication Theory*, *14*(3), 191–211.
Rowlinson, M., Booth, C., Clark, P., Delahaye, A., & Procter, S.
    (2010). Social remembering and organizational memory. *Organization Studies*, *31*(1), 69–87.
Ruling, C.
    (2011). Event institutionalization and maintenance: The Annecy animation festival 1960–2010. In B. Moeran & J. Strandgaard Pedersen (Eds.), *Negotiating values in the creative industries. Fairs, festivals and competitive events* (pp. 169–196). Cambridge: Cambridge University Press.
Saleh, F., & Wood, C.
    (1998). Motives of volunteers in multicultural events: The case of the Saskatoon Festival. *Festival Management and Event Tourism*, *5*(1/2), 59–70.
Salvador, T., Bell, G., & Anderson, K.
    (1999). Design ethnography. *Design Management Journal (Former Series)*, *10*(4), 35–41.
Sanchez-Franco, M. J., & Rondan-Cataluña, F. J.
    (2010). Virtual travel communities and customer loyalty: Customer purchase involvement and web site design. *Electronic Commerce Research and Applications*, *9*(2), 171–182.
Sandin, J.
    (2007). Netnography as a consumer education research tool. *International Journal of Consumer Research*, *31*(3), 288–294.
Sandoval, M., & Fuchs, C.
    (2010). Towards a critical theory of alternative media. *Telematics and Informatics*, *27*, 141–150.

SAS Group.
(2012). *Focus on the SAS Group 2012 – Corporate presentation*. Retrieved from http://www.sasgroup.net/SASGROUP_FACTS/CMSForeignContent/Company%20Presentation%202012%20Short%20Compressed.pdf. Accessed on September 13, 2011.

Scarles, C.
(2010). Where words fail, visuals ignite: Opportunities for visual autoethnography in tourism research. *Annals of Tourism Research, 37*(4), 905–926.

Schau, H., Muñiz, A., & Arnould, E.
(2009). How brand community practices create value. *Journal of Marketing, 73*(5), 30–51.

Schegg, R., Leibrich, A., Scaglione, M., & Ahmad, S.
(2008). An exploratory field study of Web 2.0 in Tourism. In P. O'Connor, W. Höpken & U. Gretzel (Eds.), *Information and communication technologies in tourism 2008* (pp. 152–163). New York, NY: Springer.

Schiller, D.
(2007). *How to think about information*. Urbana, IL: University of Illinois Press.

Schmallegger, D., & Carson, D.
(2008). Blogs in tourism: Changing approaches to information exchange. *Journal of Vacation Marketing, 14*(2), 99–110.

Schmallegger, D., & Carson, D.
(2009). Destination image projection on consumer-generated content Websites: A case study of the flinders ranges. *Information Technology and Tourism, 11*(2), 111–127.

Schmidt-Belz, B., Laamanen, H., Poslad, S., & Zipf, A.
(2003). Location-based mobile tourist services-first user experiences. In *Proceedings of information and communication technologies in tourism*, Ljubljana, Slovenia. Wien: Springer (pp. 115–123).

Schultz, F., Utz, S., & Göritz, A.
(2011). Is the medium the message? Perceptions of and reactions to crisis communication via twitter, blogs and traditional media. *Public Relations Review, 37*(1), 20–27.

Schultz, J.
(2011). Storytelling, sense-making. Past, present and future. In J. Schultz (Ed.), *Griffith Review* (pp. 7–10). Brisbane: Marilyn McMeniman AM.

Schwab, A., & Miner, A.
(2008). Learning in hybrid-project systems: The effects of project performance on repeated collaboration. *Academy of Management Journal, 51*(6), 1117–1149.

Schwanen, T., & Kwan, M.
(2008). The internet, mobile phone and space-time constraints. *Geoforum, 39*(3), 1362–1377.

Scott, A.
  (2000). *The cultural economy of cities*. London: Sage.
Scott, S., & Lane, V.
  (2000). A stakeholder approach to organizational identity. *Academy of Management Review, 25*(1), 43–62.
Scottish Enterprise Forth Valley.
  (2000). *The importance of tourism*. Briefing Note 5, Forth Valley Enterprise, Stirling.
Sekula, A.
  (2001). TITANIC's wake. *Art Journal, 60*(2), 26–37.
Selstad, L.
  (2007). The social anthropology of the tourist experience. Exploring the "Middle Role". *Scandinavian Journal of Hospitality and Tourism, 7*(1), 19–33.
Selwyn, T.
  (1996). *The tourist image – Myths and myth making in tourism*. Chichester, UK: Wiley.
Sengers, P., Boehner, K., Mateas, M., & Gay, G.
  (2008). The disenchantment of affect. *Personal and Ubiquitous Computing, 12*(5), 347–358.
Shandley, R., Hamal, T., & Tanase, A.
  (2006). Location shooting and the filmic destination: Transylvanian myths and the post-colonial tourism enterprise. *Journal of Tourism and Cultural Change, 4*(3), 137–158.
Shannon, C., & Weaver, W.
  (1949). *The mathematical theory of communication*. Urbana, IL: University of Illinois Press.
Sharma, D.
  (2005). *Tsunamis, manglares y economía de mercado* (F. Sastre, Trans.). Rebelión.org. Retrieved from rebelion.org/noticia.php?id = 10010. Accessed on January 14, 2005.
Shaw, D.
  (2008). *Technoculture: The key concepts*. New York, NY: Berg.
Sheldon, P.
  (1997). *Tourism information technology*. Oxford, UK: CA International.
Shih, C.
  (2009). *The Facebook era: Tapping online social networks to build better products, reach new audiences, and sell more stuff*. Boston, MA: Prentice Hall.
Shils, E.
  (1966). Mass society and its culture. In B. Berelson & M. Janowitz (Eds.), *Reader in public opinion and communication* (2nd ed., pp. 505–528). New York, NY: Free Press.

Shiva, V.
(2005). *Lecciones del tsunami para quienes menosprecian a la madre tierra.* Rebelión.org. Retrieved from rebelion.org/noticia.php?id = 10045. Accessed on January 15, 2005.

Shoaib, M.
(2001). The heart of whiteness: The allure of tourism in vertical limit and the beach. bad subjects, *54*. Retrieved from bad.eserver.org/issues/2001/54/shoaib.html

Sigala, M., Christou, E., & Gretzel, U.
(2012). *Social media in travel, tourism and hospitality: Theory, practice and cases.* Farnham: Ashgate.

Silverman, D.
(1994). *Interpreting qualitative data: Methods for analysing talk, text and interaction.* London: Sage.

Simonsen, K.
(2004). Networks, flows, and fluids – Reimagining spatial analysis? *Environment and Planning A, 36*(8), 1333–1340.

Simpson, M., Gössling, S., Scott, D., Hall, C., & Gladin, E.
(2008). *Climate change adaptation and mitigation in the tourism sector: Frameworks, tools and practices.* UNEP, University of Oxford, UNWTO, WMO: Paris, France.

Slaughter, L.
(2002). Motivations of long term volunteers at events. Paper presented at Events and Placemaking: International Event Research Conference, Sydney, July 2002.

Smith, A., & Stewart, B.
(2007). The travelling fan: Understanding the mechanisms of sport fan consumption in a sport tourism setting. *Journal of Sport and Tourism, 12*(3/4), 155–181.

Smith, M.
(2009). Development and is discontents: Ego-tripping without ethics or idea(l)s? In J. Tribe (Ed.), *Philosophical issues in tourism* (pp. 261–277). Bristol: Channel View Publications.

Smith, S.
(1990). *Dictionary of concepts in recreation and leisure studies.* Westport, CT: Greenwood Press.

Smith, T.
(2009). The social media revolution. *International Journal of Market Research, 51*(4), 559–561.

Smythe, D.
(1954). Reality as presented by television. *Public Opinion Quarterly, 18*(2), 143–156.

Snepenger, D., Snepenger, M., Dalbey, M., & Wessol, A.
(2007). Meanings and consumption characteristics of places at a tourism destination. *Journal of Travel Research, 45*(3), 310.

Sönmez, S., Apostolopoulos, Y., Yu, C., Yang, S., Mattila, A., & Yu, L.
(2006). Binge drinking and casual sex on spring break. *Annals of Tourism Research, 33*(4), 895–917.

Spagat, E.
(2010). Wave of illegals arrests rises off California. *Washington Times*, August 26. Retrieved from washingtontimes.com/news/2010/aug/26/as-borders-tighten-illegals-turn-to-sea.

Spracklen, K.
(2011). Dreaming of drams: Authenticity in Scottish whisky tourism as an expression of unresolved Habermasian rationalities. *Leisure Studies, 30*(1), 99–116.

Staiger, J.
(2005). *Media reception studies.* New York, NY: New York University Press.

Star, S., & Griesemer, J.
(1989). Institutional ecology, "translations" and boundary objects: Amateurs and professionals in Berkeley's Museum of Vertebrate Zoology, 1907–39. *Social Studies of Science, 19*(3), 387–420.

Steinman, M., & Hawkins, M.
(2010). When marketing through social media, legal risks can go viral. *Intellectual Property and Technology Law Journal, 22*(9), 1–9.

Stillman, L., & McGrath, J.
(2008). Is it Web 2.0 or is it better information and knowledge that we need? *Australian Social Work, 61*(4), 421–428.

Strathern, M.
(1996). Cutting the network. *Journal of the Royal Anthropological Institute, 2*(3), 517–535.

Strauss, A., & Corbin, J.
(1990). *Basics of qualitative research.* Newbury Park, CA: Sage.

Streitfeld, D.
(2011). Why, on the web, so much is totally awesome. *International Herald Tribune*, August 22, p. 15.

Strinati, D.
(2004). *An introduction to theories of popular culture.* New York, NY: Routledge.

Stringer, L., Dougill, A., Fraser, E., Hubacek, K., Prell, C., & Reed M.
(2006). Unpacking "participation" in the adaptive management of social–ecological systems: A critical review. *Ecology and Society, 11*(2), 39. Retrieved from http://www.ecologyandsociety.org/vol11/iss2/art39/

Sturges, D.
(1994). Communicating through crisis. *Management Communication Quarterly*, 7(3), 297.

Suchman, L. A.
(2007). *Human-machine reconfigurations: Plans and situated actions*. Cambridge: Cambridge University Press.

Sun, T., Youn, S., Wu, G., & Kuntaraporn, M.
(2006). Online word-of-mouth (or mouse): An exploration of its antecedents and consequences. *Journal of Computer-Mediated Communication, 11*(4). Article 11, 1104–1127.

Tajfel, H.
(1978). Social categorization, social identity, and social comparison. In H. Tajfel (Ed.), *Differentiation between social groups: Studies in the social psychology of intergroup relations* (pp. 61–67). London: Academic Press.

Tambini, D.
(1999). New media and democracy: The civic networking movement. *New Media Society, 1*(3), 305–329.

Tănăsescu, A.
(2006). Tourism, nationalism and post-communist Romania: The life and death of dracula park. *Journal of Tourism and Cultural Change, 4*(3), 159–178.

Tapscott, D.
(2009). *Grown up digital: How the net generation is changing your world*. New York, NY: McGraw-Hill.

Tapscott, D., & Williams, A.
(2007). *Wikinomics: How mass collaboration changes everything*. London: Atlantic Books.

Tasci, A., & Gartner, W.
(2007). Destination image and its functional relationships. *Journal of Travel Research, 45*(4), 413–425.

Taylor, J.
(2005). Engaging organization through worldview. In S. May & D. Mumby (Eds.), *Engaging organizational communication theory and research: Multiple perspectives* (pp. 197–221). Thousand Oaks, CA: Sage.

Taylor, M., & Kent, M.
(2007). Taxonomy of mediated crisis responses. *Public Relations Review, 33*(2), 140–146.

Taylor, M., & Perry, D.
(2005). Diffusion of traditional and new media tactics in crisis communication. *Public Relations Review, 31*(2), 209–217.

Terry, V.
(2001). Lobbying: Fantasy, reality or both? A health care public policy case study. *Journal of Public Affairs, 1*(3), 266–280.

The Financial.
  (2010). *SAS wins social media award for crisis communication.* Retrieved from http://finchannel.com/news_flash/Travel_Biz_News/72150_SAS_wins_social_ media_award_for_crisis_communication/. Accessed on August 24, 2011.
The Nation.
  (2006). *Filming "damaged beach".* Retrieved from nationmultimedia.com/ 2006/12/01/national/national_30020443.php. Accessed on December 1, 2006.
The-numbers.com.
  (2012a). *The-numbers.com.* Retrieved from http://www.the-numbers.com/ movies/2008/TWLIT.php. Accessed on April 23, 2013.
The-numbers.com.
  (2012b). *The-numbers.com.* Retrieved from http://www.the-numbers.com/ movies/2009/TWLI2.php. Accessed on April 23, 2013.
The-numbers.com.
  (2012c). *The-numbers.com.* Retrieved from http://www.the-numbers.com/ movies/2010/TWLI3.php. Accessed on April 23, 2013.
The-numbers.com.
  (2012d). *The-numbers.com.* Retrieved from http://www.the-numbers.com/ movie/Twilight-Saga-Breaking-Dawn-Part-1-The. Accessed on April 23, 2013.
The Onion.
  (2005). *U.S. children still traumatized one year after seeing partially exposed breast on TV.* Retrieved from theonion.com/articles/us-children-still-trauma-tized-one-year-after-seein,1285. Accessed on January 26, 2005.
The Telegraph.
  (2011). How the 2010 ash cloud caused chaos: Facts and figures. *The Telegraph.* Retrieved from http://www.telegraph.co.uk/finance/newsbysector/ transport/8531152/How-the-2010-ash-cloud-caused-chaos-facts-and-figures. html. Accessed on August 16, 2011.
Thevenot, G.
  (2007). Blogging as a social media. *Tourism and Hospitality Research, 7*(3/4), 282–289.
Thompson, S., & Sinha, R.
  (2008). Brand communities and new product adoption: The influence and limits of oppositional loyalty. *Journal of Marketing, 72*(6), 65–80.
Thrift, N.
  (2007). *Non-representational theory: Space, politics, affect.* London: Routledge.
Tooke, N., & Baker, M.
  (1996). Seeing is believing: The effect of film on visitor numbers to screened locations. *Tourism Management, 17*(2), 87–94.
Tourism Australia.
  (2011). *Tourism Australia to host the Oprah Winfrey Show in Australia.* http:// www.tourism.australia.com/en-au/news/media-releases_6092.aspx. Accessed on October 1, 2011

Travel Mole.
(2012a). *Tourist board twitter campaign spectacularly backfires*. Retrieved from http://www.travelmole.com. Accessed on July 18, 2012.

Travel Mole.
(2012b). *Hotels shun social media and online travel agents*. Retrieved from http://www.travelmole.com. Accessed on August 10, 2012.

Treuren, G., & Lane, D.
(2003). The tourism planning process in the context of organised interests, industry structure, state capacity, accumulation and sustainability. *Current Issues in Tourism*, 6(1), 1–22.

Treuren, G., & Monga, M.
(2002). Are special event volunteers different from non-SEO volunteers? Demographic characteristics of volunteers in four South Australian special event organizations. Paper presented at Events and Placemaking: International Event Research Conference, Sydney, July 2002.

Tribe, J.
(2002). The philosophic practitioner. *Annals of Tourism Research*, 29(2), 338–357.

Tribe, J.
(2006). The truth about tourism. *Annals of Tourism Research*, 33(2), 360–381.

Tribe, J.
(2008). The art of tourism. *Annals of Tourism Research*, 35(4), 924–944.

Tribe, J.
(2009). *Philosophical issues in tourism*. Bristol, UK: Channel View Publications.

Tribe, J.
(2010). Tribes, territories and networks in the tourism academy. *Annals of Tourism Research*, 37(1), 7–33.

TripAdvisor.
(2012a). *Fact sheet*. Retrieved from http://www.tripadvisor.com/PressCenter-c4-Fact_Sheet.html. Accessed on March 15, 2012.

Tsai, H., Huang, L., & Lin, C.
(2005). Emerging e-commerce development model for Taiwanese travel agencies. *Tourism Management*, 26(5), 787–796.

Tumbler.
(2012) Retrieved from http://www.tumblr.com/about

Tussyadiah, I.
(2012). A concept of location-based social network marketing. *Journal of Travel and Tourism Marketing*, 29(3), 205–220.

Tussyadiah, I., & Fesenmaier, D.
(2008). Marketing places through first-person stories' an analysis of pennsylvania roadtripper blog. *Journal of Travel and Tourism Marketing*, 25(3), 299–311.

Tussyadiah, I., & Fesenmaier, D.
(2009). Mediating tourist experiences: Access to places via shared videos. *Annals of Tourism Research, 36*(1), 24–40.

Tzanelli, R.
(2004). Constructing the "Cinematic Tourist": The "Sign Industry" of the Lord of the Rings. *Tourist Studies, 4*(1), 21–42.

Tzanelli, R.
(2006). Reel western fantasies: Portrait of a tourist imagination in The Beach (2000). *Mobilities, 1*(1), 121–142.

Tzelepi, M., & Quick, S.
(2002). The sydney organising committee for the olympic games (SOCOG) "Event leadership" training course - an effectiveness evaluation. *Event Management: An International Journal, 7*(4), 245–258.

Ulrich Beck
(2000). *The Brave New World of Work.* Cambridge: Polity Press.

Unruh, D.
(1980). The nature of social worlds. *Pacific Sociological Association, 23*(3), 271–296.

Uriely, N., & Belhassen, Y.
(2006). Drugs and risk-taking in tourism. *Annals of Tourism Research, 33*(2), 339–359.

Urry, J.
(1990). *The tourist gaze: Travel and leisure in contemporary societies.* London: Sage.

Urry, J.
(2002). *The tourist gaze* (2nd ed.). London: Sage.

Urry, J.
(2003). Social networks, travel and talk. *British Journal of Sociology, 54*(2), 155–175.

US Department of the Interior.
(2011). *U.S. Geological Survey Yearbook.* Retrieved from http://minerals.usgs. gov/minerals/pubs/commodity/iron_ore/myb1-2009-feore.pdf. Accessed on March 12, 2012.

Van der Duim, R.
(2007). Tourismscapes: An actor-network perspective. *Annals of Tourism Research, 34*(4), 961–976.

Van der Duim, R., & van Marwijk, R.
(2006). The implementation of an environmental management system for Dutch tour operators: An actor-network perspective. *Journal of Sustainable Tourism, 14*(5), 449–472.

Van der Duim, R., van Marwijk, R., Ndubi, E., & Fetene, G.
(2006). Ozi's bed and breakfast: A case of translation. *Matkailututkimus Finnish Journal of Tourism Studies, 2*(1), 41–56.

van Loon, J.
  (1997). Chronotopes: of/in the Televisualisation of the 1992 Los Angeles Riots. *Theory, Culture and Society*, *14*(2), 89–104.
Vargo, S., & Lusch, R.
  (2004). Evolving to a new dominant logic for marketing. *Journal of Marketing*, *68*, 1–17.
Vassou, A.
  (2008). *Virgin cabin crew sacked over Facebook comments*. Retrieved from http://www.computeractive.co.uk/ca/news/1910378/virgin-cabin-crew-sacked-facebook-comments. Accessed on September 3, 2010.
VECCI.
  (2012). *Facebook sacking overturned due to lack of social media policy*. Retrieved from http://www.vecci.org.au/news/Pages/Facebook_sacking_overturned.aspx?utm_source=Informz&utm_medium=eDM&utm_campaign=eDM. Accessed on January 30, 2012.
Veil, S., Buehner, T., & Palenchar, M.
  (2011). A work-in-process literature review: Incorporating social media in risk and crisis communication. *Journal of Contingencies and Crisis Management*, *19*(2), 110–122.
Viborg Andersen, K., Zinner Henriksen, H., Secher, C., & Medaglia, R.
  (2007). Costs of e-participation: The management challenges. *Transforming Government: People, Process and Policy*, *1*(1), 29–43.
Vice, S.
  (1997). *Introducing Bakhtin*. Manchester, UK: Manchester University Press.
Vickery, G., & Wunsch-Vincent, S.
  (2007). *Participative web and user-created content: Web 2.0, wikis and social networks*. Paris: OECD Publishing. Retrieved from http://puck.sourceoecd.org/vl=463338/cl=30/nw=1/rpsv/cgi-bin/fulltextew.pl?prpsv=/ij/oecdthemes/99980134/v2007n15/s1/p1l.idx. Accessed on February 25, 2010.
Visit Brussels.
  (2012). *Enter the city!* Retrieved from http://www.enterthecity.info/index.php/en/. Accessed on May 21, 2012.
Volo, S.
  (2010). Bloggers' reported tourist experiences: their utility as a tourism data source and their effect on prospective tourists. *Journal of Vacation Marketing*, *16*(4), 297–311.
Wallas, G.
  (1967). *The great society: A psychological analysis*. Lincoln: University of Nebraska Press.
Wallerstein, I.
  (1989). Culture as the ideological battleground of the modern world-system. *Hitotsubashi Journal of Social Studies*, *21*(1), 5–22.

Wang, N.
(2000). *Tourism and modernity: A sociological analysis*. Oxford: Elsevier.

Wang, Y., & Fesenmaier, D.
(2004). Towards understanding members' general participation in and active contribution to an online travel community. *Tourism Management, 25*(6), 709–722.

Wang, Y., & Fesenmaier, D.
(2006). Identifying the success factors of web-based marketing strategy: An investigation of convention and visitors bureaus in the United States. *Journal of Travel Research, 44*(3), 239–249.

Wang, Y., Yu, Q., & Fesenmaier, D.
(2002). Defining the virtual tourist community: Implications for tourism marketing. *Tourism Management, 23*(4), 407–417.

Weber, L.
(2009). *Marketing to the social web: How digital customer communities build your business*. Hoboken, NJ: Wiley.

Weick, K.
(1995). *Sensemaking in organization*. Thousand Oaks, CA: Sage.

Weil, D.
(2009). Rethinking the regulation of vulnerable work in the USA: A sector-based approach. *Journal of Industrial Relations, 51*(3), 411–430.

Weinberg, T.
(2009). *The new community rules: Marketing on the social web*. Sebastopol, CA: O'Reilly.

Weiser, M.
(1991). The computer for the 21st century. *Scientific American, 265*(3), 66–75.

Wellman, B., Boase, J., & Chen, W.
(2002). The networked nature of community: Online and offline. *IT & Society, 1*(1), 151–165.

Wellman, B., & Haythornthwaite, C.
(2002). *The internet in everyday life*. Oxford, UK: Wiley-Blackwell.

Wenger, A.
(2008). Analysis of travel bloggers' characteristics and their communication about Austria as a tourism destination. *Journal of Vacation Marketing, 14*(2), 169–176.

Whetten, D., & Mackey, A.
(2002). A social actor conception of organizational identity and its implications for the study of organizational reputation. *Business and Society, 41*(4), 393–414.

White, L.
(2010). Facebook, Friends and Photos: A snapshot into social networking for generating travel ideas. In N. Sharda (Ed.), *Tourism informatics: Visual travel recommender systems, social communities, and user interface design (e-book)* (pp. 115–129). Information Science Reference.

White, N., & White, P.
(2008). Travel as interaction: Encountering place and others. *Journal of Hospitality and Tourism Management, 15*(1), 42–48.

Williams, J.
(2009). Community, frame of reference and boundary: Three sociological concepts and their relevance for virtual worlds research. *Qualitative Sociology Review, 5*(2), 3–16.

Wilson, N.
(2011). *Seduced by Twilight: The allure and contradictory messages of the popular saga.* Jefferson, NC: McFarland & Company.

Winocur, R.
(2002). *Ciudadanos mediáticos.* Barcelona: Editorial Gedisa.

World Tourism Organization (UNWTO).
(2000). *Sustainable development of tourism, A compilation of good practices.* Madrid: World Tourism Organization.

Wright, P., & McCarthy, J.
(2008). Empathy and Experience in HCI. *Proceedings of the CHI 2008, 26th annual SIGCHI conference on human factors in computing systems,* Florence, Italy. New York, NY: ACM (pp. 637–646).

Wright, P., Wallace, J., & McCarthy, J.
(2008). Aesthetics and experience-centered design. *ACM Transactions on Computer-Human Interaction (TOCHI), 15*(4), 1–21.

Xiang, Z., & Gretzel, U.
(2010). Role of social media in online travel information search. *Tourism Management, 31*(2), 179–188.

Xie, H., Miao, L., Kuo, P.-J., & Lee, B.-Y.
(2010). Consumers' responses to ambivalent online hotel reviews: The role of perceived source credibility and pre-decisional disposition. *International Journal of Hospitality Management, 30*(1), 178–183.

Ye, Q., Law, R., & Gu, B.
(2009). The impact of online user reviews on hotel room sales. *International Journal of Hospitality Management, 28*(1), 180–182.

Yeoman, I., & McMahon-Beattie, U.
(2006). Tomorrow's tourist and the information society. *Journal of Vacation Marketing, 12*(3), 269–291.

Yin, R.
(1984). *Case study research: Design and methods.* Thousand Oaks, CA: Sage.

Yin, R.
(1994). *Case study research: Design and methods.* Thousand Oaks, CA: Sage.

Yin, R.
(2003). *Case study research: Design and methods* (3rd. ed.). Thousand Oaks, CA: Sage.

Yin, R.
(2009). *Case study research: Design and method* (4th ed.). Thousand Oaks, CA: Sage.

Yoo, K., & Gretzel, U.
(2008). What motivates consumers to write online travel reviews? *Information Technology and Tourism, 10*(4), 283–295.

Young, A., & Young, R.
(2008). Measuring the effects of film and television on tourism to screen locations: A theoretical and empirical perspective. *Journal of Travel and Tourism Marketing, 24*(2), 195–212.

Yuan, Y.-L., Gretzel, U., & Fesenmaier, D.
(2006). The role of information technology use in American convention and visitors bureaus. *Tourism Management, 27*, 326–341.

Zaichkowsky, J.
(1985). Measuring the involvement construct. *Journal of Consumer Research, 12*(3), 221–236.

Zaichkowsky, J.
(1986). Conceptualizing involvement. *Journal of Advertising, 15*(2), 4–14.

Zapico, J., Brandt, N., & Turpeinen, M.
(2010). Environmental metrics. *Journal of Industrial Ecology, 14*(5), 703–706.

Zarrella, D.
(2010). *The social media marketing book*. Farnham: O'Reilly.

Zehrer, A., Crotts, J., & Magnini, V.
(2011). The perceived usefulness of blog postings: An extension of the expectancy-disconfirmation paradigm. *Tourism Management, 32*(1), 106–113.

Zeppel, H.
(2010). Managing cultural values in sustainable tourism: Conflicts in protected areas. *Tourism and Hospitality Research, 10*(2), 93–104.

Zhang, L., Pan, B., Smith, W., & Li, X.
(2009). An exploratory study of travelers' use of online reviews and recommendations. *Information Technology and Tourism, 11*(2), 157–167.

Zhang, Z., Ye, Q., Law, R., & Li, Y.
(2010). The impact of e-word-of-mouth on the online popularity of restaurants: A comparison of consumer reviews and editor reviews. *International Journal of Hospitality Management, 29*(4), 694–700.

Zhou, Z., Jin, X.-L., Vogel, D., Fang, Y., & Chen, X.
(2011). Individual motivations and demographic differences in social virtual world uses: An exploratory investigation in Second Life. *International Journal of Electronic Commerce, 31*(3), 261–271.

ABOUT THE AUTHORS

Mads Bødker is associate professor at the Department of IT Management (Copenhagen Business School, Denmark). His primary interests are in the fields of human–computer interaction (HCI) and interaction design. Focusing on the domain of tourism, his current research attempts to challenge dominant assumptions within IT, HCI, and technical work by focusing on experiential and sensory aspects of tourism. Inspired by human geography and phenomenology, his work emphasizes the understanding of tourist places as performances and attempts to draw design inspiration from place-oriented research methods.

David Browning works as an interaction researcher and lecturer in the Polytechnic of Namibia (Windhoek, Namibia), and is interested in making meaning of and in tourist places. Motivated by rapid changes in tourist attitudes toward natural environments, he has developed a variety of methods that enable the collection of qualitative and quantitative spatial data in such infrastructure-poor places. Interpretation of this data gives rise to understandings of visitor and tourist experiences which can be used to inspire the design of new digital technologies mediating one's experience of such places.

Adriana Budeanu is assistant professor at the Department of International Economics and Management (Copenhagen Business School, Denmark), with over 10 years of experience in doing research in the area of sustainable tourism and international business, sustainable consumption and lifestyles, corporate social responsibility in tourism supply chains, and sustainable service innovation. She has teaching experience in corporate strategies for sustainable development and tourism. Her most recent research includes studies on tourist consumption and environmental awareness.

Liping Cai is professor and director of Purdue Tourism and Hospitality Research Center (Purdue University, USA). He studies service branding and consumer experiences and behaviors in tourism and hospitality. His current research includes regional branding, rural and agricultural tourism, and emerging markets. He is an author or coauthor of over 200 refereed papers, coeditor of *Bridging Tourism Theory and Practice* book series, and serves on the editorial boards of five top-ranked journals. He received Purdue University's designation of University Faculty Scholar in 2003 and has been a governor appointee on the Indiana State Tourism Council since 2004.

Elena Codeluppi holds a Ph.D. in semiotics from the University of Bologna. She has been a visiting scholar at the École Pratique des Hautes Études, Sorbonne University of Paris. She collaborates with OPERA, a research unit specialized in creative industries and social media, she is Business Development Manager of social media and web strategies at HICADV Communication Company, consultant at Fondazione Giacomo Brodolini, and trainer in several professional seminars on social media and web communication.

Richard Ek is associate professor at the Department of Service Management and Service Studies (Lund University, Sweden). In 2003 he concluded his Ph.D. at the Department of Social and Economic Geography, Lund University, on the use of spatial visions as power tools in planning and regional development, using the transnational Öresund Region as a case. He has published on such topics as critical geopolitics, biopolitics, tourism and hospitality studies, and media and communication studies. His current research interests include the biopolitics of tourism, nihilistic planning, the politics and poetics of place branding, the unsociality of social media, and the cultural imagination of nonhuman creatures in postapocalyptic capitalism.

Raslinda Mohd Ghazali is a graduate student in the School of Hospitality and Tourism Management (Purdue University, USA). She has been a faculty member at the School of Tourism, Hospitality, and Environmental Management, Universiti Utara Malaysia, Malaysia since 2003 and currently received a scholarship from the Malaysia Ministry of Higher Education to pursue her Ph.D. at Purdue. Her research interests are in tourism destination image, emotional experience, and globalization issues in tourism.

Szilvia Gyimóthy is associate professor at the Department of Culture and Global Studies (Aalborg University, Denmark). Her main field is tourism and services marketing, spanning from traditional market research, quality and satisfaction measurement to multidisciplinary customer research, including phenomenological and narrative approaches to understand experience consumption. In the past few years, she has studied communication patterns and practices of commodification, including brand mythologies, dramaturgical frameworks, and narrative reterritorialization in the context of mid-market hotels, adventure destinations, niche festivals, and meeting networks.

Anne-Marie Hede is associate professor of marketing in the School of International Business and associate dean of research and research training in the Faculty of Business and Law (Victoria University, Melbourne, Australia). She is an experienced researcher in the field of events and has undertaken a number of studies on events, using theories and models of marketing and management, to explore issues of significance to the event sector. Her research on events has been published and presented in a number of international journals and conferences.

Kristian Anders Hvass is assistant professor at the Department of International Economics and Management (Copenhagen Business School, Denmark). He holds an industrial Ph.D. from Copenhagen Business School, which focused on future airline business models. His research focuses on transportation strategy and development of business models. His current research looks at social media within the transportation field. In addition, he has an interest in applying new research methods to his field, such as qualitative comparative approaches. He has a history with the airline industry where he has been both a pilot and manager.

Pamm Kellett is associate professor in the School of Management and Marketing and coordinator of the postgraduate sport management program (Deakin University, Melbourne, Australia). She holds a Ph.D. in sport management from Griffith University (Australia). The objective of her research is to formulate and test intervention strategies that contribute to the development and optimal effectiveness of organizations in the sport and recreation sector. Ultimately, her research aims to enhance the quality of working life for those who work and participate in such organizations.

Mia Larson received her Ph.D. in business administration from the School of Business, Economics and Law at Gothenburg University, Sweden, on the topic of event management and network cooperation. She is now associate professor at the Department of Service Management and Service Studies, Campus Helsingborg (Lund University, Sweden), where she is responsible for the undergraduate service management program with a specialization in tourism. She publishes research in international journals and books, dealing with such topics as tourism development focused on pop culture tourism and coastal tourism, event and festival management, and social media.

Maria Lexhagen received her Ph.D. in business administration focusing on e-marketing and customer behavior from the School of Business, Economics and Law (Gothenburg University, Sweden). She is currently affiliated with the European Tourism Research Institute (ETOUR), Mid Sweden University as assistant professor. Her research interests include information technology use within the tourism industry, customer behavior, e-marketing, customer perceived value, social media use, and pop culture tourism such as film- and literature-induced tourism. Her scientific work is published internationally in books and journals within the areas of tourism, and marketing and information systems. She has also published popular science works.

Christine Lundberg has a Ph.D. in business administration from the School of Business, Economics and Law (Gothenburg University, Sweden), and holds a position as a researcher and senior lecturer at the European Tourism Research Institute (ETOUR) at Mid Sweden University. Her research focuses primarily on fan tourism, fandom, social media usage, servicescapes, destination development, service encounters, and employee relations. These topics have been under study in her internationally published works in journals and books. She is also an avid user of social media as a means for communicating research findings.

Toby Miller lives in Los Angeles. He is the author and editor of over 30 books and 100s of articles and chapters, which have appeared in Spanish, Chinese, German, Portuguese, Swedish, Japanese, Turkish, and English. His latest books are *Greening the Media* (Oxford, 2012, with Richard Maxwell) and *Blow Up the Humanities* (Temple, 2012). His adventures can be viewed at tobymiller.org and his podcast on iTunes or on smartphone via the "culturalstudies" application.

Fabrizio Montanari is assistant professor at the University of Modena and Reggio Emilia, Italy, where he is also scientific coordinator of OPERA, a research unit specialized in creative industries and social media. He is also lecturer at Bocconi University and Chairman of *Fondazione Nazionale della Danza Aterballetto* (www.aterballetto.it). His main research interest involves the analysis of networks, creative clusters, teams, and the use of social media by organizations operating in creative industries.

Ana María Munar is associate professor at the Department of International Economics and Management (Copenhagen Business School, Denmark). She holds an M.Sc. in political science and a Ph.D. in business and economics. Her research interests are tourism and information and communication technologies, globalization processes, destination branding, and policy and trends in tourism education. Her latest work provides insights on the impact that Web 2.0 and social media technologies have on tourism. Her articles examine the role of digital mediation on cultural change and social reproduction. She is a board member of Imagine..Creative Industries Research Center and a member of the Center for Leisure and Culture Services at Copenhagen Business School.

Can-Seng Ooi is professor and the director of the Center for Leisure and Culture Services Research (Copenhagen Business School, Denmark). His research areas include cultural tourism, destination branding, art worlds, and social media. He is a sociologist and has done comparative investigations on Denmark, Singapore, and China. He has published extensively and has contributed significantly to theoretical development in tourism studies, including the founding of the "versatile tourist," highlighting the politics and poetics of destination branding, revealing the attention structure of tourist experiences, and furthering Bakhtin's dialogism in tourism research.

Annachiara Scapolan is assistant professor at the University of Modena and Reggio Emilia, where she is also researcher of OPERA, a research unit specialized in creative industries and social media. She earned a Ph.D. in management at Ca' Foscari University of Venice, where she is lecturer of people management. Her main research areas are e-HRM, human resources management in the tourism sector and cultural industries, organization theory and design, adoption of social media, and organizational solutions and HRM practices for innovation and creativity.

Subject Index